Saving the Electoral College

Saving the Electoral College

Why the National Popular Vote Would Undermine Democracy

Robert M. Hardaway

BLOOMSBURY ACADEMIC
NEW YORK · LONDON · OXFORD · NEW DELHI · SYDNEY

BLOOMSBURY ACADEMIC
Bloomsbury Publishing Inc
1385 Broadway, New York, NY 10018, USA
50 Bedford Square, London, WC1B 3DP, UK
29 Earlsfort Terrace, Dublin 2, Ireland

BLOOMSBURY, BLOOMSBURY ACADEMIC and the Diana logo
are trademarks of Bloomsbury Publishing Plc

First published in the United States of America by ABC-CLIO 2019
Paperback edition published by Bloomsbury Academic 2024

Copyright © Bloomsbury Publishing Inc, 2024

For legal purposes the Acknowledgments on p. xvii constitute
an extension of this copyright page.

Cover photo: (Oneofmany/Dreamstime)

All rights reserved. No part of this publication may be reproduced or
transmitted in any form or by any means, electronic or mechanical,
including photocopying, recording, or any information storage or retrieval
system, without prior permission in writing from the publishers.

Bloomsbury Publishing Inc does not have any control over, or responsibility for,
any third-party websites referred to or in this book. All internet addresses given
in this book were correct at the time of going to press. The author and publisher
regret any inconvenience caused if addresses have changed or sites have
ceased to exist, but can accept no responsibility for any such changes.

Library of Congress Cataloging-in-Publication Data
Names: Hardaway, Robert M., 1946- author.
Title: Saving the electoral college: why the national popular vote would
undermine democracy / Robert M. Hardaway.
Description: Santa Barbara, California: Praeger, an imprint of ABC-CLIO, LLC, [2019] |
Includes bibliographical references and index.
Identifiers: LCCN 2019016226 (print) | LCCN 2019021749 (ebook) |
ISBN 9781440869952 (print: alk. paper) | ISBN 9781440869969 (ebook)
Subjects: LCSH: Electoral college—United States. | Presidents—United States—
Election. | Direct election—United States. | Democracy—United States.
Classification: LCC JK529 (ebook) | LCC JK529 .H375 2019 (print) |
DDC 324.6/3—dc23
LC record available at https://lccn.loc.gov/2019016226

ISBN: HB: 978-1-4408-6995-2
PB: 979-8-7651-1902-0
ePDF: 978-1-4408-6996-9
eBook: 979-8-2161-4167-9

To find out more about our authors and books visit www.bloomsbury.com
and sign up for our newsletters.

Dedicated
to
Judy Trejos

Contents

Preface		ix
Acknowledgments		xvii
Chapter 1	Introduction: John F. Kennedy's Vision of Federalism	1
Chapter 2	The Solar System of Government Power	15
Chapter 3	Electing a President: The Framers' Vision	29
Chapter 4	The Direct Election Illusion	37
Chapter 5	The National Popular Vote Interstate Compact	47
Chapter 6	The Grand Compromise and the Unit Vote: Myths and Misdirection	59
Chapter 7	Presidential Campaigns and Incentives: "That's Where the Votes Are"	65
Chapter 8	Legitimacy and Certainty	71
Chapter 9	The Recount Problem	85
Chapter 10	Myths about the Electoral College: A Response	95
Chapter 11	Reform: Proposals and Alternatives	127
Chapter 12	Conclusion: The Case for Preserving Federalism	149
Appendix A. National Popular Vote Interstate Compact: California's Bill		157

*Appendix B. Selected Provisions of the U.S. Constitution Relating
to the Electoral College* 161

Notes 163

Bibliography 183

Index 189

Preface

The facts of the matter are that the system of [direct election] will greatly increase the likelihood of a minority president. . . . [It] would break down the federal system under which most states entered the union, which provides a system of checks and balances to insure that no area or group shall obtain too much power.
—Senator John F. Kennedy[1]

This government is not completely consolidated, nor is it entirely Federal. . . . Who are the parties to it? The people—not the people as comprising one great body, but the people as composing 13 sovereignties.
—James Madison[2]

I first became interested in the Electoral College as a high school student at St. Albans School in Washington, D.C. Every Thursday evening we would meet in government class in which students would engage in mock congressional debate on an issue of national interest, proposing bills, arguing for or against them, and then voting. One of the bills proposed was to "abolish the Electoral College." I remember well one classmate of mine in that class by the name of Al Gore. Of course, none of us at that time knew the enormity that this issue would play in the future career of our classmate when he became a candidate for president in the 2000 election.

This government class debate was in large part a reenactment of a real-life debate held just a few years before in the U.S. Senate in March 1956. As documented in the Congressional Record,[3] a cadre of U.S. senators, led in part by Republican senator Everett Dirksen, had taken it upon themselves to initiate demands that since 1789 have now become a bidecade ritual—namely, to "abolish" the Electoral College. These bidecade rituals inevitably involve attacks on the Founding Fathers' plan for presidential elections and the ratification of that plan by the 13 original colonies.

At issue in the Senate debates of 1956 was Joint Resolution 31, which proposed a rewriting of major portions of the U.S. Constitution in order to impose upon the American people a so-called direct election scheme. Virtually alone against this cabal of senators was a young senator, John F. Kennedy, who in the manner of Jimmy Stewart in *Mr. Smith Goes to Washington* gave a speech in the U.S. Senate that now serves as one of the most valiant and dramatic cases for saving the Electoral College that has ever been made in U.S. history.

To one senator's tired claim that the Electoral College is somehow "undemocratic," Kennedy firmly responded that while direct election "purports to be more democratic, [it] would in fact increase the power and encourage splinter parties," with the result that presidents would be elected with only a small percentage of the popular vote.

History has shown Kennedy's concerns to be only too prescient. One might ask the exasperated voters of France, who in their 2017 direct election were told to select from a field of 11 candidates. Without the "channeling" effects of an Electoral College, the 2 established major party candidates were nudged out of the ensuing runoff by less than 2 percent of the vote, with the results that voters were faced with a choice between an extreme right-wing candidate who received less than 21 percent of the vote and an unknown maverick who received only 23 percent of the vote. Since in a runoff one candidate must by predetermined contrivance receive a majority, this is what passed as democracy despite the fact that both candidates were opposed by almost two-thirds of the electorate. In the runoff, over 600,000 voters expressed their outrage with this poor imitation of democracy by casting a *ballot blanc*—the blank ballot.

To unsubstantiated claims that because of our two-party system similar affronts to democracy could not exist in America under a French- or Russian-style direct election—that is, an election in which voters must vote directly for a candidate from a list of candidates representing a number of different parties, followed by a runoff—Kennedy understood and explained that similar affronts to democracy certainly could indeed occur in the absence of the channeling effects of the Electoral College. This is because it is the Electoral College itself that ensures the stability of a two-party system in which a true majority or substantial plurality is required to elect a president. As he explained, "the facts of the matter are that a system [of direct election] will greatly increase the likelihood of a minority president."[4] In fact, France was fortunate in 2017: under its Russian-style direct election,

Preface xi

France came within a whisker of electing a hard right-wing candidate opposed by 80 percent of the electorate. As it was, the "unknown" maverick candidate who won with only 23 percent of the vote in the first-stage election was the subject of violent countrywide demonstrations in 2018.

Perhaps even more important than how a Russian-style direct election would undermine American democracy is that without unanimous consent of all the states, *any* scheme to deprive states of equal suffrage in the Senate, *upon which the allocation of electors in the Electoral College is based,* would be *unconstitutional.* This is because Article V of the Constitution absolutely forbids the use of constitutional amendment as a means to deprive any state of its equal suffrage in the Senate—upon which the allocation of electoral votes in the Electoral College is based—without the *unanimous* consent of all the states. Consent of two-thirds of Congress and three-fourths of the states is simply not sufficient according to Article V to deprive any state of either its equal suffrage in the Senate or its representation in the Electoral College, which is based on that equal suffrage. Kennedy implicitly recognized this when he noted that states only agreed to enter the union if they were so *absolutely guaranteed* of their equal suffrage in the Senate upon which their electors are allocated in the Electoral College. He also recognized that if you tamper with the Constitution by changing "the balance of power of one of the solar system [of government power] it is necessary to consider all the others."[5]

It is beyond the scope of this short preface to set forth John F. Kennedy's major supporting arguments, facts, and history in support of saving the Electoral College. That is the purpose of the rest of this book. It will suffice here to set forth Senator Kennedy's conclusion of his dramatic plea before the Senate of the United States:

> Today we have an electoral vote system which gives both large states and small states certain advantages that offset each other. Now it is proposed that we change all this. What the effects of these various changes will be on the Federal system, the two part system, and the large-state–small-state checks and balances system, no one knows. Nevertheless, it is proposed we change the system—for an unknown, untried, but obviously precarious system which was long ago abandoned in this country, which previous Congresses have rejected, and which has been thoroughly discredited in Europe. . . . Why should we be in such a hurry to adopt a drastic constitutional amendment which most of the voters do not know we are considering? . . . The benefits which [the supporters of direct election] claim are at best speculative. There is obviously little to gain—but much to lose by tampering with the constitution.[6]

Many years after my debate with Al Gore in government class, I was asked to give a lecture to a group of visiting foreign students about the U.S. Constitution and the role it has played in making America what it is today. In the hour allotted to me I decided to limit my talk to "the two most important features of the U.S. Constitution." I enumerated them as (1) the interstate commerce clause and (2) the Electoral College. Why I listed the Electoral College on this very short list is what this book is about.

In 1994, Praeger (now a part of ABC-CLIO) published my first book on this topic, *The Electoral College and the Constitution: The Case for Preserving Federalism*. At that time, the chief threat to preserving the federalist structure of the U.S. Constitution came in the form of congressional hearings seeking to abolish by amendment the federalist structure for presidential elections as enshrined in Articles I and II of the U.S. Constitution. Most notable of these were the 1956 hearings and later the 1969 and 1979 Birch Bayh Senate hearings on a constitutional amendment to abolish the Electoral College in favor of direct election. Emboldened by the claims of pollsters that an overwhelming majority of Americans supported abolishing the Electoral College, these hearings—after exhaustive testimony by constitutional scholars—ultimately rejected any such proposed amendments after its members came to understand how such an amendment would undermine not only the federalist structure of the Constitution but also democracy itself.

For many of those not acquainted with the Founding Fathers' federalist and democratic vision of the United States of America, however, the seductive sound and siren of a Russian-style national popular vote election continues to loom large.

Since the publication of *The Electoral College and the Constitution*, however, a new threat to the federalist foundations of the Constitution has arisen in the form of a proposed National Popular Vote Interstate Compact (NPVIC). Frustrated by the rejection of proposed constitutional amendments in Congress and in particular by the need for comprehensive hearings as part of the constitutional amendment process, NPVIC advocates of a Russian-style popular vote election have come up with a scheme that they believe will, below the radar of public scrutiny, impose such a regime on the American people while avoiding the constitutional amendment process entirely.

This scheme is simplistic in its approach. Rather than abolishing the Electoral College directly by constitutional amendment, it proposes to simply create a cabal of as few as 11 states representing 270 electoral votes, willing to agree among themselves to ignore the popular vote for electors within their own states in favor of a supposed national popular

Preface xiii

vote of electors in all the states. Apparently unconcerned about the chaos that would surely ensue by attempting to impose a Russian-style direct election (a square peg) on an existing Electoral College structure (a round hole), NPVIC advocates have published a manifesto titled *Every Vote Equal,* which purports to explain how such a scheme could theoretically be imposed upon the American people by cabal. Implicit in the title of the NPVIC manifesto is that the U.S. Senate, which is inextricably tied to the Electoral College, should also be abolished, since each state is guaranteed equal suffrage in the Senate regardless of population.

The tactic of forming a cabal of states to circumvent the constitutional amendment process has the perceived advantage of avoiding the public scrutiny that would inevitably accompany any constitutional amendment process that would require a vote of two-thirds of Congress and at least three-quarters of the states. No doubt the supporters of the NPVIC are aware that whenever proposals for direct election have been proposed in Congress, the intense scrutiny that such proposals inevitably attract have always resulted in outright rejection of such schemes. A cabal of selected states, on the other hand, was thought by its supporters to require only the adoption of the NPVIC by the legislatures of as few as 11 large states representing 270 electoral votes. It thus has had the added perceived advantage of bypassing Congress entirely.

Hearings in state legislatures, on the other hand, are often if not usually conducted under the public radar. Confirmation of this can be easily tested by asking a random person on the street if he or she has ever even heard of the NPVIC. The response is very likely to be one of puzzlement. Lobbyists for the NPVIC, primarily supported by financial interests in California, rarely if ever miss an opportunity to appear at isolated and little-publicized legislative hearings in an effort to induce it to join the NPVIC cabal. Those who might believe that such a cabal could never be successful in undermining the entire structure for presidential elections should be aware that as of 2012, state legislatures representing very close to half of the 270 electoral votes necessary to elect a president have become signatories to the NPVIC.

However, on those relatively rare occasions when state legislative hearings on the NPVIC have come to the attention of concerned citizens or constitutional scholars, the NPVIC can be and has been roundly rejected as a threat to both federalism and democracy.

For example, in early March 2007, notice of a Colorado House hearing on whether to join the NPVIC cabal happened to come to the attention of both me and Jim Riley, professor of politics at Regis University. The NPVIC had already been passed in the Colorado Senate and already enjoyed preliminary support in the House committee hearing of 10–1 in favor of the bill. Professor Riley and I appeared and asked for just a full 15 minutes each to express our deep concerns about the constitutionality and efficacy of the NPVIC and how its adoption would undermine democracy in our republic.

After listening to our necessarily short presentations, the vote of the committee was reversed from 10–1 in favor of the NPVIC to 10–1 against. Only the sponsor of the bill persisted in voting for it after hearing our arguments.

This book was written in order to explain—in far more detail than what we were able to present at the House committee hearing—how the NPVIC would undermine democracy. It is hoped that the book can be distributed not just to citizens interested in what has heretofore been a process conducted below the public radar but also to legislators of states who may soon be called upon to consider adopting the NPVIC in the future. To date, many of the legislators have already been provided with the NPVIC manifesto *Every Vote Equal,* a 1,000-page tome consisting of a motley collection of disconnected political opinions, assumptions, and speculations. Those are addressed in Chapter 10.

In fact, the Electoral College serves much the same task as Parliament in the United Kingdom. It differs from a parliament only in that its powers are limited to the election of a president, with legislative powers reserved to Congress. The Founding Fathers deliberately rejected the idea of a parliament, which elects an executive leader. They did this on grounds that the executive should not be beholden to the legislature. The Electoral College was thus the Founding Fathers' way of ensuring the separation of powers so essential to a republic.

Of course, as in the case of a parliament in which a leader is chosen by the members of that parliament, it can rarely occur that a majority of members can be elected to choose a leader, which does not correlate with a hypothetical popular vote. In fact, this occurred in 1974 when the Labour Party in Great Britain lost the irrelevant popular vote but nevertheless won more seats in Parliament (the UK version of our Electoral College) and thus formed the government. As far as can be determined, there were no challenges to the legitimacy of the leader so chosen by Parliament, appeals to the United Nations, or demands that the United Kingdom's entire parliamentary system that evolved over 1,000 years and provided a model for parliamentary democracies around the world should be dismantled.

Legitimacy and certainty in presidential elections are discussed in Chapter 8, but such claims about legitimacy often remind me of claims in the sports world that a particular football team's win is not legitimate if it didn't accrue the most yardage even while piling up the most points.

Preface xv

Because the NPVIC is based on using the creation of a cabal to impose a direct election on the American people, the first four chapters are directed toward reviewing the weaknesses of that system. The remaining chapters consider the added problems and anomalies of attempting by cabal to impose that system on top of an Electoral College structure.

The content of this book has been organized in such a way to accommodate those who may not have time to read the book from cover to cover. For those, Chapter 1 may serve as a brief summary of all the major points addressed in the book. The remaining chapters address in detail a particular feature or issue related to the NPVIC. Because some of the points, historical examples, and references may be relevant in a variety of different contexts, some of these references and historical examples may be repeated in separate chapters.

For those interested in the history of past threats to our federal system of government, Chapter 11 briefly reviews those threats. Because that history has not changed since the publication of my *The Electoral College and the Constitution,* this chapter is adapted from that previous publication, including verbatim passages, as is Chapter 12, which sets forth recommendations for sound but modest housekeeping amendments to the Electoral College system that would not undermine the federalist vision of the Founding Fathers.

Acknowledgments

I wish to thank my dedicated student assistants at the University of Denver Sturm College of Law. Without their research, this book would not have been possible. Adam Cribari, Lukas Dregne, Haylee Knight, Elizabeth Partlow, Sarah Quigley, Judy Trejos, Joseph Stark, and Laura Yeager all worked many hours compiling research, finding sources, editing, and contributing to this book—both written and in lively discussion. I also thank Judy Trejos for her valuable editing assistance. However, the opinions and conclusions expressed in the text do not necessarily reflect those of my assistants, and any errors are mine alone.

I would also like to thank my hard-working secretaries, Sarah Brunswick and Nick Williams, at the University of Denver Sturm College of Law who spent countless hours incorporating the work feedback from my student assistants into this book. Each of them went above and beyond their responsibilities to help this book come to fruition.

Additionally, I would like to thank Dean Bruce Smith of the University of Denver Sturm College of Law. Without the financial support of the University of Denver Sturm College of Law, this book would not have been possible.

CHAPTER ONE

Introduction
John F. Kennedy's Vision of Federalism

> Direct election would break down the federal system under which most states entered the union, which provides a system of checks and balances to insure that no area or group shall obtain too much power.
>
> —John F. Kennedy

It is a rare presidential election that does not trigger demands by the losing party to abolish the Electoral College, particularly when the loser in the Electoral College wins the hypothetical popular vote as calculated by various media outlets. Since 1789, this has happened in 4 out of 56 presidential elections—in 1888, 1960,[1] 2000, and 2016. After the 1960 election, for example, when the *New York Times* and the Congressional Quarterly announced that Richard Nixon had won the popular vote despite losing in the Electoral College to John F. Kennedy,[2] it was outraged Republicans who felt cheated by the Electoral College and demanded the abolition of it. In 2016, it was outraged Democrats who felt that they had been so cheated.

Since the 1789 election of George Washington by the Electoral College, there have been between 500 and 700 serious proposals to abolish the Electoral College—depending on how one defines "serious."[3] (In 1808, U.S. senator James Hillhouse proposed that retiring senators choose a president by drawing colored balls from a box.)

One of the first proposals to abolish the Electoral College came in the final hot days of the 1787 Constitutional Convention itself. The bedraggled, tired, and very hot delegates had left to the end of the deliberations the contentious question of how states would be represented in any proposed national legislature. Small states feared that delegates from such large states as New York and Pennsylvania would try to bully them into giving up the right of equal representation in the Senate that they had enjoyed under the Articles of Confederation. Rhode Island refused to send any delegates at all, and tiny Delaware only sent delegates with letters making it clear that they were to walk out and form their own country the moment any big-state bullies suggested that they give up their right to equal representation in any new proposed legislature or in the election of a president.

By this time, it was generally conceded that there was very little hope of uniting all the 13 colonies into one cohesive union. Even an exasperated George Washington, who had only reluctantly agreed to moderate the convention in the first place, thought there was little chance of forming a single united country and a cohesive union and "despaired of seeing a favorable issue to the proceedings of the convention and do therefore repent having had any agency in this business."[4] The larger states had already hedged their bets and formed their own amalgamations or incipient nations and even imposed tariffs and customs barriers and boundaries on their neighboring states.[5] The smaller states were also contemplating going their own way and thus were not inclined to be marginalized in a union dominated by arrogant big-state bullies. In this contentious environment, small-state delegates such as Gunning Bedford were announcing that they would instead form their confederations and amalgamations with foreign powers and "find some ally of better honor and good faith who will take them by the hand and do them justice."[6] Much to the glee of King George III, the 13 colonies were breaking apart, leading the royal adviser to advise his king that the desperate former colonists would very soon "openly concert measures for entering into something like their former connections to Great Britain."[7]

As delegate Luther Martin later recalled, "We were on the verge of dissolution, scarce held together by a hair."[8] It was only now that realistic delegates, including the large state delegates, began to realize that the only way *all of the colonies*—especially the smaller ones—could ever be induced to join a common union was if they were offered equal representation in one of two houses of a national legislature (the Senate) as well as concomitant weight in presidential elections that reflected that equal representation in the Senate.

Introduction

Like the advocates of Russian-style direct election today, big-state bullies at the convention—particularly Rufus King—resisted any such concession to the small states. As feared by the smaller states, he demanded that representation in the national legislature as well as the concomitant though modest extra weight that equal representation gave to small states in presidential elections be based on population alone.

In retrospect, it can now be fairly said that the bellowing of Rufus King and a few other big-state delegates stands as the very first attempt in American history to abolish—in the cradle—the entire federalist concept ingrained in what we now call the Electoral College. Had it succeeded, there can be little doubt that the North American continent would now consist of as many separate nation-states as now exist in South America.

Fortunately for the united republic under which Americans today are privileged to thrive in a manner unknown to much of the rest of the world, Rufus King's bellowing proposal for a direct election based on a national popular vote, while duly considered by all the delegates, was never adopted by the Constitutional Convention of 1787. Instead, just as hope for a truly united republic seemed most forlorn, the Founding Fathers agreed to a Grand Compromise that would bind all the colonies scarce held together by a hair into an indivisible United States of America. The two great prongs of this Grand Compromise are now reflected in the two most important federalist principles in the U.S. Constitution:

Article I, Section 3, which establishes a Senate composed of "two Senators from each state" regardless of population; and

Article II, Section 1, Clause 2, which allocates to each state a number of electors, to be appointed in "such manner as the Legislature thereof may direct, equal to the whole number of Senators and Representatives to which the state may be entitled in the Congress."

The latter provision thus enshrines the federalist principle that *the two senators each states is allocated, regardless of population within that state, shall be reflected in the weight which each such state shall be given in the presidential election process.* It does so by giving every state a minimum of three electoral votes: one based on representation in the House regardless of population and two additional electoral votes based on the two senators to which each state was entitled regardless of population.

It is fashionable today among some men and women on the street to take for granted that Americans today live in a united country and that the federalist institutions created by the Framers in order to *form* that union— the Senate and the Electoral College—are now anachronistic. Citing the mantra of *Every Vote Equal,* they demand the abolition of not only the U.S. Senate but also the Electoral College, which allocates presidential voting weight based upon equal state suffrage in the Senate. Unfortunately, pollsters who claim to find popular support for such demands rarely mention to the people polled that Article V of the Constitution *guarantees* to each state in the union that no such amendment can ever be enacted without the *unanimous agreement of every state in the union.* The wording of the last sentence in Article V is quite clear: "*[N]o state without its consent shall be deprived of its equal suffrage in the Senate.*" Article II is also equally clear that the weight given to each state in the presidential election process shall in turn be based on the number of electors "equal to the whole number of Senators and Representatives to which the state may be entitled in the Congress." Without this guarantee that no state without its consent would *ever* be deprived of that equal suffrage in the Senate, which provides the basis for every state's weight in the presidential election process, the United States of America would simply never have been created. Article II therefore remains the *only* provision in the Constitution that cannot be amended by the regular constitutional amendment process (which requires approval of only two-thirds of Congress and three-quarters of the states).

To be sure, this extra weight granted to the smaller states is modest, but it is also both clear and constitutionally sacrosanct: a state with a small population base, such as Delaware or Wyoming, is entitled to *the same two extra presidential electors* based on equal suffrage in the Senate as such large-population states as California or New York. It was precisely this constitutional dimension to which John F. Kennedy was referring in his famous defense of the Electoral College when he noted that "direct election would break down the federal system under which most states entered the union."[9]

The federal system of which Kennedy spoke is of course the Electoral College, which is the presidential election formula based on the Grand Compromise. Without the one state, one vote concession made to the small states at the Constitutional Convention, there would have been no Constitution and no United States of America. Instead, as George Washington feared and George III hoped, there would have been in its stead various amalgamations, alliances, rump nations, and, most probable of all, a return of at least some of the states to the embrace of the king of England. Difficult as it is today to imagine such an outcome had the bellowing demands by Rufus King for a direct election been heeded, one has only to look upon the creation of numerous nation-states in South America to realize how close the North American continent came to a similar conglomeration of separate nation-states.

Introduction 5

Like so many constitutional scholars, John Kennedy understood clearly the intricate connection between the Article I provision providing for equal state suffrage in the Senate, the Article II allocation of two electors to each state based on such equal suffrage, and, not least, the Article V guarantee to every state of equal suffrage, which is in turn reflected in the Article II allocation of electors.

Democracy and Federalism

While it is true that the Founding Fathers' concession to the small states of equal suffrage in the Senate and modest extra voting power in presidential elections achieved the herculean task of uniting 13 contentious colonies into one federalist union, it would be unfair to suggest that this was the Framers' only reason for creating both the Senate and its sister institution of the Electoral College. Equally important was the Framers' vision of successful self-government. Implicit in the allocation to states of electoral votes based on equal suffrage was the notion that no government of a large continental landmass could long survive if support for its leaders could be concentrated in just one *region* of the country. John F. Kennedy's observation that the "Electoral College provides a system of checks and balances to insure that no *area* . . . shall obtain too much power" reflects this vision.

A simple hypothetical illustrates. Imagine that in 1950s America there was no Electoral College and that presidential elections were conducted under a Russian-style direct election based on a national popular vote. A staunch segregationist presidential candidate might be able to win such a national election by winning an overwhelming majority of the popular votes in a single region (say, in the South)—despite being opposed by majorities in all other regions of the country. Under the Electoral College, by contrast, a successful presidential candidate must secure *broad* support across several regions, not just *deep* support in a single region.

The Framers' vision also reflects a fundamental understanding of how multiple candidates and parties can best be whittled down to one candidate who can achieve the support of a majority or substantial plurality of voters. One of the least successful systems for achieving such a democratic result has been shown to be the so-called direct election. The Russian election of 1993 revealed the undemocratic consequences of such a system. In that election, dozens of parties put forth candidates. The fascist-oriented candidate Vladimir Zhirinovsky received 23 percent of the vote, while the Stalinist Communist Party candidate received 11 percent. Had the more moderate People's Choice party not narrowly edged out the

Stalinist party candidate by 2 percent, the hapless Russian voters would have been faced with the choice in a runoff of either a Stalinist or a hard-core fascist—despite the fact that *two-thirds of the electorate strongly opposed both of these candidates.*

The 2017 French election also revealed the democratic hazards of such national popular vote elections: the two major mainstream party candidates received 19 percent each, while two maverick candidates, Emmanuel Macron and the hard right-wing party of Marine Le Pen won 23 percent and 21 percent, respectively. In the ensuing runoff, hapless French voters were presented with a bizarre choice between a political upstart and a hard-right candidate. Enraged French voters expressed their outrage with such a Russian-style direct election system by casting over 600,000 *ballot blancs* (blank ballots).

American apologists for such Russian-style election systems claim that in an American direct presidential election such undemocratic outcomes might not occur because we have a two-party system, and thus we would not be plagued with such undemocratic outcomes in which a candidate opposed by two-thirds of the electorate is elected. The irony of such a defense of Russian-style elections is that it is the *Electoral College system itself that created the very two-party system that the apologists seek to destroy.* Party candidates with little broad national support soon come face-to-face with Article II's constitutional requirement that a candidate must first receive a plurality of popular votes in any state before receiving any electoral votes. This gives such minor party candidates an incentive to seek compromise with a major party, often seeking and obtaining concessions in return for support. This process was played out several months before the 1932 presidential election. Polls showed socialist candidate Norman Thomas enjoying support from 7 percent of the electorate. As election day drew closer, however, Thomas gained platform concessions from the Democratic Party in return for support. By election day, support for Thomas was down to less than 1 percent. Under a Russian-style direct election, Thomas and numerous other parties would have so split the national vote that even with a runoff, a candidate could have won despite being opposed by a majority of the electorate. In other words, the Electoral College does a far better job of winnowing the field than arbitrary runoffs. As one witness testified at the 1977 Birch Bayh Senate hearings in response to a question as to why a direct election would undermine democracy,

> There is no reason under your proposed [direct election] system . . . why [a large percentage of votes would not be garnered] by 15 or 20 parties. I can name 4 or 5 of them: Wallacites, Henry and George; McCarthyites, Eugene

Introduction 7

and Joseph; socialists, Trotskyites, Communists, black militants, green militants, purple militants. . . . It's not hard to create the French Chamber of Deputies in a multiparty system. We've seen it happen everywhere. It can be done by fiddling with the constitutional structure that undergirds and constrains and channels the two party system. . . . Every minority party would have no reason for the chastening constraint of the need to win in the first election. . . . We would simply create a multiparty system.[10]

In the end, the prospect of endless runoffs and recounts in every state, the creation of an unstable multiparty system, and, not least, the undemocratic consequences of what would inevitably follow "fiddling with the constitutional structure" so appalled the Birch Bayh Senate committee that had begun on such a high notion of national popular vote that it mercifully let die the proposed bill to abolish the Electoral College.

It should also be noted that the two-party system is not enshrined in the Constitution. Indeed, the Electoral College allows flexibility and adaptability in the forming and creation of major parties—witness the demise of the Federalist Party and the replacement of the Whig Party by the Republican Party of Abraham Lincoln. As recently as 1992, polls taken just several months before the presidential election showed that Ross Perot would have received 33 percent of the vote, the Republican Bush would have received 28 percent, and the Democrat Clinton would have received just 24 percent. Had it not been for the Electoral College, which effectively channeled support for Perot to the two other major parties, a direct election system might have engendered the same outrage as the 2017 French presidential election.

The breakdown of a two-party system that ensures that a winner achieve a majority or substantial plurality of votes would be further complicated by a national recount—particularly when no federal legislation exists for preempting all state recount laws. One of the great benefits of the Electoral College is that even in the rare election where the electoral count is close, recounts are isolated to a single state (as in Florida in the 2000 election). Even in the unlikely event that if a federal law could be constitutionally constructed to strike down all state recount laws, such a national recount would require recounts in all 50 states. Court cases and extensive appeals would inevitably follow.

If Americans were traumatized and allies were alarmed at the chaotic spectacle of the seemingly endless recounts, court dramas, and appeals in Florida in the aftermath of the 2000 election, one can only imagine the damage that would have occurred to the body politic had that trauma and uncertainty been magnified by a factor of 50.

In the 1960 presidential election in which the popular vote was so close that even the newspapers and the Congressional Quarterly could not agree on who won the popular vote, the trauma of 50 different state recounts and appeals was averted only by the fact that the Electoral College gave John Kennedy a comfortable margin in the Electoral College. This rendered moot any difference of opinion as to how the national popular vote should be tabulated.

Once these constitutional parameters and federalist foundations of the Electoral College have been noted and understood by those who are wont to rewrite the Constitution, it can be more easily understood why the Framers' vision of perpetual union and federalism as represented by the Electoral College has held up over the past two and a quarter centuries. It has done so in the face of hundreds of political assaults and partisan attempts to undermine it by various machinations and schemes (see Chapter 11). An example of the latter has understandably come in the form not of a proposed constitutional amendment—which for the reasons already noted has consistently been defeated in the halls of Congress, and for good reason—but rather a scheme that purports to undermine the Framers' federalist vision by means of an interstate cabal. It is in response to that scheme that this book is written.

The National Popular Vote Interstate Compact

No doubt frustrated by the constitutional obstacles which the Founding Fathers created in order to preserve states' equal suffrage in the Senate and the modest extra weight thereby granted to the small states in presidential elections in order to induce them to join the union, partisan advocates and self-appointed "reformers" have long sought an alternative means of undermining the Framers' vision by looking for ways to circumvent the constitutional amendment process entirely.

On February 23, 2006, an advocacy group calling itself National Popular Vote! held a press conference in Washington, D.C., to present the first edition of their National Popular Vote Interstate Compact (NPVIC)[11] manifesto titled *Every Vote Equal: A State-Based Plan for Electing the President by National Popular Vote*. Financially backed by a California millionaire named John Koza, by 2012 this group had successfully lobbied for adoption of the NPVIC in state legislatures representing close to half the electoral votes required to elect the president. It now stands as the greatest threat to the federalist structure of the U.S. Constitution since the Birch Bayh Senate hearings of 1979.

Introduction 9

Impressive as this manifesto publication is in terms of sheer weight—its fourth edition comes to 1,059 pages—the content consists of an unorganized assortment of repetitive partisan and political rants accompanied by voluminous charts and graphs purporting to justify its transparent agenda of imposing a Russian-style direct election on the United States. The manifesto proposes to do so in an indirect way by bypassing not only the people's representatives in the U.S. Congress but also states. Most of its invective, however, is in fact directed toward the unit-rule electoral allocation system employed by all states except Nebraska and Maine. The unit rule is a legislative choice made by each state individually to allocate all its electoral votes to the candidate who gets the most votes in that state. Very little of its content is directed toward the constitutional problems associated with its ultimate agenda.

Ironically, had the NPVIC merely sought by means of interstate compact to obligate signatory states to abandon the unit vote, it could have achieved its purported goals without undermining the federalist and democratic foundations of the Electoral College. Instead, the NPVIC seeks to deprive nonsignatory states of the weight given to them under Article II of the Constitution by rendering irrelevant their voting weight in the Electoral College.

The text of the NPVIC is set forth in its entirety in Appendix A and is discussed in detail in Chapter 5; however, stripped to its essence, the NPVIC may be summarized as follows:

Each state that signs on to the NPVIC forms a cabal with as few as 11 other states representing 270 electoral votes under which it binds the legislatures of each signatory state to refuse to cast its electoral votes in accordance with an elector slate elected by the popular vote of that state if that state's popular vote somehow differs from a so-called total national popular vote. Instead, the signatory legislature appoints an unnamed entity to tally the popular votes for electors as reported by chief election officials of all the states, including nonsignatory states, and then send to the Electoral College an electoral slate associated with that national popular vote tally. Amazingly, it also provides that popular votes cast in other states for unpledged electors are to be totally ignored, thus leaving disenfranchised any voters who so cast their votes.[12]

An example illustrates how signatory states of this cabal might act in an actual presidential election. Assume that in a hypothetical election between, say, Obama and Trump, an overwhelming majority of California voters cast their ballots for Obama, but certain unnamed chief election officers of *other* states proclaim that the so-called popular votes for Trump electors in all the states slightly exceeded those cast for Obama electors. Under the terms of the NPVIC cabal, the California legislature would be obligated under the terms of the cabal to defy the will of the people of California and instead cast its electoral votes for Trump, thereby giving him the election. If California voters become enraged at what they perceive as their disenfranchisement and demand that California withdraw from the cabal and cast its electoral votes in accordance with the will of the people of California, NPVIC lawyers would doubtless claim that the California legislature is forbidden to do so by the terms of the NPVIC and file injunctions to enforce it—despite the fact that Article II of the Constitution gives to every state the power to allocate its electoral votes as it sees fit without limitation or restriction other than doing so in accordance with the due process and equal protection clauses of the Fifth and Fourteenth Amendments.[13]

If both the summary and example seem confusing, it highlights why the chapters that follow are necessary to unravel in detail how supporters of the NPVIC hope that it would work to undermine and circumvent the constitutional system for presidential elections. For purposes of this introduction, only a few brief points are here noted:

1. The very premise of the NPVIC is clear from the title of its manifesto, *Every Vote Equal*. This title both acknowledges and implies the *intricate* connection between the Constitution's guarantee to the states of equal suffrage in the Senate and the weight that equal suffrage in the Senate gives to the states in presidential elections. In other words, the title of the NPVIC's manifesto *Every Vote Equal* suggests an agenda that requires *at a minimum* the abolition of the U.S. Senate. This is because it is the equal suffrage of each state in the Senate that on its face violates the principle of every vote equal. (This is why voters in Wyoming, which has two senators, carry far greater weight in both the Senate and the Electoral College than voters in California, which has a far greater population.) It will be recalled that Article II grants to each state two presidential electors based on the number of its senators. It is for that reason that supporters of Ralph Nader in the 2000 election advocated for abolition of the U.S. Senate and why current reformers and politicians today demand abolition of the U.S. Senate along with the sister institution to which it is connected, the Electoral College. Presumably, would-be reformers such as Alexandra Ocasio-Cortez who advocate abolition of the Electoral College understand that abolishing it would of necessity mean abolishing the U.S. Senate. This is because the modest extra weight accorded to some states in the Electoral College is based on its equal suffrage in the Senate.[14]

2. Under the NPVIC, a cabal of at least 11 states, but consisting of at least enough states to represent 270 electoral votes, could render the electoral votes of nonsignatory states—along with their modest extra weight in the

Introduction 11

Electoral College guaranteed to them in Article II—completely moot and irrelevant. In fact, once the unnamed entity empowered by the NPVIC to conduct a tally of the popular votes in all the states as recorded by chief election officials, there would be no reason for electors from nonsignatory states to meet at all. As a consequence, the smaller states would be effectively deprived of all the modest extra weight in the Electoral College guaranteed to them by Article I, Article II, and Article V.

3. For the same reason that abolishing the U.S. Senate would require unanimous agreement of all the states in accordance with Article V, the NPVIC would also require unanimous agreement of all the states inasmuch as it purports to deprive nonsignatory states of the modest extra weight guaranteed to them in the Electoral College. It does so by excluding them from the electoral process entirely by rendering *irrelevant all their electoral votes,* including their electoral votes based on equal suffrage in the Senate. The NPVIC does so by casting its own electoral votes as one unit in the manner of a cartel in direct violation of the compact clause of the Constitution.[15] According to the Supreme Court decision in *U.S. Steel v. Multistate Tax Commission,*[16] states are strictly forbidden to create compacts, agreements, or cabals that give a compact member political power it could not exercise but for the compact—in this case determining in advance what system shall be employed to elect a president as well as restricting the signatory states of their right to allocate electoral votes in any way they wish. (See Chapter 10 below for a full discussion.)

4. Whatever the merits of a constitutional amendment to abolish the equal suffrage of the states in the Senate (along with the extra weight accorded to small states based on the equal suffrage), it cannot be done by attempting to fit a round peg (the NPVIC scheme) into a very square hole (the Electoral College). If a Russian-style direct election is to be imposed on the American people, it must be done by constitutional amendment and ratified by every state in accordance with Article V.

5. The entity on which the NPVIC purports to rely to recount the national popular vote is apparently the media. This is apparently based on the expectation (or hope) of NPVIC supporters that if the NPVIC was ever actually adopted by states representing 270 electoral votes, Congress might be tempted not only to overthrow the recounts laws of all 50 states by preemptive federal legislation but also establish a national entity or institution charged with conducting a recount in all 50 states. This is surely putting the cart before the horse: any law purporting to overthrow every state's current recount laws must be passed before any state considers throwing its electoral votes to a candidate who failed to win the popular vote in its state.

6. Weak as the undemocratic Russian-style direct voting systems are in producing a winner supported by a majority of voters (witness the Russian and recent French elections), that weakness becomes even more extreme and

undemocratic if there is no provision for a runoff between at least the top two vote getters. The NPVIC cannot even provide for such a runoff, since it is based on the Electoral College structure—and of course there is no provision for a runoff in the Electoral College. (Under the U.S. Constitution, Article II, Section 3, any candidate who fails to achieve a majority of electoral votes in the presidential election is thrown into the House of Representatives.) At least under a Russian-style direct election the chances are that a winning candidate might receive the support of as much as a third of the electorate (as in the 2017 French presidential election). Without a runoff provision, however, there would be nothing to prevent a candidate from winning with as little as 10 percent of the one and final vote. This would be particularly likely when the abolition of the Electoral College inevitably leads to the kind of multiparty system that plagues such countries as Russia and France. Even in parliamentary systems such as exist in the United Kingdom, the parliament performs the same function as the Electoral College does under the American constitutional system. Just as American electors elect the president, the winning party in parliamentary elections chooses the prime minister. The only difference between the UK Parliament and the American Electoral College is that the constitutional Framers wanted to bifurcate the responsibilities of a parliament by giving to Congress the power to enact legislation and giving the Electoral College the power to elect the president. They did so in the interest of separation of powers so as to not leave the president beholden to the legislature. Occasionally a party in the United Kingdom wins a majority of seats in Parliament even while losing the national popular vote for that party. That occurred in 1974 when the Labour Party lost the national popular vote but nevertheless won a majority of parliamentary seats, enabling it to elect the prime minister. Occasionally this occurs as well in the Electoral College, as it has done four times in the last two and a quarter centuries. However, in both the United Kingdom and the United States, this has not been considered a cause to abandon a democratic system in favor of a Russian-style direct election that inevitably creates a multiparty system leading to the election of leaders opposed by a majority of the electorate.

Nevertheless, both the American Electoral College and the UK "electoral college" (Parliament) channel political support in a way that spares their respective countries the undemocratic features and dangers of a Russian or French multiparty system. The Electoral College has done a somewhat better job of this, generally featuring two major parties, while the UK parliamentary system often has to cope with three or even four. This sometimes requires UK parties to form unstable, unwieldy, and often temporary coalitions in order to govern—an outcome that the Electoral College happily spares the United States. Under the American constitutional system,

Introduction 13

such accommodation of minor parties generally takes place *before* the election rather than after—as was the case when the Democratic Party accommodated some features of the socialist platform prior to the 1932 and 1936 presidential elections.

The NPVIC under the Radar of Public Scrutiny

The seductively titled national popular vote banner of the NPVIC sounds enticingly democratic. When scrutinized, however, its undemocratic foundations are revealed. This is why it has been so roundly rejected once those implications and ramifications are understood. This occurred on March 3, 2007, when well-paid NPVIC lobbyists attempted to push the NPVIC through the Colorado legislature. Having breezed through the upper Senate chamber, under the public radar and without scrutiny, the NPVIC finally faced scrutiny in a House committee. Enjoying 10–1 support going into committee, it was finally met with the opposition of both this author and Professor Jim Riley, professor of Politics at Regis University. At the House committee hearing, both this author and Professor Riley were asked to compress the arguments and points set forth in this book into but 15 minutes of testimony each. The result was a dramatic reversal of the support the NPVIC had enjoyed going into the committee. Appalled by both the constitutional issues exposed and the intractable recount problems of the NPVIC, the actual final vote in committee was a resounding 10–1 *against* the NPVIC bill. Only the lone vote of the bill's actual sponsor kept the rejection from being unanimous.

Unfortunately, however, neither this author nor Professor Riley have the resources to attend legislative committee hearings in every state house in the country to oppose the NPVIC and set forth the points made in this book. Without financial support, this has left but a relative handful of committed constitutional lawyers[17] and political scientists to oppose a vast army of well-financed lobbyists attempting to relentlessly push through the NPVIC in enough legislatures to form a cabal of states representing 270 electoral votes.

In the chapters that follow, readers can enjoy the luxury of reading in detail the points and arguments set forth only briefly in this introduction. Chapter 2 relates the political and historical background that led to the creation of the Electoral College. Chapter 3 outlines the Grand Compromise at the Constitutional Convention that created the Electoral College as the foundation of the United States of America. Chapter 4 addresses the direct election illusion that underpins much of the misunderstanding of how the Electoral College actually works. Chapter 5 reviews and analyzes the NPVIC. Chapter 6 reviews the history of the unit vote that pervades so many of the current issues relating to the Electoral College. Chapter 7 addresses the way in which the Electoral College affects how presidential candidates' campaigns are conducted and how that differs from how campaigns would be conducted under the NPVIC. Chapter 8 addresses how the Electoral College differs from the NPVIC in the degree to which each provides certainty and legitimacy to presidential elections. Chapter 9 addresses the recount problem that would arise under the NPVIC. Chapter 10 responds to the many myths that have been created over the years about the Electoral College. Chapter 11 reviews the hundreds of attempts made since 1789 to undermine the federalist foundations of the Electoral College and why they have failed so abysmally; and finally, Chapter 12 submits conclusions and recommendations about how the Electoral College could be adapted to modern America without destroying the federalist and democratic foundations upon which it is based.

CHAPTER TWO

The Solar System of Government Power

> [W]e are talking about . . . a whole solar system of government power. If it is proposed to change the balance of power of one of the elements of the solar system, it is necessary to consider the others.
> —John F. Kennedy[1]

Perhaps no institution of the U.S. government is more misunderstood or maligned than the Electoral College. And yet it is this one venerable institution, enshrined in Article II of the U.S. Constitution, that is responsible more than any other for the success of the United States, the freedoms its citizens enjoy, its stable institutions of government, and its prosperity. Over the course of history, the American people have become accustomed to and expect the orderly transition of power that has made America the envy of the world. It is taken for granted that on election night as Americans turn on their televisions to watch the returns, as the clock strikes midnight a new president will have been chosen, and the country can return to its normal life.

There have been exceptions to these peaceful transitions, of course, the major one occurring in 1860 when the southern states refused to accept the Electoral College's clear-cut choice of Abraham Lincoln as president. A lesser exception, but still a dangerous one at the time, came during the presidential election of 1876, when massive vote fraud and intimidation of African Americans at the polls in several southern states threatened a second civil war. In the end it took a controversial bipartisan commission to select a president.

Since that time America has been largely free of the kind of succession traumas that have brought down so many civilizations of the past. Even in the election of 1960, when the popular vote was so close that by estimate a national recount across the entire nation would have taken many months if not years to conduct and weave its way through the courts of 50 separate states, Americans were mercifully spared such a succession crisis by a decisive 303–216 margin for John F. Kennedy in the Electoral College. Most Americans didn't even notice, because despite the razor-thin margin in the popular vote (which would have triggered a national recount under a Russian-style popular vote system), Richard Nixon didn't bother to challenge the result or even demand a recount since the electoral vote was so decisive. In the very rare election in which the Electoral College vote has itself been close—as in the 2000 election—the recounts and court cases were isolated to a single state, thus sparing the nation a succession trauma that would have been 50 times as great if such recounts had to be conducted in over 174,252 precincts in all 50 states of the United States.[2]

So why, with such a track record of success for the Founding Fathers' vision for the selection of a president to head the executive branch of government, does every election reignite calls for reform? Part of the answer lies in the demagogic predilections of some in the popular media to characterize popularly elected electors as walking anachronisms. A Herblock cartoon in the *Washington Post* depicted an elector as "an old fuddy-duddy in colonial knee britches and powdered wig with an ear to a trumpet, saying 'don't expect me to get this right, bub.'"[3] Some journalists, with little or no analysis of the history, background, or constitutional structure of the Electoral College have called it "an archaic ritual."[4] A hastily assembled "commission" has derided it as "archaic, undemocratic, complex, ambiguous, indirect, and dangerous."[5] It is none of these. Even the Founding Fathers have not been spared journalists' vilification, being called elitist and "undemocratic" thinkers.[6] Meanwhile, pollsters purport to confirm that an overwhelming percentage of Americans want to abolish the Electoral College by asking such questions as should the president be elected by the popular vote of all Americans? A 2012 manifesto titled *Every Vote Equal,* in support of the National Popular Vote Interstate Compact (NPVIC), claims that a 2007 national poll "showed that 72%" of Americans supported a scheme to establish a national popular vote,[7] even if it meant evading the inconvenient process of passing a constitutional amendment.

With such overwhelming public support for a Russian-style[8] nationwide popular vote, one might fairly ask why a constitutional amendment abolishing the college is not currently being adopted. It might also be asked why every single one of these constitutional amendment proposals submitted in the past 200 years has failed miserably. Is it because the majority of members of Congress since 1791 have been incorrigibly and horribly corrupt or self-serving? Hardly. The simple answer is that while the simplistic phrase national popular vote may be seductively alluring—especially to the man or woman in the street—when congressional representatives from both sides of the aisle have closely and rationally considered abolition of the Electoral College, in the end they have always concluded that its implementation would undermine the very federalist and democratic foundations of our constitutional system.

Today, those who have been frustrated by the lack of success in promulgating a constitutional amendment have been attracted to a plan that promises to evade the constitutional amendment process. It has done this by proposing that states form a cabal to enter into a compact to evade the intent and purpose of the constitutional plan for conducting presidential elections by binding signatory states to ignore the popular vote of the people within their respective states and instead send a slate of electors pledged to the candidate whose electors in all the states have received what various newspapers tally as a nationwide national popular vote. This is the NPVIC scheme currently being submitted to state legislatures around the country.

Supporters of this latter scheme inevitably assume that such a nationwide tally can be accomplished by an unnamed entity who simply conducts a tally of votes across the country for a particular candidate's electors as released by the chief election officer in each state, procure an adding machine, and then *unofficially* add them up. If only it were that simple. Unfortunately, such an assumption betrays a basic misunderstanding of how the Electoral College system actually works. For example, in the 1960 election, the voters of Alabama elected a Democratic slate consisting of five electors pledged to Kennedy and six unpledged electors who ultimately cast their electoral votes for Senator Harry Byrd of West Virginia. Since voters in Alabama could vote for unpledged electors on the Democratic slate, the newspapers' unofficial national popular vote count differed from that calculated by the Congressional Quarterly. Some newspapers, which later committed to the narrative that Kennedy had won the popular vote, decided to include in their national popular vote count *all* the votes cast for electors on the Alabama Democratic slate, which included votes cast for the unpledged electors who later voted for Senator Byrd in the Electoral College. Other newspapers and the Congressional Quarterly (the institution that most closely resembled a national official vote-counting body) begged to differ, reasonably concluding that only five-elevenths of the votes cast for the electors on the Democratic slate should be allocated to Kennedy. This difference in counting popular votes resulted in the Congressional Quarterly concluding that Nixon had won the (irrelevant) national popular vote.

One of the many problems with the NPVIC plan, discussed in more detail in later chapters, is that it does not provide for an official national body that would have the authority to conduct a conclusive tally for the national popular vote. Absent such a body, any close presidential election conducted under the NPVIC plan would inevitably result in being decided by the courts rather than by the American people.

Because the NPVIC approach necessarily depends upon the efficacy of a national popular vote plan, it is necessary to consider, first, the efficacy of a national popular vote election under the Constitution and, second, the NPVIC plan for achieving that result without going through the inconvenient process of amending the Constitution.

Constitutional Origins of the Electoral College

During the five years following America's independence from Great Britain, it appeared that the colonies were dissolving into what George Washington sadly described as "thirteen sovereignties pulling against each other."[9] A weak Confederation Congress operating under the Articles of Confederation billed itself as a "firm league of friendship"[10] under which each state would retain its own sovereignty and independence. Like the Holy Roman Empire, which Voltaire noted was "neither holy, Roman, nor an empire," the Articles of Confederation was neither a league, nor firm, nor very friendly.[11] States began to set up protective and retaliatory tariffs against each other, while others attempted to form separate amalgamations and confederations. Maryland invited Virginia, Pennsylvania, and Delaware to form an alliance to protect it from other states, and four states south of Virginia began negotiating to set up a four-state nation as a counterweight. America was breaking apart, and trade and commerce came almost to a halt. These developments led a royal adviser to King George III to gloat that within months the economy in America would surely collapse and that the desperate former colonists would "openly concert measures for entering into something like their former connections to Great Britain."[12]

Alarmed by America's impending breakup, economic collapse, and not least the whispers in some quarters of some states seeking to reestablish political connections to Great Britain, James Madison and Alexander

The Solar System of Government Power   19

Hamilton arranged for a rump meeting of 12 bedraggled delegates at George Mann's Tavern in Annapolis, Maryland, in August 1786 to discuss matters pertaining to trade and commerce among the states. Although all 13 states had been invited to send representatives, only 5 states bothered to send anyone. When it became obvious that little if anything of consequence could be decided with so few states represented, all but Hamilton and Madison consumed their mugs of ale and prepared to go home.

It was at this most pivotal moment in American history that Alexander Hamilton, probably with mug in hand, leaped on a table and in a booming voice quoted from a parenthesis in the written instructions to the New Jersey delegate to the effect that he was authorized not only to discuss matters of trade but also "other important matters." As historians have since noted, "Never has a parenthesis in a state paper served a grander historic end."[13]

As the retreating delegates came back to down a final mug, Madison relinquished the floor completely to Hamilton. The delegates to this Annapolis Convention unanimously issued its proclamation that

> [A] convention of all the states be held at Philadelphia on the second Monday of May next, to take in consideration the situation in the United States, to devise such provisions as shall appear necessary to render the Constitution of the Federal government adequate to the exigencies of the Union, and to report such an act for the purpose of the United States [Confederation] Congress.[14]

The Two-Pronged Grand Compromise That Created a Nation

When on May 3, 1787, James Madison arrived in Philadelphia to find that not a single other delegate had yet arrived, he must have had an apprehension that this Constitutional Convention would fare no better than the ill-fated Annapolis Convention held the year before. By May 13 a few curious delegates had begun to arrive. To Madison's chagrin, however, even George Washington begged off attending, using the excuse that he had promised his revolutionary comrades in arms that he would attend their Society of Cincinnati Convocation, which had been scheduled at the same time. It was only after Madison's annoyingly persistent and repeated pleas that Washington finally relented and reluctantly agreed to attend Madison's so-called Constitutional Convention. Nevertheless, Washington's reluctance revealed that he was skeptical as to what if anything might be realistically achieved. (How Washington's comrades in arms took this last-minute snub is not recorded in the history books, but presumably they got over it.)

Washington's skepticism was well founded. For one thing, the Confederation Congress's commission to the convention made it clear that only very minor amendments or modifications to the Articles of Confederation would be authorized. Delegate John Lansing later asked, "Is it probable that the states will adopt and ratify a scheme which they have never authorized us to propose?"[15] And Hamilton's codelegate from New York, Robert Yates, had made it clear in advance that under no circumstances would his state agree to any amendment to the Articles of Confederation that would inhibit in any way his state's right to impose lucrative tariffs on any sister states transporting goods through New York. Rhode Island refused outright to send a single delegate to the convention, suspicious that the big states would seek to bully it and the other small states to give up the right of equal representation in Congress that they enjoyed in the Confederation Congress. (And Rhode Island was right.) At the last moment, Delaware reluctantly agreed to send a delegate to the convention, but only with signed and sealed credentials in hand that absolutely "forbade the delegate's participation in any attempt to change the 'one state, one vote' provision of the Articles of Confederation."[16] Along these same lines, the renowned patriot Patrick Henry, who though elected as a delegate outright, refused to attend, saying that "he smelt a rat." (Some historians might agree that like Rhode Island, he was right too.)

Thomas Jefferson had a convenient excuse for not attending, as he was serving as a minister to France and was not inclined to make the long sea trip back for such a dubious convocation that, in light of the small states' adamancy in preserving their right of equal representation, seemed to promise little more than an exercise in futility. John Adams, who as minister to London might have enjoyed a late spring sail back to Philadelphia to escape the constant abuse he was enduring in London, nevertheless declined to do so. And John Hancock, whose daring bold signature on the Declaration of Independence had inspired the American Revolution, conveniently begged off attending the convention on grounds of a sudden attack of gout.

Aside from Madison and Hamilton, few of the motley crew of drenched delegates who actually made it to the convention would be considered household names today, with the exception of Benjamin Franklin. Now 81, Franklin's performance at the convention has since been derided by historians as being "so feeble that his speeches were read by a close colleague; his ideas made no impression, though he was heard with respect due to his years of fame."[17] George Washington did finally agree to preside but rarely participated in debate except by frowns or grunts—though he

The Solar System of Government Power

did express his thought that any constitution that the convention might come up with was unlikely to last 20 years.

In the end, 19 delegates failed to appear at all, and average daily attendance never exceeded the 29 who convened on May 25. Apart from Franklin, it was a very young group of men: Jonathan Dayton of New Jersey was 26, Hamilton had just turned 30, and Madison was 34.

By late May, many of the basic principles of the Constitution, including the separation of powers into three branches of government, had been hammered out. But when the dreaded question arose as to how representatives to the legislative branch would be chosen, the outraged Delaware delegate warned that even the slightest suggestion by other delegates that the small states might lose their equal voting power in Congress would trigger his state's immediate departure from the convention. This was enough to table that troublesome question while the remaining elements of the Constitution were worked out, but the issue remained as a dark cloud over the entire proceedings during the weeks that followed.

By June 29, however, the issue of congressional representation could not be further avoided or tabled. As feared, the proposal by the delegates from the large states of New York and Pennsylvania that congressional representation be made on a principle of every vote equal and based on population rather than on the principle of one state, one vote triggered emotional outbursts not just from the small-state delegates but also from some of the other large state delegates who feared that such a departure from their commission would doom from the outset any constitution that they might devise.

A massive walkout now threatened, and as delegate Luther Martin later recalled, "We were on the verge of dissolution, scarce held together by a hair."[18] The convention now split into two warring factions, with delegate Morris declaring in exasperation that if a compromise could not somehow be worked out to unite the country, "the sword will. . . . The scene of horror attending civil commotion cannot be described."[19] Hugh Williamson of South Carolina warned that "if no compromise should take place, what will be the consequence? A secession, I foresee, will take place. It we do not come to some agreement among ourselves, some foreign sword will probably do the work for us."[20] It now appeared that the United States of America would die an ignominious death in the womb before it could even be born—and there seemed to be no prospect for a compromise that could save it. An exasperated George Washington now despaired of "seeing a favorable issue to the proceedings of the convention and do therefore repent having had any agency in this business."[21] If he had left at this point, what little prospect remained of an agreement on a constitution that would have united the country would have evaporated with his departure. The whole idea of a United States of America would be over.

As delegates from states both large and small now prepared to go home in failure, there still appeared little prospect of a compromise. The small-state delegates and their supporters from the large states remained adamant. John Rutledge bellowed that "the little states are fixed! They have repeatedly and solemnly declared themselves to be so! All that the larger states then have to do is to decide whether they will yield or not!"[22] A disgusted Gunning Bedford charged that the large states were seeking to have an "enormous and monstrous influence" and the "larger states proceed as if our eyes were already perfectly blinded. Impartiality with them is already out of the question."[23] Ominously, Bedford now threatened that if the large states persisted in taking away the "every state equal" rights, the small states "will find some foreign ally of more honor and good faith who will take them by the hand and do them justice."[24]

Nevertheless, most of the large-state delegates also remained intransigent. Like NPVIC advocates, who to this day persist in wanting to impose their "every vote equal"[25] demand, large-state delegate Rufus King raged that he was "filled with astonishment" that the small states would not be willing to sacrifice for the good of all the "phantom of state sovereignty!"[26] Hamilton even proposed mooting the entire issue by getting rid of states altogether and instead just drawing arbitrary provincial lines across the country from which representatives would be elected based on population alone.[27]

Even as the delegates prepared to leave the convention in despair, a last-minute compromise was proposed that was hoped just *might* unite the nation if both warring factions could agree. Why not accommodate both the large states *and* the small states? Why not split the proposed new Congress into *two* houses: a lower house—a "House of Representatives"—in which the big states would be allowed to predominate with their larger populations and an upper house to be called the "Senate" that would preserve the "every state equal" principle that the small states demanded? The fact that neither warring faction was entirely satisfied with this formula boded well for its ultimate adoption as a compromise, but the small states were still reluctant to sign on for two reasons.

First, they wanted the "every state equal" principle to be reflected in the executive branch as well as the in legislative branch of constitutional government. Thus, when it came to allocating the number of presidential electors to each state, they insisted that every state's allotment should be based not just on the number of representatives it was entitled to in the House but also on the number of senators to which each state was entitled

The Solar System of Government Power

in the Senate. Of course, this would also mean that the citizens of the smaller states would have a disproportionate influence on legislation in the Senate and would blatantly violate the "every vote equal" principle demanded by Rufus King—and today by advocates of the NPVIC.

Second, mindful of the amendment procedure set forth in the first part of Article V whereby any provision of the Constitution could be abrogated or amended by a vote of two-thirds of both houses and three-quarters of the states, the small states could envisage a future rampaging Rufus King orchestrating a future abolition of Article I, Section 3, which provided that the Senate would be composed of two senators from each state, regardless of the population of that state, and Article I, Section 2, Clause 3, which guaranteed that every state would be entitled to at least one representative regardless of population—a total of a *minimum* of three presidential electors. These two provisions taken together guaranteed that even the smallest state would be entitled to three electors in the Electoral College while also preserving the "one state, one vote" principle in the presidential election process.

With the rest of the Constitution coming together and the creation of the United States of America hanging in the balance, the convention addressed both of these final concerns in the following way. First, the "one state, one vote" principle was to be enshrined in Article II, Section 1, Clause 2, which provided that "Each state shall appoint, in such manner as the Legislatures thereof may direct, a number of electors equal to the whole number of Senators and Representatives to which the state may be entitled in the Congress." Second, in order to address the small states' concern that a future Congress might attempt to abolish by future amendment their entitlement to equal representation in the Senate, the last sentence of Article V was to provide that the principle of one state, one vote in the presidential election process could not be abrogated by the regular Article V amendment process but only by the *unanimous* consent of *all* the states: "no state, without its consent, shall be deprived of its equal suffrage in the Senate."

These final provisions enshrined the principle of one state, one vote into what is now called the Grand Compromise that united a nation and consisted of two interrelated prongs: first, that every state, regardless of population shall be entitled to equal representation in the Senate, which cannot be abrogated except by unanimous consent of all the states, and second, that each state's equal representation in the Senate shall be reflected in the minimum number of three presidential electors.

As the great constitutional historian Max Farrand has observed, the Grand Compromise *was not just to accommodate the small states in the* legislature; rather the "method of electing the President was a compromise." Nevertheless, it has become fashionable among NPVIC advocates to deny that any such Grand Compromise ever took place or was ever intended to extend to the method of electing the president. This denial is puzzling given that two electoral votes were allocated to the states *based on representation in the Senate*. Presumably NPVIC advocates perceive the very existence of the Grand Compromise as an obstacle to imposing a Russian-style election system on the United States. But it should be clear that the second prong of the Grand Compromise is in fact dependent on the first. Can it be imagined that the small states would ever have agreed to an electoral allocation that deprived them of the two electors allocated to them by virtue of their equal suffrage in the Senate? The fact that they did not speaks volumes.

It therefore follows that *abolishing the "one state, one vote" principle in the Electoral College—by, say, trying to abolish it in favor of a national popular vote—would also require unanimous consent of each state in the union, not just a two-thirds majority in Congress and ratification of three-fourths of the states.* The NPVIC would adopt such a plan by means of a cabal of selected states that would agree to effectively deprive the smaller states of their modest extra weight in the Electoral College by rendering their electoral votes meaningless. Once the NPVIC cabal agrees to cast its 270 electoral votes in concert, the electors of the nonsignatory states might just as well stay at home and not vote at all.

John Kennedy's Defense of the Electoral College

John F. Kennedy's valiant defense of the Electoral College in which he stated that if it is attempted to change the balance of power in one of the elements of the solar system of government power it is "necessary to consider the others" now comes into focus: the abolition of the Electoral College in favor of a so-called national popular vote cannot be accomplished unless all the other elements are reconsidered as well. This includes the Constitution's guarantee to each state of equal suffrage in the Senate, which in turn not only grants to each state a minimum of three presidential electors but also backs up that guarantee by providing that no state can be deprived of this right without the unanimous consent of all the states.

As a practical matter, as John Kennedy surely devised, such a comprehensive and drastic rewriting of both Article I and Article II of the Constitution could only be accomplished by calling for a new convention of the states, as provided in Article V. Before considering such a drastic rewriting of the Constitution by a newly convened convention—basically from scratch—a few caveats are in order.

First, all the old contentious issues that plagued the delegates of the 1789 convention would be reignited. Delegates from the large states might again demand representation by population alone and the abolition of the Senate. Today, supporters of a national popular vote would no doubt insist upon implementation of their antifederalist principle of "every vote equal" (the very title of the 2012 NPVIC manifesto),[28] which if actually imposed would mean the abolition of the U.S. Senate. It might be recalled that in the 2000 presidential election, supporters of Ralph Nader did actually propose the abolition of the U.S. Senate for this reason—correctly observing, of course, that the Senate violates the principle of "every vote equal" by giving citizens of the smaller states great voting power per voter. On October 8, 2018, NBC national security reporter Ken Dilanian tweeted "The idea that North Dakota and New York get the same representation in the Senate has to change."[29] Of course, the only change that would accomplish this result is the abolition of the U.S. Senate, which would in turn deprive states of their electoral weight in the Electoral College based on Senate representation.

Even more worrisome, if a new convention was convened, so many of the rights enshrined in the Constitution would then be "up for grabs." For example, polls today reveal that a large percentage of the population would support abolishing the First Amendment[30] or at least severely limiting it. Rights under the Fifth, Fourteenth, and Sixth Amendments would also surely come under attack from some quarters. How many people today would really support the rule that a murderer should go free if the constable stumbles?

Of course, the supporters of the NPVIC might very well walk back the title of their manifesto, claiming that it doesn't really mean what is says and that it did not mean to suggest that, for example, the U.S. Senate should be abolished. (A convenient concession, given that its abolition would require unanimous support from all the states.) And how many Americans would actually support abolishing the U.S. Senate, even though it blatantly violates the principle of every vote equal?

The Founding Fathers' Federalist Vision

Understanding the constitutional Framers' federalist vision is only the first step in evaluating the merits of current attacks on the Electoral College as an institution. It was never envisioned that the United States of America would be governed by a monolithic and centralized government structure ruling from the top down as was the case with the monarchies ruling Europe. The very essence of federalism was to recognize that while some government responsibilities such as national defense should be centralized, other more localized and geographic interests should be accommodated. Balancing these national and local interests can be challenging and often complex. It is known as federalism. The U.S. Constitution largely accomplishes this balancing through the Tenth Amendment, which preserves to the states all the sovereign powers of a nation-state except those powers specifically delegated to the national government in the Constitution.

Nations that master this critical balancing between local and national powers tend to endure. Those with too much centralized government power, such as the Soviet Union, do not long survive; those in which local power unduly predominates are torn apart from within, as in Yugoslavia and Somalia.

It was for this reason that the Founding Fathers rejected all suggestions for abolishing the states and implementing a top-down central government with a division of the national state into political subdivisions. It was also for this reason that the convention delegates rejected outright not only proposals to abolish the states but also a proposal for a national direct popular vote election. (Only Robert Morris of Pennsylvania proposed such a popular vote scheme, and his state was the only one to vote for it.)[31] Rather, the federalist vision was to involve the states, including the small states, in the selection of the president by *leaving it up to each state* to determine how best to exercise their choice for national executive.

Article II does exactly that in the simplest possible terms: "Each state shall appoint, in such manner as the legislature thereof may direct, a number of electors, equal to the whole number of Senators and Representatives to which the state may be entitled in Congress." There is, of course, no Electoral College mentioned in text of the Constitution—just a provision that the electors chosen by the states shall meet to choose the president.

For some years after the promulgation of the Constitution, many elected state legislatures chose the electors themselves, but by 1876 every state in the nation had decided to delegate to the citizens of their respective states to choose in open and fairly conducted elections electors based on an elector's pledge to vote for the candidate of the voter's choice. Far from being complex, this process is quite simple and direct.[32]

Left unmentioned in the Constitution is the role of electors. Do a state's Article II powers extend to allowing popularly elected electors to vote on their own whim, or can a state require by law that electors cast their vote in accordance with the pledge they gave to the voters? In answering this question, some wishing to cast discredit on the Electoral College as an institution refer to Alexander Hamilton's remark in Federalist No. 68 to the effect that electors should be "men most capable to analyzing the qualities adapted to the nation."[33] Presumably this gives Electoral College opponents the ammunition it needs to make the case that the Electoral College is somehow undemocratic because it suggests that the decision to elect the president is delegated to the "old fuddy-duddies in colonial knee britches and powdered wigs." In fact, there have been only a handful of electors in all of American history who have failed to cast their electoral vote in accordance with the will of the voters who elected them, and such violations have never had an effect on any election. This is in accordance with Madison's view of the Electoral College that it is a vehicle whereby "the president is now to be elected by the people."[34] It may also be recalled that great as Hamilton's influence was on the future financial integrity of the federal government, his other opinions such as states should be abolished or the president should be elected for life are hardly grounds for interpreting the intent of the Framers—especially since the Framers never mentioned the role of electors. Such matters were left *exclusively* to the states in Article II.

Because Article II also provides that a president can only be elected by a majority vote of electors, it was assumed by most delegates that elections by a majority of electors would rarely happen—which is why Article II provides that where no such majority is achieved, the election of the president would be referred to the House of Representatives. (Such a reference to the House has been necessary in only two presidential elections—those of 1800 and 1824.)[35] It was therefore assumed that the typical election would go to the House, which would elect a president in the same way as leaders are chosen in parliamentary democracies. However, it was also hoped that most elections would not go to the House, since the Electoral College was envisioned as a parliament—the only difference being that the Electoral College's powers were limited to electing a president and, unlike parliament, were given no legislative powers. The purpose of having the Electoral College rather than Congress choose the president was that this was thought necessary to preserve the separation of powers, since a president chosen by the legislature would necessarily be beholden to the legislature in a way that would blur that critical separation of powers between the branches.

One criticism of the Electoral College is that it can result in the election of a president who, while winning the electoral vote, fails to win the popular vote. This happened in the elections of 1888, 1960, 2000, and 2016. However, this is not an unusual result in the great parliamentary democracies of the world. It happened in 1974, for example, when Labour lost the popular vote but nevertheless formed the government of the United Kingdom when three more members of its party were elected to Parliament. As far as can be determined, there were no outcries at the time about the prime minister being the wrong prime minister, no appeals to the United Nations, and no claims that the elected prime minister was not legitimate.

But if reformers are ever able to overturn the Founding Fathers' vision of federalism and democracy, the question remains whether a popular vote election would be a good thing or perhaps more democratic. It follows that the next step in answering that question is to understand how the Electoral College works and has worked in practice and then finally consider the efficacy of achieving the so-called popular vote election by a backdoor method espoused by those who advocate a compact among the states to avoid the inconvenience of going through the process of passing a constitutional amendment.

CHAPTER THREE

Electing a President
The Framers' Vision

The [Framers'] method of electing the president was a compromise.
—Max Ferrand[1]

It has been noted that Article II, Section 1(2), provides that "each state shall appoint, in such manner as the legislatures thereof may direct, a number of electors, equal to the whole number of Senators and Representatives to which the state may be entitled in the Congress."

The U.S. Supreme Court, in the case *McPherson v. Blacker,*[2] interpreted this language as conferring "plenary power to the state legislatures in the manner of appointment of electors." In 1874 the U.S. Senate Committee on Privileges and Elections confirmed that "The appointment of these electors is thus placed absolutely and wholly with the legislatures of the several states. They may be chosen by the legislature, or the legislature may provide that they shall be elected by the people at large."[3]

Implicit in this constitutional provision is a fundamental principle of federalism: the federal government confers to the states the power to determine the manner in which electors are chosen, and the states then exercise that power as the legislatures thereof see fit. In the first few elections after the ratification of the Constitution, most state legislatures chose to elect the electors themselves. Gradually, however, a few states began delegating the appointment of electors to the people by means of a direct popular election. By 1829, all but nine states had followed suit, and by 1832, only one state persisted in legislative appointment of electors. By 1880, all states provided for direct popular election of electors. What voters see on most ballots today in those states is the name of the presidential candidate (in big bold letters) and in tiny letters below "electors for." Some states have even dispensed with the reference to "electors for" and list only the name of the candidate. This has misled some voters into thinking that they are actually voting for a presidential candidate rather than an elector pledged to vote for that candidate.

In other respects, however, state legislatures have differed widely in how they allocate electors. Shortly after the Twelfth Amendment to the Constitution was ratified—which ensured that both the president and vice president were elected on the same ticket—states began implementing the now controversial unit-vote rule. Under this plan, a state allocates all its electoral votes to the candidate whose electoral slate received a plurality of popular votes in that state. Any candidate who received less than a plurality receives not a single electoral vote regardless of how many popular votes he received. Most states have now adopted this method of elector allocation in the belief that it gives their state an enhanced influence on the election. As Thomas Jefferson observed in reluctantly supporting the unit-vote rule over the district vote system (under which one electoral vote would be allocated to the popular vote winner in each congressional district), "If 10 states . . . choose by general ticket, it is worse than folly for the other six not to do it." Today, only Maine and Nebraska now allocate their electors by congressional district rather than on a unit-vote "winner take all" basis.[4]

Despite the apparent unfairness of the unit-vote system, individual states have shown reluctance to abandon it, as it gives other states that do not abandon it a disproportionate effect on the electoral vote. This is one area in which a compact between all the states to allocate their electoral votes by the same percentage as the popular vote in their state would make sense. It would not in any way undermine the federalist structure of American government while virtually guaranteeing that no president would ever be elected who did not receive a popular vote majority. Unfortunately, advocates of the National Popular Vote Interstate Compact (NPVIC) have taken an entirely different direction. They seek to involve as few as 11 states to ignore entirely the popular votes within their states and revert to the barbaric 1876 practice of letting the legislatures of the compact states determine which candidate to cast their electoral vote for. In the case of the NPVIC scheme, state signatories to the scheme would allocate electoral votes based on unofficial newspaper tallies of purported popular votes as reported by the chief election officer of each state. (Chapter 5 lays out in more detail the terms of this NPVIC scheme.)

Electing a President

States have also varied widely in whether to select presidential candidates by convention or by popular vote primaries. As late as 1917 only 17 states were holding popular vote primaries, and by 1968 only 15 states conducted primaries. Today almost all states conduct primaries, with the result that in most cases a party's nominee is known well before that party's convention.

States also vary on the requirements for being placed on the ballot. The preelection process has become a virtual labyrinth in many states, with each state promulgating its own complex rules, laws, and political procedures. When so-called political reform groups and organizations criticize the Electoral College system as being too complex, they would be well to concentrate on simplifying and unifying the exceedingly complex maze of preelection procedures for nominating presidential candidates. Indeed, the process of electing a president in the Electoral College is probably the least complex of the entire election process.

Given Article II's plenary grant to states to appoint electors, there is very little constitutional room left for any federal involvement at all in the presidential election process. The Twelfth Amendment does provide that the president of the U.S. Senate will conduct a largely ceremonial recount of the electors' combined signed vote tallies after they have been transferred to him by the electors. Article II, Section 2(4), also gives Congress the power to determine the date for appointing electors as well as the date when choosing electors—which it has done. Title 5, Section 7, of the U.S. Code[5] now provides that the electors shall meet on the first Monday after the second Wednesday in December to cast their votes. Though a possible intrusion on the plenary power of the states, Sections 3 and 15 of Title 3 of the U.S. Code also purports to set forth federal requirements that state governors must certify electoral tallies before they are transferred to the Senate president for vote tally confirmation while simultaneously claiming the right of Congress to reject those certifications if any vote is not considered by Congress to have been "regularly given."[6] In 1968, a congressional dispute over whether a Richard Nixon elector's vote for George Wallace was regularly given has left open the ambiguous question of whether the U.S. Code, Section 15, does indeed unconstitutionally invade the plenary power of the states to appoint electors under Article II.[7]

Aside from these purely formalistic federal statutory provisions, the only substantive constitutional limitations on the states' Article II power are to be found in the Fifteenth Amendment (forbidding both federal and state abridgments of the right to vote on account of race or color), and the Fourteenth Amendment (forbidding denial of equal protection of the laws to all citizens). Except for those constitutional limitations, the states' plenary power to appoint electors remains inviolate.

Why an Electoral College?

Although it is not uncommon for appellate judges to cite and rely upon legislative history to support their judicial decisions, many others recognize that relying upon such history can be problematic, if not unsound. Legislators may profess entirely different reasons for why they support or oppose a piece of legislation such that none of those statements can be dispositive of the drafter's intent. This is true of statements of the constitutional drafters, which often conflict. It has been previously noted that while Alexander Hamilton in Federalist No. 68 urged ratification of the constitutional plan for appointment of electors as a design for ensuring that an election be made "by men most capable of analyzing the qualities adapted to the nation,"[8] James Madison viewed that same design as ensuring that the president would be chosen "by the people at large."[9]

Indeed, so concerned was Madison that future interpreters of the Constitution might misuse statements made by the Framers by failing to take into account the circumstances of the cited assertion—such as that the assertion was made in the spirit of compromise or accommodation—that he convinced the convention to issue the republic's first gag order. This order decreed that "nothing spoken in the House be printed, or otherwise published or communicated without leave."[10] Jefferson, who was having to sit out the convention in Paris and was obviously frustrated by being cut out of all discussion, complained bitterly: "I am sorry that they began their deliberations by so abominable a precedent as that of tying the tongues of their members."[11] Madison nevertheless stuck to his guns, later justifying his order by noting that "no Constitution would ever have been adopted by the Convention if the debate had been made public."[12]

When it comes to gleaning the Framers' intent in creating the Electoral College in Article II, it is perhaps a blessing that we have precious little in the way of statements or speeches as to what was actually on their minds. Instead, such intent is best gleaned by considering the entire Constitution in context. It may be recalled that the whole question of representation in Congress was only decided in the hectic final days of the convention as part of the two-pronged Grand Compromise and that the second prong included provision for equal state representation in the Senate in the formula for allocating presidential electors in Article II. While it is fashionable today to deny that the Electoral College was part of the Grand Compromise that enabled 13 unfriendly states to unite as a federal republic, it is not the label we give to the Framers' plan but rather the text of the Constitution itself that confirms that such a compromise did indeed take place. That compromise gave to the small states not only equal representation in the Senate but also the weight which that equal representation in the Senate gave *to the small states in electing the president.* So important was this provision to the small states that they demanded that it be guaranteed in Article V, which provides that no state can be deprived of equal suffrage in the Senate—which in turn gave the smaller states modest extra weight in the Electoral College—without the consent *of every state in the union.*

The greatest concern of the delegates of the small states was their fear of being overwhelmed by the relatively large populations in the large states. Implicit in this concern was that the election of the president should reflect not only the *deep* support that a candidate might enjoy in any particular region of the new country but also *broad* support across the *entire* country and in more than one region.

It is the fashion of many of those today who advocate abolition of the Electoral College to disparage the Framers as "elitist, undemocratic thinkers"[13] for rejecting outright the idea of direct popular vote election. But by reading the entire Constitution in context and recognizing the unifying federalist principles embedded therein, it is clear that the Grand Compromise did indeed reflect that the Framers' federalist and democratic vision for the new nation was thereby vindicated.

By way of illustration, consider how Russian-style direct election might have played out in past elections. In the 1950s, segregationist sentiment was strong in the southern states. (Some may recall Alabama governor George Wallace defiantly standing before the television cameras declaring "segregation now, segregation tomorrow, segregation forever!")[14] If a segregationist presidential candidate at that time enjoyed such overwhelming popular support in the South that he could eke out a popular vote victory across the entire country, he might be elected nationwide despite having very little support in other regions of the country.

The Electoral College, of course, prevents such an outcome by ensuring that a successful candidate has broad support across several regions of the country, not just overwhelming support in only one.

Ensuring Majority Support for a Presidential Candidate

The notion of a majority is more slippery than the man in the street might imagine, and the Framers understood this. Advocates of National Popular Vote are fond of claiming that a direct popular vote election is more democratic and more likely to ensure that a candidate is elected by a majority of voters. As will be seen, the exact opposite is the case.

Both Article II and the Twelfth Amendment provide that a president shall be elected by the Electoral College only in the unlikely circumstance that the final tally of electoral votes would constitute a "majority of the whole number of electors appointed."[15] The Framers apparently did not believe it likely that most presidential elections would be decided by a majority of electors. They apparently assumed that the election of George Washington would be the exception that would prove the rule. For this reason, no provision was made for a runoff in either Article II or the Twelfth Amendment. Doubtless anticipating the undemocratic result of a direct election followed by a runoff (as today occurs in such countries as France and Russia), the election was instead to be referred to people's representatives in the House of Representatives. There, each state would have precisely *one vote* to cast from a list of the three candidates who received the *most* votes in the Electoral College—again preserving the cherished principle of one state, one vote implicit in the Grand Compromise.

The Electoral College was to serve as a strong incentive for candidates and splinter parties to coalesce and compromise prior to a presidential election. The Framers doubtless foresaw that a direct popular vote election with Russian-style runoffs would result in an unstable government and the proliferation of small splinter parties.

Creating a Federalist Nation

Perhaps no single provision of the Constitution is as significant and critical to the establishment of a national union as the last sentence of Article V, which guarantees that no state without its consent can be deprived of its equal suffrage in the Senate. Implicit in that guarantee is that no state shall likewise be deprived of the influence it exerts in the Electoral College by virtue of its equal suffrage in the Senate. As recognized by John F. Kennedy in his valiant defense of the Electoral College,[16] without that guarantee the smaller states never would have signed on to the Constitution, much less ratified it. Kennedy recognized that without that guarantee, there would be no United States of America today, only a geographical landmass consisting of numerous smaller amalgamations and nation-states such as have evolved in South America.

It will be recalled that Delaware delegate Gunning Bedford reacted in righteous anger at Rufus King's suggestion that the small states should give up the weight they demanded in both the Senate and the Electoral College: "I do not gentlemen, trust you."[17] The delegates and citizens of

Electing a President

the smaller states knew that once they ratified the Constitution they would still remain under the Damocles Sword of the first sentence of Article V, which set forth the standard process for amending the Constitution.[18] That sentence permitted a majority of two-thirds in the Congress and the ratification of three-fourths of the states to deprive the small states not only of the equal suffrage in the Senate but also of their weight in the Electoral College, which was based on the allocation to each state of a minimum of one elector based on its representation in the House (regardless of population) and two electors in the Senate (regardless of population). In order to preserve this guarantee absolutely inviolate, the small-state delegates insisted that it could not be abrogated by the standard amendment procedure but only by the *unanimous vote of each and every state in the union.*

They were both wise and prescient to do so. Without this Article V guarantee, the small-state delegates foresaw that the Article II allocation of presidential electors based on equal suffrage in the Senate would prove worthless in the face of countless anticipated partisan onslaughts to abrogate it by constitutional amendment. It was Rufus King who first inspired this fear of future onslaughts by attempting to bully the small states into giving up their right to equal suffrage in the Senate. After many hundreds of subsequent onslaughts over the past 200 years, supporters of Ralph Nader in the 2000 election made the threat explicit by demanding outright abolition of the U.S. Senate.[19] More explicit still were the demands by members of Congress such as Alexandria Ocasio-Cortez, who in 2018 demanded the abolition of the Electoral College.[20] Since 2007, the most dangerous threat to both the U.S. Senate and the Electoral College has come in the form of the NPVIC.

CHAPTER FOUR

The Direct Election Illusion

[Direct election], while purporting to be more democratic would increase the power and encourage [extremist] splinter parties. . . . I should hate to see the abolition of state lines. . . . The presidential election is determined on the basis of 48 separate units. I think the election should be decided in each one of them.

—Senator John F. Kennedy[1]

This government is not completely consolidated, nor is it entirely federal. . . . Who are the parties to it? The people—not as people comprising one great body, but the people comprising 13 sovereignties.

—James Madison[2]

It has been noted that there have been over 500 political attempts to abolish the Electoral College since the ratification of the U.S. Constitution. These reform proposals have ranged from the labyrinthine to the bizarre. In 1808 Senator James Hillhouse proposed choosing a president by drawing colored balls from a box.[3] In 1964 Senator Lazarus Powell proposed that electors choose a president by lottery.[4] In the 1820s the so-called District Plan was popular and enjoyed a revival of interest in the 1950s. Senator Paul Douglas denounced the plan as an obvious attempt to "deliver the cities bound hand and foot, into the power of the rural sections of the country."[5] Professor John Dixon denounced the plan, claiming that if it were implemented, "we shall have gerrymandered the presidency."[6] These attempts have tried to ride a wave of public opinion polls purporting to show that most Americans wish the Electoral College to be abrogated in favor of a national popular vote.

In 1978, the Twentieth Century Fund enlisted the contributions of a distinguished panel of Americans to study the Electoral College and make recommendations.[7] Members of this task force included such distinguished historians as Arthur Schlesinger and Jeane Kirkpatrick (later to be U.S. representative to the United Nations). Although it considered a national popular vote plan, the study revealed not only that plan's dangers and impracticability but also its potential violation of the Constitution. In the end the final recommendation was to implement a complex hybrid plan whereby the winner of the national popular vote would get a bonus of 102 extra electoral votes. Despite being notable for having conducted the most in-depth study of the Electoral College system in American history, its plan too was ultimately thrown upon the rubbish heap of discarded plans—and ignored.

In 1969, yet another ambitious assault on the Electoral College was launched in Congress under an umbrella of relentless invective. One representative bellowed that the Electoral College was "barbarous" and "dangerous."[8] In 1970, this assault was finally stemmed by the testimony of America's most eminent historians, including Theodore White and Clinton Rossiter. The latter testified that "[w]e should hesitate before replacing [the Electoral College] for a neat one that will blow up in our faces."[9] In the end, however, it was the whole runoff feature of the direct election proposal that gave even its original advocates pause, raising the specter of endless runoffs in the style of banana republic elections. "Everyone is very much scared of the run-off feature,"[10] confessed one legislative aide. Americans were simply too accustomed to having one national election, knowing the winner on election night, and returning to normal life the next day. It also didn't help the cause of abolition when minority groups testified that direct election would have a "disastrous effect . . . on black people."[11]

A 1981 study by Peirce and Longley has traced public support for the Electoral College going back to 1945.[12] The study shows that by 1967, 58 percent of Americans were in favor of abolishing the Electoral College.[13] This percentage increased to a high of 81 percent in 1968, falling back to 75 percent by 1981.[14]

Perhaps more revealing was the breakdown of opinion by political orientation. In 1981, Republicans favored abolition by 79 percent, far higher than the percentage of Democrats who favored abolition.[15] (This was almost certainly because of Republicans' lingering memories of their loss in 1960 in which John F. Kennedy won the electoral vote but, according to the Congressional Quarterly, lost the popular vote.) A 1987 American Bar Association poll revealed that while 69 percent of lawyers favored its

The Direct Election Illusion 39

repeal, political scientists and constitutional scholars continued to passionately support it.[16]

Among demographic groups, the study revealed that while whites favored abolition by 79 percent, a majority of African Americans did not favor abolition.[17] This latter result may be explained by the observation by black leaders that abolishing the Electoral College would result in racial discrimination against African Americans. As Vernon Jordan (president of the National Urban League, one of the leading civil rights organizations) testified at the 1979 congressional hearings, "Take away the Electoral College and the importance of being black melts away. Blacks, instead of being crucial to victory in major states, simply become 10 percent of the electorate, with reduced impact."[18]

Depending upon which particular group feels aggrieved, it has been claimed that the Electoral College discriminates against large states,[19] states with large voter turnout,[20] northern African Americans,[21] southern African Americans,[22] Mexican Americans,[23] Mormons,[24] and homosexuals.[25] It has been claimed that the college unfairly favors Jews,[26] suburbanites,[27] Italians, and a variety of economic interests.[28]

It is difficult to credit any of these claims, however, since prior to 1960 the only election in which the electoral winner did not win the popular vote was in 1888. In 1960 it was Republicans who claimed discrimination, and in 2000 and 2016 it was Democrats. In the 1980s Democrats claimed that Republicans had an electoral lock on the South and Midwest, and later Republicans claimed that Democrats had a lock on the large coastal states of California and New York. But the real problem with such claims is that demographics and political orientations change. The fact is that over time the Electoral College favors no one group or political party.

Criticism of the Electoral College

Aside from such spurious criticism as "[electors] are old fuddy-dudd[ies] in colonial knee britches and powdered wigs with an ear to a trumpet,"[29] the most prevalent criticism is that voters in different states do not have precisely the same voting power in electing the president. A voter in North Dakota who votes for three electors on a party slate (two of whom are based on that state's two senators) does indeed have greater voting power than a voter in California who also votes for electors, two of whom are also based on its two senators. This has given scholars of mathematics a field day in proving the obvious. John Banzhaf's oft-quoted "One Man, 3.312 Votes: A Mathematical Analysis of the Electoral

College"[30] spawned a veritable plethora of mathematical sequels by equally renowned mathematical scholars,[31] capped by the most recent of these sequels, *Every Vote Equal,* the manifesto of the National Popular Vote Interstate Compact (NPVIC).[32]

Of course, all of these studies prove no more than what the Framers would have freely conceded: voting power for president is not the same in every state. This is because Article II allocates electors based on the number of representatives and senators to which each state is entitled. On average, once or twice *a century* this disparity in voting power has indeed resulted in a presidential candidate winning the electoral vote but narrowly losing the hypothetical national popular vote—as sometimes happens in all the great parliamentary democracies of the world.[33] (As happened in 1974 when the Labour Party lost the national popular vote but nevertheless won three more seats in Parliament, which enabled it to form the government and elect the prime minister.)[34]

Doubtless the Framers would have made the very same concession with regard to their constitutional Article II formula for representation of the states in the U.S. Senate. Perhaps the reason why there are no equally esoteric mathematical studies showing that voters in small states have disproportionate voting power in the Senate where legislation is continuously and systematically passed *every week* or so, and which directly affects all Americans on a *daily basis,* is that a fourth grade schoolkid could figure that out in minutes using chalk on a blackboard. Does it follow, then, that all legislation passed by the Senate and confirmations of Supreme Court justices are illegitimate?

Given the fact that voting disparity in the Senate affects Americans on a virtually daily basis and that voting disparity in presidential elections does so only once or twice a century, one may wonder why the "every vote equal" advocates prefer to devote all their energies toward abolishing the Electoral College rather than on first abolishing the U.S. Senate. After all, if they were first successful in abolishing the U.S. Senate, the small states' extra weight in presidential voting power would automatically disappear as well. Is not trying to abolish the Electoral College before abolishing the U.S. Senate putting the cart before the horse?

While the answer to that question would be best posed to the NPVIC advocates themselves, speculation suggests several answers they might give.

First, the U.S. Senate is much more visible on a daily basis to most Americans. It is a rare television program or newspaper article that does not report daily on important legislation pending in Congress. The Senate itself is also the focus of confirmation of presidential nominations for office, including Supreme Court nominations, and ratification of international treaties. Senators themselves, as distinguished members of the upper house, generally are regarded as enjoying greater prestige than mere representatives, not least because there are far fewer senators, with even New York and California being entitled to only two each. Senators are often regarded as the closest things to aristocrats that a republican form of government has to offer. Being elected to the Senate has been considered as stepping-stone on the political ladder to a presidential candidacy. The Senate is a hallowed national institution, while fuddy-duddy electors are envisioned as being decked in knee breeches and powdered wigs who offer a poor comparison to the distinguished and polished senators. In most elections, the electors' meetings held after the presidential election are mentioned as little more than a footnote on the back pages of the newspapers. In the rare election in which their votes do not coincide with the newspapers' tallies of the hypothetical popular vote, they are vilified by the losing party whose members have been known to hurl epithets and threats at them and in 2016 conducted demonstrations in front of their homes.[35] In short, NPVIC advocates doubtless view the Senate as too big an institution to target. Far easier to go after the softer target of fuddy-duddies in breeches and wigs.

Second, the Senate is not only too big a target but is also one that is well protected by the last sentence of Article V of the Constitution, which provides that the equal suffrage of the states embodied in the Senate cannot be abrogated except by *unanimous* consent of all the states. Despite the protestations of some NPVIC advocates that small states would gladly give up their privileged role in a federalist republic, the facts do not bear this out. In 1979 when Electoral College abolitionists mounted their most ambitious assaults on the Electoral College, two-thirds of the senators from the smallest states voted against a constitutional amendment for a direct election,[36] doubtless being fully aware that abolition of the Electoral College would be the first step toward abolishing the Senate itself.

In the NPVIC manifesto *Every Vote Equal*, NPVIC advocates have gone on record as giving their own answer to this question. It sets forth "Myth 9.4.5: Equal representation of the states in the Senate is threatened by the national popular vote plan." It then purports to rebut this myth by asserting that "enactment of the National Popular Vote Compact has no bearing on the federal constitutional provisions establishing equal representation of the states in the Senate."[37]

This rebuttal appears to ignore that the Article II allocation of electoral votes to the states is *based* on each state's representation in the U.S. Senate. Abolishing this Article II allocation formula would necessarily deprive not just small states but all states of their weight in presidential elections. This is because the number of electors to which a state is entitled is based on the number of senators each state is entitled to in the Senate.

As renowned historian Arthur Schlesinger has so eloquently pointed out, "should an abstract standard of equity require the abolition of large-state advantages in presidential elections, *then surely it requires the abolition of the small state advantage in the Senate.*"[38] Without the small-state advantage in the Senate, there would be no need for the Senate to exist at all. Indeed, the only reason it exists is that it was the key feature of the Grand Compromise that unified the nation.

It follows therefore that any attempt to abolish the Electoral College, replace it with a direct election scheme, or alter the number of electors to which a state is entitled in Article II would require the acquiescence of *every state in the union* pursuant to Article V. This is because Article V forbids depriving any state of its equal representation in the Senate except by unanimous consent of all the states, and it is precisely the small-state advantage in the Senate that in turn determines the number of electors to which a state is entitled in the Electoral College.

The Concept of Majority

The very notion of majority is elusive. It is rare that any one person in a largely populated society rises to the level of being favored for top leadership above all other candidates combined. In American history, it is probably safe to say that only George Washington enjoyed that status in America's first presidential election. In most cases, however, the existence of only one candidate is indicative of an authoritarian society in which choice is influenced more by fear than free will—witness the "elections" in some communist and fascist nations of the past in which the leader is purportedly chosen by 99.8 percent of the vote.

It is beyond the scope of this book to review in detail the various stages in which an array of presidential candidates is whittled down to but one, two, or three candidates in which only one candidate has any realistic chance of being elected by a majority or substantial plurality.[39]

Suffice it to say, the first stage is self-selective: a candidate simply steps forward and announces her or his candidacy. If the person's name is not already widely known, the candidate faces the challenge of organizing support and raising money to advertise her or his candidacy.

The intermediate stage is the more complex and varies widely by jurisdiction and state. Typical methods of culling candidates down to a manageable handful that can fit on a ballot, such as imposing a requirement of obtaining a requisite number of signatures or support shown in prior elections, are the subject of complex legislation in most states. The means favored in most jurisdictions is to require nomination by one of the major political parties or by a minor political party that received a certain percentage of the vote in previous elections.[40]

It is the final culling stage with which the Article II Grand Compromise was concerned. It has been suggested that the Framers did not consider the possibility of the formation of political parties when devising the constitutional plan for allocation of electors. This seems unlikely given that political parties had evolved in the parliamentary system of the mother country, and the Framers' did envision that most presidential elections would be referred to the House of Representatives in the likely event that no candidate received a majority of electoral votes in the Electoral College. What can be said is that the Framers clearly hoped that their plan would ensure that a majority, or at least a substantial plurality of voters, would elect the president, for it was upon that basis that the stability and success of the republic would depend.

Whatever their hope, however, their constitutional plan succeeded beyond any conceivable realistic expectation they might have had. With only two exceptions—the elections of 1800 and 1824—every president elected in American history has won a majority of electoral votes. The legitimacy of those elections has never been successfully challenged[41]—a rare exception in a world where most governments and civilizations ultimately collapse due to internal civil strife over succession.

Into the teeth of this constitutional success story comes the claim that a so-called direct Russian-style popular election could do better. It is instructive to examine how such elections have fared in countries that have employed them.

As noted in the preface and Chapter 1, a prime example is the Russian popular vote election conducted on December 14, 1993. With no Electoral College system in place to cull the final candidates to but two or three, dozens of parties put forth candidates, and 13 parties received a significant number of votes. The fascist-oriented Liberal Democratic Party of Russia led by Vladimir Zhirinovsky received 23 percent of the vote. (Despite its name, this party's platform included blaming Jews for starting past wars and advocating the military takeover of Finland, Poland, and even Alaska.) The reformist People's Choice party received 13 percent, edging out the Communist Party by less than 2 percent. Unlike the Electoral College of the U.S. Constitution, the Russian popular vote system dictated that there be a runoff between the two top vote getters (the very scheme that finally convinced the Electoral College abolitionists in the U.S. House of

Representatives to back off in 1979). Thus, a swing of less than 2 percent of the vote would have meant that voters in a runoff would have had to choose between a hard-line fascist and a hard-line communist—despite the fact that two-thirds of the electorate adamantly opposed both of those candidates! Of course, in the subsequent runoff between the two of them, one of these two extremist parties could claim the majority. For National Popular Vote advocates, this result is what would pass as a democratic outcome.

The 2017 French presidential election also revealed the hazards for democracy inherent in a popular vote election. In an 11-party field, the vote was so splintered that the 2 major parties received only 19 percent each, while two maverick candidates, Emmanuel Macron and the hard right-wing party of Marine Le Pen, won 23 percent and 21 percent, respectively. To the alarm of much of the world, this catapulted the extremist right-winger Le Pen into the final second-round runoff even though she had received only 21 percent of the votes in the first round. So disgusted was the French electorate with this final choice (65 percent opposed both of the runoff candidates) that in the second round the highest vote getter was the *ballot blanc* (the blank ballot), which received 600,000 votes. This result may reasonably be interpreted as a protest vote against a popular vote system that can propel even a small extremist party to the final round. Again, this is what NPVIC supporters claim passes for democracy, even while asserting that such an outcome surely could not occur in a popular vote election in the United States, since the two major parties—Democratic and Republican—are so ensconced in our political system.

Hardly.

Those who express such an illusion may wish to consider the polls in the months leading up to the 1992 U.S. presidential election, which showed that had that election been held on May 18, 1992, interloper Ross Perot would have received 33 percent of the popular vote, Bush 28 percent, and Clinton 24 percent. A Democratic candidate would not even have appeared on the ballot. Fortunately for the nation, the Electoral College spared the country the humiliating election spectacle that France endured in 2017. When Perot realized that he had no chance of winning a majority of electoral votes (which would have thrown the election into the House, where the majority party would elect the president), he decided to drop out of the race despite leading in the popular vote polls.

Nevertheless, direct vote advocates continue to claim that resort to a rerunoff would be a relatively rare occurrence in a popular vote election. This assumption is apparently based on the fact that since 1860, no

The Direct Election Illusion 45

winning presidential candidate has ever received less than 40 percent of the vote. What this fails to take into account, however, is that *these consistently large pluralities and majorities are the result of the very Electoral College system they seek to destroy.*

The truth of this was most starkly revealed in the 1977 congressional hearings on the Electoral College conducted by Senator Birch Bayh. A former member of the Socialist Party testified before the committee:

> One thing we all had in common was an absolute detestation of the Electoral College. . . . We knew we had [no] chance to win any states. Whereas [with a direct popular election] we would have made hay while the sun shined [sic] during the autumn. We always started with 5 or 6% who said they were for Norman Thomas. . . . About the third week in October it was down to 2 percent; on the first day of November it was down to 1 per cent . . . and on [election day] it was down to about 150,000 votes.[42]

When Senator Bayh inquired how this would affect a runoff under a popular vote election, the socialist responded without hesitation: "[U]nder your proposed system . . . I believe that the 20 percent would be gathered by 15 or 20 parties. I can name 4 or 5 of them: Wallacites, Henry and George; McCarthyites, Eugene and Joseph; Socialists, Trotskyites, Communists, black militants, yellow militants, green militants, purple militants."[43] The witness further explained: "It is not hard to create the French Chamber of Deputies in a multiparty system. We've seen it happen everywhere. It can be done by fiddling with the constitutional structure that undergirds and constrains and channels the two-party system."[44]

One need only look at the dynamics of multiparty systems in which it is rare than any one candidate can achieve the majority cherished by the NPVIC advocates. This means that in order to form a government these countries must endure lengthy negotiations to form a governing coalition, which more often than not proves unstable. In Italy, citizens have had to endure 65 governments in 70 years, or an average of 1 unstable government approximately every 13 months. The 2013 elections in Italy produced no less than 3 successive governments during which unstable coalitions collapsed on a regular basis and new ones formed as small parties were perpetually bribed with promises of a minister or two.

The genius of the Framers in creating the Electoral College was in creating a system in which negotiations between parties occur *before* an election rather than after, when small or even extreme parties can exact concessions out of all proportion to the popular vote they received. In 1936, socialists reached an accommodation with the Democratic Party.

They obtained important concessions *prior* to the election and then proceeded to cast their ballot for the party that best represented their interests.

Thus, the Electoral College promotes compromise, accommodation, and stability. So-called popular vote systems do the opposite, virtually guaranteeing that a leader will be elected who enjoys only minority support of the people—and by so doing *undermine democracy*.

After Senator Bayh was educated by the Electoral College witnesses at the Senate hearings in 1979, senators backed off because they began to realize the genius of the Framers' vision of the Electoral College. They finally understood the dangers to democracy of adopting Russian-style popular vote elections. Not least, they finally appreciated the French-style horrors of endless runoffs and instability. For this they deserve the thanks of the republic.

In the face of yet more demagogic calls to undermine the system that has served the republic so well for over 250 years and become the envy of the world, increased vigilance and education (most of all) will be required.

CHAPTER FIVE

The National Popular Vote Interstate Compact

> He who knows only his side of the case, knows little of that . . . but wrong opinions . . . gradually yield to fact and argument.
> —John Stuart Mill[1]

Previous chapters have summarized the many attempts to undermine the Framers' federalist vision for electing the executive branch of government. The most recent and ambitious attempt to do so by initiating a constitutional amendment process occurred during the 1977 congressional hearings on the Electoral College conducted by Senator Birch Bayh.[2] As described in the previous chapter, momentum for such an attack on the Electoral College was initially carried by such simplistic slogans as "national popular vote" and "every vote equal"—until, that is, the implications and potential disastrous consequences of such an amendment were explained in the waning days of the hearings. While the major constitutional and federalist weaknesses will be explained in detail in the chapters that follow, the primary weaknesses of direct election ones may be summarized here as follows:

1. If implemented without unanimous consent of *all* the states, it would violate Article V's guarantee to all the states the right of equal representation in the Senate and the concomitant weight that Article II grants each state in presidential elections.
2. It would often produce the election of a candidate who did not receive a majority or even a significant plurality of the votes cast, just as such systems produce in countries such as Russia and France.

3. By reducing the states to mere provincial subdivisions of the central government, it would, in the words of John F. Kennedy, "break down the federal system under which most states entered the union, which provides a system of checks and balances to ensure that no area or group obtains too much power."[3]

4. It would permit the election of a president who, while enjoying overwhelming support in one particular geographic region, received but little support in other regions.

5. It would focus the attention of candidates on the great centers of population to the detriment of engagement with less populated heartland states and regions.

6. In the case of a close election, it would require recounts and litigation in 50 states and over 114,000 precincts rather than in just 1 state (as occurred in 2000).

7. It would transform the two-party system into a multiparty system along the lines of Russia or Italy in which countless runoffs over a protracted period of time would be required to make a final selection.

8. It would disenfranchise millions of voters in states that present voters with ballots listing only the names of electors and not the names of presidential candidate.

Although all of these weaknesses weighed heavily when it came to a final vote in the Bayh hearings, it was the hazards and uncertainties of the run-off provisions that gave the 1977 Senate committee the final pause to pull back and affirm the Framers' original vision for presidential elections.

Perhaps in acknowledgment that once the true ramifications of such tampering with the Framers' vision have ultimately been revealed in previous attempts to abolish the Electoral College, those determined to impose such a system have in recent years turned to advocating a scheme to accomplish the same result as a constitutional amendment but by a judo-type means of turning the Constitution against itself.

Financed by a group calling itself the National Popular Vote!,[4] it is funded by financial interests in California determined to avoid any need to submit their plan to Congress. Lobbyists generously financing by these interests have tried to recruit states one by one by introducing in the legislatures of each state a proposed National Popular Vote Interstate Compact (NPVIC).[5]

NPVIC agents have appeared at these hearings under the radar of public scrutiny. Since no organized group has yet appeared to oppose these tactics, state legislatures representing upwards of 130 electoral votes have to date become signatories to this scheme. Should anyone doubt the lack of public scrutiny, or even of public knowledge of this scheme, one need

The National Popular Vote Interstate Compact

only go on the street and ask the first person who appears whether they have ever heard of it.

In one of the few state legislative hearings that came to the attention of a political scientist or constitutional scholar, an attempt to push through the NPVIC in Colorado in 2007 ended with a 10–1 vote against it in a Colorado House Committee Hearing. This vote was most remarkable for the fact that the bill had enjoyed preliminary support of 10–1 in its favor. After listening to the arguments set forth by this author and Professor Jim Riley, the vote was reversed to 10–1 *against* the Compact Bill.[6]

Provisions of the NPVIC Bill

The premise of the NPVIC purports to be based on Article II, Section 1(2), which provides that "each state shall appoint, in such manner as the Legislature thereof may direct, a number of electors." It was precisely this clause that in the early days of the republic led many legislatures to reserve for themselves the privilege of appointing electors to represent the state in the Electoral College. Very gradually over many decades, this notoriously undemocratic practice gave way to delegating the power of appointment to the people of the state to select by popular vote. The premise of the NPVIC is that there is therefore nothing to prevent states from forming a cabal among themselves to appoint electors in any way they please—in this case agreeing among themselves that they will ignore the popular vote of the people within their state and instead appoint an elector slate pledged to vote for the purported national popular vote winner.

The complete text of the "Agreement among the States to Elect the President by National Popular Vote" (the NPVIC) is set forth in Appendix A, but the main provisions are as follow:

III-1: "Prior to the time set by law for the meeting and voting of the presidential electors, the chief election officer of each member state shall determine the number of votes for each presidential slate in each state of the United States . . . in which votes have been cast by popular election and shall add such votes together to produce a national poplar vote total" for each presidential slate.

III-2: The chief election officer of each member state shall designate the presidential slate with the largest national popular vote total as the "national popular vote winner."

III-3: The presidential elector certifying official of each member state shall certify the appointment in that official's own state of the elector slate nominated in that state in association with the popular vote winner.[7]

The NPVIC is apparently not being submitted to legislatures as a self-contained plan. Rather, the NPVIC manifesto *Every Vote Equal*[8] sets forth a number of bills that it hopes would be passed by Congress in order to accommodate its scheme. For example, in Section 9.15 (concerning national recounts) the manifesto suggests that the viability and efficacy of its scheme would be contingent on Congress passing a plethora of special bills, including a complete overhaul of U.S. Code Title 3. It even suggests a title to the bill it proposes: the "Presidential Election Recount Act of ___."[9]

None of this has kept NPVIC lobbyists from pressuring state legislatures to sign on to the NPVIC without any assurance that such a proposed overhaul of Title 3 of the U.S. Code would ever actually be passed by Congress. Since the NPVIC would only take effect when states representing 270 electoral votes become signatories (which could be as few as 11 states), one might wonder what the basis is for assuming that congressional representatives of as many as 38 of the remaining states would vote for such a bill accommodating the very scheme they declined to sign on to.

Preliminary Textual Issues

Section III-1 of the Compact Bill provides that "the chief election officer of each member state shall determine the number of votes for each presidential slate . . . and shall add such votes together to produce a national popular vote total." This clause appears to empower some unnamed entity to conduct an official *national* vote tally of the popular vote returns reported by 50 different chief election officers. Implicit in this failure to appoint such a person is the assumption that conducting such a national vote tally is only a purely ministerial task involving nothing more than receiving the popular vote count from the chief election officer of each state, going to the nearest drug store to buy a calculator, and then adding the numbers up to get a final national vote tally. It is here that the first problem arises with trying to impose a direct election scheme (a round peg) into the Electoral College structure (a square peg).

It has already been noted that states may differ in how they present slates of electors on the ballot provided to voters. The right of states to do so is freely conceded by the NPVIC: Article II, Section 1(2), is quite clear in granting plenary powers to each state to appoint electors as they see fit. One example of how a state is empowered by the Constitution to present electoral slates to voters is the way in which Alabama presented the Democratic elector slate to voters in the 1960 presidential election. That slate

The National Popular Vote Interstate Compact

listed the names of 11 electors but did not indicate for whom any of those electors would vote in the Electoral College. In a previous primary, 5 of those electors had run on a platform of supporting Kennedy, but 6 had indicated that they did not intend to vote for him in the Electoral College. In the event, while the Democratic slate received the most votes, only 5 of the electors listed on the Democratic slate of electors voted for Kennedy in the Electoral College, while the remaining 6 cast their electoral votes for Senator Harry Byrd of West Virginia.

The question of how to apportion the popular votes cast for these 11 electors never became an issue, because yet again the Electoral College saved the nation from a constitutional crisis: Kennedy's comfortable national margin of victory in the Electoral College rendered moot and irrelevant the purely hypothetical question of who *would* have won a popular vote election had such an NPVIC scheme been in effect.

However, had the NPVIC scheme been in effect in that election, its unnamed entity or unnamed person (a newspaper perhaps?) would have been charged with buying a calculator and conducting a tally of the popular votes reported by the chief election officers of all 50 states. He/she or it would have then been faced with making a threshold decision prior to counting a single popular vote: How do I count the popular votes cast for the unpledged electors on the Democratic slate? Do I count the votes cast for the Democratic slate as popular votes cast for Senator Byrd (since a majority of the Democratic electors voted for Byrd in the Electoral College rather than for Kennedy)? Or do I count the popular votes cast for those six anti-Kennedy electors as popular votes for Kennedy?

If the NPVIC had been in effect in the 1960 election, a threshold decision as to how to count the popular votes for the unpledged *Democratic* electors in Alabama *would have decided who won the national presidential election.* If one were to count as popular votes for Kennedy *all* the votes for the Democratic slate (despite the fact that six of the electors were anti-Kennedy), then when added to the so-called national popular vote total for Kennedy a newspaper could conclude that Kennedy won the popular vote. The Congressional Quarterly, however, and most newspapers including the *New York Times* more rationally allocated to Kennedy only five-elevenths of the popular votes cast for the Democratic slate of electors. In doing so, it concluded that Richard Nixon had won the ephemeral (and irrelevant) nationwide popular vote.

Because the Congressional Quarterly's method of counting the popular votes in 1960 led to the conclusion that Nixon won the popular vote, that election has been included on a list of four presidential elections conducted since 1789 in which the electoral winner did not win the most popular votes. To this day, however, there are those who persist in perpetuating what has become an urban legend—that Kennedy won the popular vote. They do so by counting the popular votes cast for the anti-Kennedy electors on the Democratic slate as popular votes for Kennedy. If this method were the more rational, this would leave only three elections since 1789 in which the electoral vote winner did not win the popular vote: the elections of 1888, 2000, and 2016, or an average of once every 75 years. (It should be recalled that for elections conducted prior to 1880 no comparison between electoral and national popular votes would be meaningful, since some states had their legislatures, rather than voters, choose electors.)

This more rational method of tabulating the national popular vote was also followed by the major newspapers of the time, including the *New York Times,* which concluded that Nixon had won the popular vote. Unfortunately, such an election-deciding decision could not have been made by just anyone who happened to be in possession of a calculator. But who? The NPVIC doesn't say, despite the fact that this decision would have decided the winner of the presidential election in 1960.

Why does the NPVIC not designate an entity or person who would be empowered to make such a critical decision prior adding up the popular vote tallies reported by 50 different chief election officials? Here the answer is simple: such a person or entity would have to be a national or federal entity acting under the authority of the United States, and *no cabal of states has the constitutional power to appoint such a federal official or body charged with such responsibility.*

This is but one example of how the attempt by the NPVIC to impose the round peg of direct election into the square peg of the existing Electoral College structure fails in dramatic fashion. If supporters of a Russian-style direct election had instead successfully taken the traditional and legitimate course of amending the Constitution and abolishing the Electoral College outright—which its supporters assert claim could be easily done, given what they claim is overwhelming public support for direct election—such anomalies would never arise. While a direct election created by constitutional amendment would have its own problems, the NPVIC would create chaos, particularly in close elections such as the 1960 presidential election.

In 1960 several of the newspapers undertook the task of doing what the NPVIC would have an unnamed person or entity perform—namely, deciding how to count votes for unpledged electors and nationwide popular votes. There was, of course, no national or federal entity, then or now, charged with that responsibility, since the popular vote was (and is) entirely irrelevant to who won the election. Not surprisingly, the newspapers came

The National Popular Vote Interstate Compact

up with entirely different tallies of who won the national popular vote. More recently, some newspapers have expressed concern that Kennedy's iconic legacy might be tainted by a tally showing he had lost the popular vote. In order to calculate the popular votes in a way that would show that Kennedy won the popular vote, these newspapers have suggested that *all* the popular votes for the Democratic slate in Alabama should be attributed to Kennedy—despite the fact that six of the unpledged Alabama electors cast their electoral votes for Senator Byrd. By so doing, their tally shows Kennedy winning the total national popular vote. However, most newspapers in 1960, including the *New York Times,* tallied only five-elevenths of the popular vote cast for the Democratic slate to Kennedy, reasoning that there was no rational reason to include votes for Senator Byrd as votes for Kennedy.[10] This resulted in a national popular vote tally showing that Nixon had indeed won the national popular vote. This method of counting was also confirmed at the time by the Congressional Quarterly, the closest thing to a federal vote counting entity—although even that entity was not given any official responsibility by any federal statute or law to count the (irrelevant) national popular votes.

More recently, yet a third manner of counting the popular votes for the anti-Kennedy electors has been suggested. In 2013, Dr. Steven Allen wrote an article titled "JFK's Popular Vote Victory: The Myth" in which he cited a 1988 letter to the *New York Review of Books* by George Mason University's Gordon Tulloch responding to review of a book by Doris Kearns Goodwin by Francis Russell:

> Personally, I would suggest that we simply discard all these votes in the popular total on grounds that we can't tell what these voters thought. Another possibility would be to divide the popular vote cast for these eleven electors in the same ratio as the popular vote in the earlier primary. Either of these corrections would lead to Nixon having more popular votes nationally than Kennedy.[11]

Today, of course, we can cavalierly offer numerous speculations about how the popular votes in Alabama *could* have been counted, since the Electoral College mercifully rendered that question moot in 1960. To even attempt to do so, however, risks missing the main point, which is not which method of counting might have been better but rather that *any* attempt to do so under the NPVIC regime would be largely illusory and would certainly lead to litigation and chaos.

The NPVIC manifesto appears to recognize this, conceding that in states that present voters with ballots listing only the names of electors on the ballot and not names of presidential candidates "there would be no way to associate the vote counts of the various presidential electors with the national (popular) vote tally."[12] The 1,000-page NPVIC manifesto *Every Vote Equal* devotes only a single paragraph to resolving this NPVIC anomaly. Ironically, its draconian solution to this anomaly is to disenfranchise all the voters in such states by disregarding their votes entirely, referring to the NPVIC's provision that limits the counting of popular votes to those cast in a statewide popular election—presumably an election in a state that presents voters with the actual names of candidates, not just the names of electors. Apparently, the irony of the NPVIC manifesto proposing to disregard 1 million votes is best hidden by burying it in one short paragraph in a 1,000-page tome. As a practical matter, of course, the NPVIC has no other choice: how can popular votes *ever* be tabulated for candidates whose names are not even on the ballots?

A constitutional amendment providing for direct election and the abolition of the Electoral College would avoid this anomaly. But the NPVIC has instead chosen the course of creating a state cabal to circumvent the constitutional process rather than proposing a constitutional amendment.

Undemocratic Implications of Imposing NPVIC on Noncontracting States

The Russian and French elections have revealed the most undemocratic implications of imposing on a nation the seductively sounding national popular vote. As described in detail in Chapter 3, such elections reveal the direct election illusion that so often results in the election of a candidate opposed by the vast majority of voters. What is claimed as a redeeming feature, the so-called runoff, does little to instill confidence in the integrity of such a voting system—witness the French runoff election of 2017 in which the largest vote getter was the *ballot blanc* (the blank ballot) by which 600,000 outraged voters expressed their undisguised disgust for a voting system that produced a winner opposed by two-thirds of the electorate.

It will be recalled that the prospect of extended runoffs was the final nail in the coffin of the last major effort to impose a direct vote on the nation—namely, the 1977 Bayh congressional hearings. Americans are simply not prepared to trash an election system that has almost always provided a prompt winner and allows the country to return to normal on Wednesday morning after the first Tuesday in November of an election year. Doubtless the exhausted voters of direct election nations who are again and again faced with extended runoff elections and minority

The National Popular Vote Interstate Compact

winners wonder why their systems cannot duplicate this feat of certainty and normalcy.

Whatever the shortcomings of the runoff system, it can in some instances at least reduce the possibility of producing a winner opposed by the majority of the electorate. It is in this respect that the NPVIC provides no safeguards whatsoever. At least in the French runoff elections, the chances of a candidate being elected with less 23 percent of the vote was prevented by a runoff. But the NPVIC provides for no runoff whatsoever, thus leaving open the possibility that a candidate could be elected by as little as 5 percent of the vote. It should be recalled that the Electoral College as now constituted permits no such undemocratic result. This is because Article II provides that if no candidate receives a majority of votes in the Electoral College, the election is referred to the House of Representatives, where election is made in the same manner as in parliamentary democracies.

As previously noted, the NPVIC is fond of assuming that if it is imposed on the American people, the two-party system will continue to prevail—thus ensuring a winner with substantial public support. Indeed, for an election or two it might even do so by its own momentum. But as senators in the 1977 Bayh Senate hearings on the Electoral College learned to their dismay, the imposition of direct popular vote would very quickly transform the country into a multiparty nation along the lines of Italy, Russia, or France. It will be recalled that dozens of parties participated in the 1993 Russian election (including 13 major parties receiving a significant number of votes), with the result that voters in the subsequence second-round election came within a whisker of being asked to choose between a left-wing and a right-wing extremist.[13] That the Russian election system ultimately resulted in the authoritarian government we see today also does little to recommend it as a sound democratic process. Historians may recall that in the popular vote elections in Germany during the 1930s Adolf Hitler never received more than 30 percent or so of the popular vote but was nevertheless able to leverage that minority vote into an absolute dictatorship.

Unfortunately, this is a common feature of so-called direct elections in which small but better organized and financed parties can indeed win as much as 20–30 percent of the vote and thus win a trip to the final rounds—and even win in a runoff despite being opposed by the vast majority of voters.

It may be presumed that NPVIC advocates would prefer a constitutional amendment that could include a provision for runoffs to at least reduce the chances of a candidate being elected who is opposed by the vast majority of voters. NPVIC even contemplates this, stating in IV-4 that "This agreement shall terminate if the Electoral College is abolished." It has been cynically suggested that the NPVIC is being proposed not on the basis of its merits but instead as a means of causing so much disruption in future elections that it will lead to an outcry for a constitutional amendment.

Unfortunately for such advocates, the NPVIC itself cannot provide for a runoff, since it has chosen to avoid the constitutional amendment process entirely, choosing instead to shackle its scheme to the Electoral College structure by forming a cabal to allocate its electoral votes to a hypothetical popular vote winner. Under this scheme there is simply no room for runoffs, appointment of a federal entity to conduct national vote tallies, or even a national process of conducting recounts.

The NPVIC's Intractable Recount Problem

The Tenth Amendment of the U.S. Constitution guarantees to the states that all "powers not delegated to the United States by the Constitution, nor prohibited by it to the states, are reserved to the States." Thus, the states retain all the powers of a sovereign state except those that are specifically delegated to the federal government.[14] They are therefore free to exercise not only those retained powers but also those plenary powers specifically granted to them by Article II 1(2) to "appoint, in such manner as the Legislatures thereof may direct, a number of electors." Since 1880, all states have exercised this power by providing that electors shall be appointed by the popular vote of people within their respective states and in accordance therewith have promulgated such legislation as it deems proper to regulate the manner and procedures in which electors are chosen. This power includes providing for the terms and circumstances under which recounts of statewide elections shall take place.

States vary widely in this respect. New Hampshire, for example, permits candidates to call for a recount if the margin is within 20 percent.[15] Others, such as Alabama, provide for automatic recounts if the margin is 0.5 percent of votes. Still others require a losing candidate within a certain margin, such as 2 percent, to request the recount and sometimes to pay the costs of such recount.

A glance at the records of the margin of vote in past presidential elections reveals that in 44 of 49 presidential elections, the margin has been sufficient to qualify for a recount in at least one state, such as New Hampshire, and the national margin in about one in five presidential elections has been less than 2 percent. The election of James Garfield in 1880 was

.09 percent, and the election of George Bush in 2000 was .51 percent. It has already been noted that the margin of popular votes in 1960 was so narrow that the virtual popular vote could not even be finally determined, contingent as it was on how to count the popular votes for the split slate of Democratic electors.

Given the frequency with which the popular vote in past presidential elections was within the margin of error for triggering a recount in at least 1 state, it is difficult to imagine a more chaotic horror than an NPVIC direct election in which some states conduct recounts and others do not. The spectacle becomes even more disturbing when one considers that under the NPVIC, as few as 11 states—though almost certainly less than all the states—would even agree to a national popular vote at all. With less than all the states having signed the NPVIC, what would prevent the nonparticipant states from declining to engage in any national recount at all—especially if its favored candidate had already won? Given these circumstances, how could any legitimate national recount ever be conducted?

The NPVIC manifesto responds that *if* a number of federal laws were passed, these intractable problems might somewhat be mitigated. It expresses the hope that "enactment of the National Popular Vote compact would provide impetus for the states to review and modify their laws regarding timely recounts in presidential elections."[16]

The real problem, however, is that such hopes are not a substitute for an actual federal national vote recount law, which would make uniform all the recount laws of all the states and provide for a national entity to recount the votes. The fact is, however, that no interstate compact, league, or combination has the constitutional power to enact such federal laws. A constitutional amendment might conceivably be able to do so by essentially rewriting and amending major portions of the Constitution. But a cabal, an amalgamation, or combinations of any sort do not and cannot.

The Compact Clause of the U.S. Constitution

The compact clause of the Constitution Article I, 10(3)—not to be confused with the NPVIC—provides that "No State shall, without the Consent of Congress . . . enter into any Agreement or Compact with another State." In *U.S. Steel Corp. vs. Multistate Tax Comm'n*[17] the Supreme Court held that any compact or agreement between states is illegal without congressional approval if it (1) gives a member state political power that it could not exercise but for the compact and thereby "encroach(es) upon the supremacy of the United States,"[18] (2) gives delegates sovereign power to another entity, or (3) does not allow a member to withdraw at any time.

The NPVIC manages to violate all three of these constitutional prohibitions.

First, it purports to give a cabal of states the power to conduct a national tally of national popular votes and to make such decisions as to how to count those votes in a way that could affect the national presidential election—such as how to allocate popular votes cast for unpledged electors. This is a power no state other than the state listing only electors would have but for the powers it would gain under the compact and thus directly infringes upon the supremacy of the United States.

Second, the NPVIC does delegate signatory states' sovereign power to an unnamed entity charged with responsibility for conducting a national tally of popular votes and for making decisions as to whether to count votes cast in states that list only electors on the ballot and not the names of presidential candidates.

Third, the NPVIC sets strict limits on when states can withdraw from it in direct violation of the Supreme Court's requirement that any such compact must allow member states to withdraw at any time.

While the compact clause has been held not to forbid various housekeeping agreements between states such as those to settle water rights or create interstate commissions to develop uniformity of certain states and tax laws, no compact between the states has *ever* been approved that encroaches upon federal sovereignty as the NPVIC purports to do.

Finally and most seriously, the NPVIC would effectively deprive all nonsignatory states of the two electoral votes to which it is constitutionally entitled by virtue of its equal representation in the Senate, which entitlement is guaranteed by Article V and subject to abrogation only by unanimous consent of all the states. The cabal created by the NPVIC does so by rendering *all* the electoral votes of nonsignatory states irrelevant once the cabal has cast its electoral votes based on popular votes alone.

CHAPTER SIX

The Grand Compromise and the Unit Vote

Myths and Misdirection

The National Popular Vote Interstate Compact (NPVIC) manifesto *Every Vote Equal*[1] cavalierly dismisses as myths any concerns expressed about the disruption to federalism and democracy that would follow any attempt to implement the NPVIC. Each myth is then purportedly refuted by contradictions, half-truths, and non sequiturs having little or no relevance to the substance of the purported myth.

For example, to the myth that the "distribution of political influence envisioned by the Great Compromise would be upset by a national popular vote,"[2] the manifesto argues first that the NPVIC is "state legislation and therefore would have no effect on the formula in the U.S. Constitution for allocating electoral votes among the states."[3] Two sentences later it asserts that "the balance of power in the choice of president has been dramatically changed by state legislation in the past—most notably the widespread adoption of the winner-take-all rule."[4]

These two sentences alone reveal not only contradiction but also misdirection. First, state legislation either can or cannot affect the states' balance of power in presidential elections. Both cannot be true. Second, the decision of an individual state to adopt such a winner-take-all rule cannot be equated with a compact or conspiracy[5] between states to do so in concert.

The first sentence quoted states a half-truth. Legislation promulgated within an individual state and affecting only that state cannot affect the formula for allocating electoral votes among the states, and any legislation purporting to do so would indeed be unconstitutional on its face. The NPVIC purports to create a cabal such as would bind signatories to a scheme that no state could enact individually. How such a combination in violation of the compact clause would affect the constitutional allocation of power among the states for election among the states has been described in detail in Chapter 2: the NPVIC would effectively deprive each state of the electoral votes to which it is entitled by virtue of its equal representation in the Senate. This entitlement is guaranteed by both Article II, Section 1(2), and Article V and is subject to abrogation only by unanimous consent of all the states.

Rather than addressing this unassailable point, the NPVIC myth breakers nevertheless purport to refute it by changing the subject entirely to the issue of the unit-vote rule, which has been adopted by all states except Maine and Nebraska. Under this rule (often called the "general ticket system"), a state chooses to cast *all* its electoral votes to the candidate whose elector slate won the most popular votes in that state. According to some cynics, it was James Madison himself who switched his support from a district system (in which each congressional district voted for an elector) to the unit-vote system in the 1800 election because he thought the district system would favor Thomas Jefferson.[6] Although Jefferson did favor the district system, he was perhaps the first to recognize that if all the other states "choose . . . by general ticket, it is folly and worse for the [other states] not to do it."[7]

Jefferson's reasoning is not difficult to comprehend when considering the following hypothetical: assume a state is allocated 12 electoral votes (10 electors for each House representative and 2 for each Senate representative); assume further that candidate A won the popular vote in six of the congressional districts and that candidate B won the vote in four of the congressional districts and also won the statewide vote by a margin of 60–40 percent. Under most variations of the district vote system, the state in question would send 6 electors pledged to candidate A to the Electoral College and 6 electors for candidate B (1 for each congressional district won and 2 for winning the statewide vote)—for a *net* impact of the state's vote in the Electoral College of precisely *zero*. Under the unit-vote system, *all* 12 electoral votes would go for candidate B, dramatically increasing that state's impact on the presidential election.

Under the proportional system advocated by some reformers,[8] a state's electoral votes would be cast in proportion to the popular votes cast in the state. In the example above, this would mean that if electoral votes are rounded off to the nearest whole vote, the state would cast 7 electoral

The Grand Compromise and the Unit Vote 61

votes for candidate B and 5 electoral votes for candidate A—this time for a net impact in the Electoral College of 2 votes for candidate B. If every state adopted the proportional system, this would mean that the electoral vote would very closely track the national popular vote and reduce the odds—although not completely eliminate the possibility—that any candidate could be elected in the Electoral College without winning the national popular vote. (Had this plan been in effect in 1880 and 1896, it would have elected popular vote losers Winfield Scott Hancock and William Jennings Bryan.)[9] For this reason, another reform proposal would allow for fractional electoral voting. In the example above, this would mean that candidate A would receive 7.2 electoral votes and candidate B 4.8 electoral votes. If every state adopted this system, it would virtually guarantee that no candidate would ever be elected without winning the popular vote. But understandably, no state would want to adopt this system alone. In the above example, the net impact of a state's electoral votes would be 2.4 votes depending on how many decimal points out the fraction would be calculated. Some proportional proposals have advocated rounding off each electoral vote to the nearest one thousandth of 1 electoral vote.[10] Senator Henry Cabot Lodge ridiculed such a plan by noting that "Even the cleverest surgeon cannot divide one man up—proportionately or otherwise—and expect him to live."[11] (Of course, the problem of carving up a human being could be easily avoided by adopting yet another proposal for electoral reform, namely the automatic plan by which electoral votes are awarded only on paper without the need to appoint actual human electors.)[12]

Consequently, it is no wonder that ever since Jefferson first noted that it would be "folly and worse" for any state to *not* adopt the unit-vote system if other states were adopting it, all but Maine and Nebraska *have* adopted it. At least two other states—Colorado and California—have attempted to adopt similar plans by public referendum, but all such proposals have been defeated by voters or legislators in their respective states.[13] Understandably, California Democrats who now consider that state a lock to give their presidential candidate a huge bloc of 55 votes in the Electoral College were not keen on sharing even a single one of those 55 votes with a Republican candidate under either a district or proportional plan.

When in 1950 a bill was introduced in the Senate to amend the Constitution to require all states to adopt the proportional system in casting its electoral votes,[14] it was recognized that such a constitutional mandate would be the functional equivalent of a national popular vote election. As such, it would carry with it all the undemocratic features of a national popular vote—namely, it would result in countless runoffs, allow for election of a candidate opposed by a majority of the people, encourage factionalism, discourage compromise, lead to the creation of an unstable multiparty system, and magnify the ambiguity and delay in close elections by requiring problematic recounts in all 50 states and over 100,000 precincts. It did, however, have one redeeming feature: unlike the NPVIC, it would not have violated the Article V guarantee to the states the right to two electors based on their equal representation in the Senate and thus would not have required agreement by every state in the union to this amendment to the Constitution. In any case, outraged senators killed the proportional bill for a variety of reasons. As noted, Senator Henry Cabot Lodge objected that "Even the cleverest surgeon cannot divide one man up—proportionately or otherwise—and expect him to live."[15] Democrat Paul Douglas fumed that if the "Republican Party succeeds in having the Gossett resolution adopted that would put an end . . . to the civil rights issue from national politics. . . . No surer method of introducing confusion and lack of confidence in our electoral system could be devised."[16] Senator John F. Kennedy observed that the proportional plan "has been discredited in the past and promises only doubt and danger for the future. . . . There is obviously little to gain—but much to lose by tampering with the Constitution."[17]

Even those who supported the proportional plan, such as Senator Ed Gossett, managed to undermine their own bill by claiming that one advantage of the proportional plan was that it would lessen the influence of African Americans and Jews.[18] This view coincided with a critic of the plan who *opposed* it for precisely the same reasons: "If the Gossett Plan goes through, the [African American] and the vote of any other minority or national, or religious group will no longer be important. . . . The Gusset plan is anti-urban, anti-northern, and anti-liberal."[19]

The fact that the unit-vote system has been adopted by most states, however, is hardly a rebuttal to the fact that on its face the NPVIC would violate the Article V guarantee to every state of two electoral votes for each senator and the weight that those two electoral votes gives to each state in the Electoral College. If supporters of the NPVIC really believe that it is the unit vote adopted by most states that is the problem rather than the Electoral College itself, it is unfortunate that they have not directed their considerable resources and energies to proposing an interstate compact by which signatory states would agree to abandon the unit-vote rule in favor of either a district or proportional plan that would closely track the national popular vote. While such a compact would carry all the undemocratic features of a direct vote plan that have been previously described, it would at least pass muster under Article V, since it would not deprive the states of their two electors based on equal representation in the Senate. Unlike the NPVIC, it could also conceivably pass muster under the Article I, Section 10(2), compact clause, since by retaining the basic element of the Grand Compromise it would not alter federal structure. (See Chapter 10 on the compact clause.)

CHAPTER SEVEN

Presidential Campaigns and Incentives

"That's Where the Votes Are"

The Grand Compromise at the Constitutional Convention of 1787 that united 13 disparate colonies into the United States of America was achieved only by granting to all states the right of equal representation in the Senate and the concomitant allocation of presidential electors based on that equal representation.[1] This right was so integral to forming the union that these states made it an absolute precondition for joining.[2] But this was not enough to allay their suspicions of a future bait and switch. Delegate Gunning Bedford spoke for all the states that had demanded equal representation when he stated frankly to all those whose promises of equal representation had been made to induce them to agree to the Grand Compromise, "I do not, gentlemen, trust you."[3] So lacking in trust that some future attempt might not be made to deprive them not only of their right to equal representation in the Senate but also of the electors allocated to them based on that equal representation, they insisted on a *specific* provision that would not allow even the regular amendment process to take away those rights. It is the very last clause of Article V that does so by absolutely forbidding the taking away of a state's equal representation in the Senate upon which the allocation of electors' votes is based unless those rights are abrogated by unanimous consent of every state in the union. In light of the numerous attempts since then to deprive states of their electoral votes based on equal representation in the Senate, it now appears that their lack of trust was well founded. The National Popular

Vote Interstate Compact (NPVIC) is only the latest of those attempts to do so, mostly by those groups whose political motivations are only too transparent and whose vision only too narrow and short-sighted.[4]

When one considers the potential consequences of a national popular vote, one must treat its premise as a pure hypothetical. It is hypothetical in that it assumes that every state in the union would agree to being deprived of the weight in the presidential election process granted to it by virtue of its guarantee of two electoral votes based on equal representation in the Senate. But unlikely as it is that *every state in the union* would give up the very guarantee that formed the touchstone of the Grand Compromise and the Constitution, it is at least theoretically possible that all the states, even all the smaller states, might do so. It is therefore incumbent to consider the possibility of the NPVIC reaching a critical mass of signatory states but also somehow passing constitutional muster.

The NPVIC manifesto asserts that it is a myth that "the current system ensures that presidential candidates reach out to every state."[5] Like most of the long litany of myths that the 1056 page NPVIC manifesto purports to debunk, it misstates a very valid and critical objection to the NPVIC. First, no advocate or preserving federalism has ever claimed that the current system ensures that a presidential candidate must reach out to every state. It is true that in the 2012 presidential election "campaign field offices were heavily concentrated in the twelve states where the presidential and vice presidential candidates held postconvention general-election campaign evens."[6] But under the present system even the states with the smallest populations are allocated three electoral votes, which gives them a disproportionate voting weight in the Electoral College—a disproportion that the NPVIC manifesto reviles since it is violates the "every vote equal" principle by giving every state the right of equal representation in the Senate regardless of population. This means that even the smallest states can deliver more presidential voting weight than they could if their voting weight was measured solely on the basis of population. This in turn makes a small state a greater attraction for a candidate to campaign in than would be the case under a direct election scheme. This is especially true if the state has adopted the unit-vote rule.

What defenders of the Framers' constitutional plan *have* claimed is nothing more than the obvious—namely, under a national popular vote scheme, however constructed, there would be every incentive for candidates to concentrate campaigning efforts where there are the greatest concentrations of population—Los Angeles, New York, and Chicago.

Like the answer attributed to bank robber Willie Sutton when asked why he robbed banks ("that's where the money is"), candidates having to

Presidential Campaigns and Incentives 67

operate under a national popular vote scheme would be certain to concentrate their campaign efforts in areas of the greatest concentrations of population because that's where the votes are. If a candidate giving a campaign stump speech can expect to draw people from a radius of 20 miles, would he or she be more likely to schedule that event in the middle of Los Angeles or in the wilds of Alaska? Would a candidate expect to reach more people broadcasting an ad on a television station reaching all the inhabitants of Manhattan or all the inhabitants of a small town in North Dakota? Which campaign ad would provide the biggest bang for the buck?

The NPVIC manifesto recognizes the disproportionate weight small states have in the Electoral College but dismisses this as only a "theoretical" advantage that "does not in practice translate into political influence."[7] This is a puzzling dismissal given that the very premise of *Every Vote Equal* is that this smaller state advantage in both the Senate and the Electoral College justifies abrogating and gutting the entire constitutional plan for presidential elections that has worked so well for over two centuries. If the small-state advantage is so inconsequential, why does it justify such an untested upheaval of the Framers' plan for presidential elections?

It is true that under the current constitutional system candidates focus more of their attention on the big population states than those with a small population,[8] but this would be even truer under the NPVIC scheme simply because that's where the votes are. Although presidential campaigns can be hideously expensive, funds are never unlimited, so choices must be made as to where limited funds can be spent to have the most impact. The notion that under an NPVIC election scheme candidates will be rushing to sparsely populated areas to spend their available campaign funds is speculation unsupported by facts or logic.

Having trivialized the small-state advantage in the Electoral College that it previously reviled, the manifesto resorts to two additional explanations as to why, under the current constitutional plan, candidates tend to concentrate their campaign efforts in the large-population states and why the NPVIC scheme candidates would stop ignoring the small states.

The first is the manifesto's recurrent bogeyman: the unit vote.[9] Since the largest-population states are allocated the most electoral votes, the argument goes that when they become battleground states by virtue of the political parties being closely divided there, candidates tend to spend a disproportionate amount of their campaign energies in those states. This is undoubtedly true where each candidate has a chance of winning all of them. The manifesto gushes about the lucky voters in battleground states such as Ohio who are treated to "every method of communication (including television, radio, newspapers, magazines, direct mail, billboards telephone and the internet)."[10]

If the unit vote truly is the problem, then a more rational interstate compact would be directed toward getting states to agree to award their electoral votes on a proportional basis. Such a compact would surely pass constitutional muster, since it would not be in direct violation of Article V guaranteeing equal representation in the Senate and on the weight that equal representation carries in the Electoral College. It also brings us full circle to the merits of the proportional plan discussed in the previous chapter. It is simply recalled here that great attention has already been given to such a plan by Congress on numerous occasions and was ultimately rejected, highlighted by John F. Kennedy's observation in referring to the unit vote: "If it is proposed to change the balance of power of one of the elements of the solar system [of government power], it is necessary to consider the others."[11]

The manifesto's second explanation as to why the NPVIC scheme would send candidates scurrying to spend campaign money in sparsely populated hinterlands is that it would eliminate that political species known as the supposed ignored state. The reason for candidates ignoring such a state is that "presidential candidates have no incentive to visit, advertise in, organize in, poll in, or pay any attention to voters in states where they are comfortably ahead or hopelessly behind."[12] It is these voters, the manifesto claims, who are the unlucky voters. Professor John A. Tures claims that because of the unit-vote system adopted by most states, "The South is largely disenfranchised by the Electoral College."[13] How being spared television advertisements, junk mail, and unsolicited phone calls is the equivalent of being denied the right to vote is not fully explained.

The puzzling nature of this rationale becomes apparent if we carry its premise to its logical conclusion by applying it to the nation as a whole under an NPVIC scheme. According to NPVIC theory, if one candidate was far ahead in the national polls, neither party would ever spend a dime on campaigning: the candidate who was behind in the polls wouldn't spend any time campaigning or spending because he or she would be so sure to lose; the candidate ahead in the polls wouldn't spend a dime either since he or she was so far ahead in the polls. If any of this were really true, it might provide an instant remedy to the problem of excessive (or indeed any) spending in presidential campaigns, but it strains credulity to imagine that such a nationwide election could be conducted without a single penny being spent by either party or candidate.

Presidential Campaigns and Incentives   69

Since in the real world neither party has unlimited campaign funds, it is rational for a candidate to spend money where he or she thinks it will have the most impact, but that would be true regardless of how an election was structured.

The NPVIC theory also seems premised on one additional assumption—namely, voters in an ignored state would somehow suffer from being spared the barrage of television campaign advertisements, junk mail, and unsolicited telephone calls during the presidential campaign season. The bulk of campaign funds now go toward the most despised of all types of political advertising, namely television,[14] the bulk of which are either negative in nature, distort opponents' actual views, or take them out of context. Certainly very little in the way of constructive or useful knowledge is to be gained by such irritating commercials especially in ignored states, where the NPVIC theory suggests that voters have presumably made up their minds and will not be converted by yet more irritating or fatuous commercials. It is no wonder that candidates who spend the most on commercials are often the losers in elections.[15]

It is true that such commercials can play an important part in the early phases of the election process, particularly in primaries where name recognition can be key.[16] It is fair to say, however, that by the time the two major parties have selected their candidate, name recognition is not the problem. While voters in ignored states may not have the same opportunity to attend live campaign events in which a candidate appears in the flesh to give a stump speech, such events can only be attended by a very small percentage of a state's population, and the lack of such opportunity to attend such an event may be a small price to pay for not having to endure the barrage of commercials, unsolicited calls, and endless junk e-mails asking for contributions.

It might also be noted that in other democratic countries such as Great Britain, the campaign season and opportunity for barraging the public with mindless commercials is far more limited, and the voters there do not seem to feel deprived.[17]

Lucky them.

CHAPTER EIGHT

Legitimacy and Certainty

Every four or five presidential elections, the popular vote margin has been close enough to trigger recounts in at least one state and in many cases numerous states.[1] The 1960 election provides perhaps the most illustrative example of what could happen in any of these close elections had a Russian-style national popular vote election system been in effect.

According to the Congressional Quarterly, Richard Nixon won the national popular vote in that election by less than two-tenths of 1 percent.[2] (Some years later, some newspapers even began to claim that John F. Kennedy had won the popular vote by an even less margin but only by adding votes cast in Alabama for electors who voted for Senator Harry Byrd into the Kennedy popular vote column.)[3]

Fortunately for the nation and the stability of the U.S. government at a time of grave threat of international thermonuclear war, the very tricky question of who won the popular vote did not throw the country into a constitutional crisis. An election that could have resulted in interminable recounts, exhaustive litigation and appeals in courts of every state, and uncertainty as to which person would have his finger on the nuclear button did not do so. Instead, it resulted in a certain and clear cut decision: Kennedy was proclaimed and accepted as the undisputed winner of the election by virtue of his decisive 303–219 in the Electoral College. There were no postelection riots in the streets, no violent protests that Kennedy was not the legitimate winner, no foreign attempts to take advantage of internal civil unrest in the United States, and no appeals to the United Nations. Rather, the election played out precisely as envisioned by the Framers: the result was decisive and accepted by the people, and life returned to normal the day after the election.

Nevertheless, in light of the overwhelming evidence of massive vote fraud in Chicago,[4] there were many who expected Nixon to contest the election and demand a recount of the votes in Illinois. A recount showing that he had won the most popular votes in that state would have given him the Illinois electoral votes that had been allocated to Kennedy. Many have since explained Nixon's failure to do so as an indication of his magnanimity and concern for the welfare of his country that otherwise would have been thrown into turmoil by such a contest. Whatever Nixon's magnanimous motivations may or may not have been, however, the most compelling reason for not contesting the election was simple electoral math: his advisers presumably told him that even if he won all of Illinois's electoral votes by exposing the massive vote fraud committed by the Chicago political machine, it would not have changed the final electoral result. Kennedy would still have won the vote in the Electoral College even if he lost all of Illinois's electoral votes (though by a smaller margin of electoral votes).

It turns out that the true heroes of an election that might otherwise have thrown the nation into a cataclysmic convulsion was not Nixon's magnanimity. It was the Framers of the Constitution, in particular those Framers who not only conceived of the Grand Compromise but also implemented it in the form of specific provisions in Article I, II, and V. These three provisions, which taken together allocated to the small states a minimum of three electoral votes, *guarantee* that the minimum of three electoral votes based on equal representation in the Senate could only be abrogated by the agreement of every state in the union.

Because the likelihood of all 50 states agreeing to deprive the small states of their modest but important advantage in the Electoral College is so remote, it is tempting to dismiss that possibility as inconceivable. Of the 50 states in which the National Popular Vote Interstate Compact (NPVIC) has been introduced, two chambers of at least 11 states have already refused to sign, and in two others both chambers have failed to sign in a single session.[5] However, because the promoters of the NPVIC are apparently sufficiently convinced that the NPVIC could actually be implemented into law, they are willing to continue to spend millions to attempt to ram it through state legislatures under the public radar. For this reason it is instructive to consider how the NPVIC might have played out had it been in effect in previous elections such as the 1960 presidential election.

First, if the NPVIC had been in effect in that election, either Nixon or Kennedy would surely have contested the election results because of the incredible margin in the popular vote—less than two-tenths of one

Legitimacy and Certainty

percentage point. Without the Electoral College, a national recount would have been necessary in every precinct in every state of the union, since a change of even a handful of votes anywhere in over 100,000 precincts could alter the entire election result. For Americans traumatized by the 2000 election in which a recount and court appeals were necessary in a single state (Florida), it is difficult to even imagine that trauma magnified by a factor of 50 in which similar recounts and court appeals would have to be undertaken in every state in the union and the District of Columbia.

Second, although the NPVIC does not bother to define "chief election officials," whom it charges with the task of making a final tally of national popular votes, it is unlikely that even if these unnamed officials could somehow be identified they would all agree on a final vote tally. Presumably the chief election officers of states in which Nixon had clearly won the popular vote would have chosen to adopt the Congressional Quarterly's method of counting the popular votes. This method of making a final tabulation did not assign to Kennedy the popular vote cast for five of the Alabama electors' pledge to Senator Byrd. This resulted in a final total national popular vote tally in favor of Nixon. Other chief election officers in states in which Kennedy had clearly won the popular vote would presumably have chosen to follow the method of counting popular votes adopted by some newspapers. These newspapers reasoned that although the Democratic elector slate in Alabama included five electors pledged to Byrd, the Democratic slate taken as a whole received more popular votes than Nixon. Thus, presto, all the popular votes for the Democratic slate should be included in the final tally for Kennedy, since he was a Democrat and Byrd had no chance of winning the national election—despite the fact that five of the electors on that slate were in fact pledged to Byrd rather than Kennedy. By such a creative method of counting the popular vote, with the additional votes being accorded to Kennedy by pretending they were cast for him instead of Byrd, a number of newspapers calculated a final slender popular vote margin for Kennedy. Even today the average man in the street has come to believe that Kennedy won the popular vote, testament to the assumption that in 1960 at least some of the 50 chief election officers would have adopted this alternative method of counting the popular votes. Indeed, the election of Kennedy rather than Nixon would have depended upon which method was adopted. However, the fact that these two alternative methods existed at all reveals that the NPVIC's simplistic notion that all these 50 chief election officers have to do is obtain a calculator and "calculate the total number of popular votes from each state"[6] is at best illusory.

In Chapter 9, it is noted that the NPVIC manifesto *Every Vote Equal* suggests that the problem of which method to use to count the popular vote would be resolved by simply ignoring the votes for Alabama's unpledged electors. Aside from the draconian nature of a solution requiring the disenfranchisement of up to 1 million voters, the suggested the NPVIC solution fails to resolve how to force the chief election officers of the nonsignatory states to use any particular method of counting the popular votes.

In the unlikely circumstance that 50 chief election officers agreed on how to count the popular vote in 1960, the popular vote loser in 1960 would certainly have demanded a recount in every precinct in every state in the land. Not explained by the NPVIC is how 50 simultaneous Florida-style recounts, court trials, and appeals could take place prior to the date set by federal law for the Electoral College. Federal law has set the first Monday after the second Wednesday in the month of December following the election of electors on the Tuesday next after the first Monday in November in every fourth year as the deadline for casting electoral votes in the Electoral College.[7] In lieu of any explanation in the text of the NPVIC itself, the *Every Vote Equal* manifesto suggests a litany of proposed federal statutes that, if passed by Congress, might address the problem that the NPVIC itself creates. On the one hand, the manifesto dismisses the whole idea of a national recount by claiming that "the possibility of conducting a timely recount of a presidential election is largely an illusion"[8]—citing the short period of time between election day and the meeting of the Electoral College. On the other hand, it acknowledges the need for a national recount in close elections and proposes a series of statutes that might make a national recount feasible.[9]

This obfuscation misses the point. The 2000 recount of the popular votes in Florida showed not only that a recount is possible during the time between election day and the meeting of the Electoral College but also that such a recount has actually occurred.[10] In fact, television preserved for posterity the process of conducting the Florida recount in excruciating detail in the days following the election. If Florida managed to conduct recounts, it is not clear why other states would be incapable of doing so. The point is not whether such recounts are feasible—they clearly are—but that such recounts, if conducted on a national basis, would have to be conducted in every state, thus magnifying the trauma of the recount process by a factor of 50. (The whole problem of conducting recounts in some states but not others when trying to conduct a so-called national recount is set forth in the following chapter.)

The Certainty Principle

Americans have been spoiled by over 200 years of peaceful elections in which almost all cases have produced an immediate, clear-cut, and undisputed presidential winner even in such razor-thin elections as the 1960 election. Two exceptions generally prove the rule: the elections of 1876 and 2000.

The election of 1876, a favorite topic of political history journals, has been variously described as "the master fraud of the century,"[11] "the stolen election,"[12] "injustice and fraud," "a confidence game,"[13] and worse.[14] NPVIC advocates have even tried to include it on a list of "wrong winner" elections in which the popular vote winner was not the same as the electoral vote winner. In fact, this election was *sui generis*[15] and one that would have been disputed regardless of the election system in place. It took place at a time when the nation was still recovering from the trauma of the American Civil War, and emotions and wounds in both the North and the South still ran deep. In the South, resentment of Reconstruction and federal troops in their midst energized the redeemers of the Democratic Party, who were anxious to follow up on the Mississippi Revolution of 1875 that emboldened whites—most notoriously the Klu Klux Klan—to step up their attacks on African Americans. As one historian recorded, "Whites used threats, floggings, and outright murder to keep blacks away from the polls."[16] Northerners were no less passionate, as a typical Republican campaigner ranted that "Every man that shot Union soldiers was a Democrat. . . . Every man that loves slavery better than liberty was a Democrat. . . . The man that assassinated Lincoln was a Democrat. . . . Every arm that is lacking, every limb that is gone . . . is a souvenir of a Democrat!"[17] Enraged Republicans supporting Rutherford Hayes for president charged that the Democrat nominee, Samuel Tilden, even favored reparations for the former southern slaveholders to compensate them for "war damage."[18]

Although Tilden appeared to be the electoral winner on a tide of electoral votes in the Old South—particularly in Florida, Louisiana, and South Carolina—a second civil war now threatened in this heated political environment. When evidence of the massive intimidation of African Americans in those states came to the attention of the *New York Times,* its political writers quickly did some calculations and determined that if the fraud and intimidation revealed that Hayes had won the popular vote in those states, he would win the nationwide electoral vote in the Electoral College. Amid additional reports of flagrant vote buying and bribery, a second civil war was only averted when representatives of both parties agreed to the appointment of a bipartisan commission consisting of two Republicans, two Democrats, and a fifth member to be chosen jointly by the other four.

Had it been necessary for this commission to reexamine the votes in all the states, it is doubtful if any rational or acceptable conclusion could have been reached, at least not in any acceptable time period. Fortunately, the Framers of the Constitution had ensured that in such cases the problem of resolving challenges would be isolated to just a few states. In the end, the commission was persuaded that the evidence of intimidation of blacks in the states cited was simply too great and that the reported results in those states should be discounted. The commission declared the Republican Hayes the winner.

By all accounts, the conduct of both political parties was shameful and inexcusable. In elections in which intimidation, fraud, corruption, and bribery are endemic, no system of election can provide a certain and undisputed outcome. But the Electoral College certainly comes the closest. Even so, Hayes was obliged without fanfare to sneak into the White House through the backdoor on March 3, 1877, and take the oath of office in a private ceremony. As unsatisfactory as the outcome was, some small comfort may be found in the fact that compared to the state of the nation just a few years before in which over half a million Americans were being slaughtered en masse, the disputed election of 1876 can count not a single killing in the course of its final resolution. Nevertheless, NPVIC proponents continue to cite the 1876 election as an example of the election of the wrong president by comparing the electoral vote to an invalid and much-disputed popular vote.

The disputed 2000 election provides another example of how the Electoral College averted both a constitutional crisis and civil upheaval. That election was one of the rarest of elections in which the margin of victory in the Electoral College was itself very narrow and turned upon the allocation of electoral votes in a single state—Florida.

In the end, the election of 2000 was resolved by the Supreme Court when it finally upheld the most recent recount conducted prior to the meeting of the Electoral College and put an end to what threatened to become an interminable stream of yet more recounts that would have provided no additional certainty.[19] Not surprisingly, and depending on what method was employed for counting different formats of ballots including the notorious butterfly ballot, each recount provided slightly different results each time it was conducted. In the meantime, America needed a president, on time and in accordance with what the Constitution required.

Legitimacy and Certainty 77

The 2000 election also provides a microcosm of how the election might have been resolved under a Russian-style popular vote election. The so-called popular vote was close enough to trigger recounts in some but not all states. The NPVIC does not provide a mechanism for a hypothetical national recount and instead relies upon the hope that some future Congress might promulgate statutes to do so. The passage of any future bill purporting to do so would be unconstitutional on its face, as it impinges upon Article II's delegation to each state the plenary power to allocate its electoral votes in any way in which it sees fit. It would also mean abrogating all state recount laws, including in states that decline to join the NPVIC conspiracy of states. In so doing it would also violate the Tenth Amendment, which preserves to each state all of the sovereign powers except those it specifically delegates to the federal government. Nevertheless, it is instructive to envision how such hypothetical bills, even if somehow passing constitutional muster, would play out in an election such as the 2000 election.

First, a hypothetical national recount would require that recounts be conducted not just in a single state, as in Florida in the 2000 election, but in *every* state. This in turn would require recounts in each state's electoral districts, precincts, and hamlets, which could number well over 100,000. As in Florida, this would in turn generate lawsuits and court appeals in each of those states and also assumes that every hamlet, every precinct, and every state from North Dakota to Alaska had the same bureaucratic infrastructure, resources, and judicial infrastructure as Florida that would enable it to do so in the time frame required by federal law. Given the nightmare that such a scenario presents, it highlights yet again how wise the Framers were in leaving the entire matter of choosing electors to the states rather than trying to impose a monolithic federal structure from on high *upon* the states. Indeed, had the Framers chosen to do so, it would have necessitated revising elements of the entire structure of federalism embedded in virtually every other provision of the Constitution.

Historical Lessons

The history of civilizations is largely the study of the leaders of those civilizations. The fall of these civilizations reveals a fatal defect common to almost all: the failure to provide for the orderly transition of power from one leader to the next. History is littered with the carcasses of nations that collapsed less because of external threats than from the weaknesses created by internal rivalries for political power. Even in those instances where civilizations fell due to external forces, that fall can be traced in most cases to internal divisions in the conquered state.

The Roman Empire provides the most illustrative example. Rome thrived during a period in which it recognized the fatal defects of the monarchist model, which often led to tyranny. Instead, over years of trial and error the empire created a republic in which powers were separated and an internal political structure was created, largely by custom, whereby power was limited and succession took place according to procedures agreed upon *in advance* to ensure legitimacy and certainty in the matter of succession. Its one fatal flaw was its failure to memorialize those procedures in the form of a written constitution. This left the Roman Republic subject to the predations of military leaders who were able to seize personal power by resort to brute physical force outside the limits of the political structures that had been developed during the period of the republic. This in turn resulted in the reversion to the monarchism model in which succession is based primarily on a ruler's ability to provide a suitable male heir. Failing that, which was often the case, power again resided in those able to marshal the great physical force until the monarchist model could again be reinstated. While the Roman Empire that resulted under this model continued to exist and even expand for several hundred years pursuant to the deep-state bureaucratic infrastructure created during the republic, the civil wars for succession that it generated ultimately so undermined the strength of the empire that it ultimately fell to outside forces.

The monarchist model has persisted in the world even up to the present day—witness North Korea—because of the one single advantage it bestowed in providing the stability necessary to create and preserve a complex civilization, namely certainty in the manner of succession. As long as a leader produced a male heir that all the citizenry would recognize as legitimate, civil war could be avoided. The Roman Empire could survive even such tyrants as a Nero and Caligula under such a model. What it could not ultimately survive was the civil wars that followed any breakdown in the certainty, acceptance, and legitimacy of succession.

In 1135 a devastating and destructive civil war broke out in England when King Henry I could not produce a male heir, leaving a daughter, Matilda, as his only heir. When a more distant male relative, Stephen, contested the throne, the country was thrown into a violent civil war in which "the earth bare no corn, for the entire land was laid waste." The average villager of the time probably cared little about whether Stephen or Matilda was on the throne or which of the two was more qualified, but what he would certainly have cared about was the laying waste to his fields, the killing of his livestock, the burning of his home, and the raping of his wife and daughters by the rampaging armies of each side.

Legitimacy and Certainty 79

The ancient Athenians are credited with implementing one of the first alternative systems to the monarchist model—namely, a democratic vote of the people. But even this system, made possible only by the simplicity and certainty of counting the votes in a civic assembly, was dependent on advance acceptance of the citizenry of whatever the result might be. Even then, the acceptance of the result was dependent upon absolute confidence in the integrity of the process.

The 1960 presidential election provides a modern example of the importance of the certainty principle. That election could have degenerated into a constitutional crisis and civil upheaval triggered by endless recounts, litigation, and appeals. That it did not can be attributed to how it was instead quietly and routinely resolved in the Electoral College. Even more remarkable is that this peaceable resolution occurred almost without the knowledge of the average American. Only those Americans who happened to read the back pages of newspapers on the day after the third Wednesday after the first Monday of November would know that the president had been duly elected in the Electoral College.

In 2006 a disputed election in Mexico resulted in massive street protests and threats of civil war because of the lack of confidence in the integrity of a system charged with the almost insurmountable task of counting the popular vote.

In 2007, a disputed presidential election in Kenya incited massive disruptions that virtually shut off all commerce and threatened bloodshed.

In 1876 the United States was spared the threat of upheaval and civil war by the last-minute agreement of Tilden and Hayes to abide by the decision of a five-person commission. No doubt the raw memories of the recent slaughter of the American Civil War tempered what might otherwise have resulted in calls for yet more death and bloody destruction of the kind endured by the Roman Empire and by the English in 1135.

Civil commotion in the United States was averted in 2000 due to the Electoral College, helped by the grudging, last-minute, narrow but ultimately decisive acceptance of the Supreme Court's decision to resolve the dispute by resort to legal and constitutional principles. But the survival of a republic should not depend on such narrow escapes from chaos. Only by giving the highest priority to preserving the integrity of the election process can the certainty principle of democracy be preserved.

Despite these lessons from history, self-proclaimed electoral reformers continue to give certainty of result a very low priority. Typical of the considerations given much higher priority by many politicians is convenience. Oblivious to the very real dangers of a disputed election and eager

Absentee Ballots

First among these is the emasculation of the most sacred and personal aspects of the voting process. In the past, those who were unable to go to a voting station were entitled to obtain absentee ballots. These included railroad workers, military personnel serving abroad or outside their home districts, and those with medical disabilities who obtained a doctor's notarized statement affirming their physical inability to travel to a polling station. Today, virtually anyone can obtain such a ballot and for virtually any reason. "I'd rather stay home and watch the hockey game" or "I really don't like to go out in the rain or wait in line" will suffice. In many cases, no reason at all is even asked for.

As a result of such ill-conceived legislative measures, incidents of absentee voting fraud have skyrocketed in recent years.[20] Although endemic, a few examples reveal the tip of the iceberg. In 1998, a Pennsylvania congressman was convicted of absentee ballot racketeering in a nursing home, which involved the forging of absentee ballots in the names of nursing home residents. In other cases absentee ballots were collected from nursing homes, and only selected ones were dropped off in the mail or the ballot receptacle. In the 1997 Miami mayoral race, it was revealed that hundreds of absentee ballots were forged, prompting a Pulitzer Prize–winning series in the *Miami Herald* to conclude that "absentee voting has led to massive fraud."[21]

In 2003, the Indiana Supreme Court overturned a mayoral primary election after finding "pervasive fraud" that it termed a "'textbook' example of the chicanery that can attend the absentee vote cast by mail."[22] In 2011 a man was convicted for voting in the names of 10 people, 4 of whom were actually deceased.[23]

These examples are by no means isolated. To date, the U.S. Justice Department has prosecuted massive absentee vote fraud in dozens of states, including but not limited to Arkansas, Missouri, North Carolina, Oklahoma, Pennsylvania, and South Carolina.[24]

The fact that absentee voting fraud is causing so many Americans to lose confidence in the integrity of their elections poses a grave risk to achieving the kind of certainty necessary to prevent the constitutional crisis and civil commotion that come with disputed elections. Other countries have had to learn this the hard way.

Legitimacy and Certainty   81

In 2004, the presidential election in Ukraine was marred by wide-spread absentee ballot fraud. Thousands of absentee ballots disappeared from warehouses, only to reappear in voting bins shortly before the election. A total of 1.5 million absentee ballots were cast, far exceeding the number of real voters in the country. So flagrant were the absentee ballot frauds that 800,000 Ukrainians braved the freezing cold to encircle the parliament and other government buildings to threaten violence if absentee ballot laws were not reformed. To its credit, the parliament did just that, ordering a new election and reforming the absentee ballot laws to limit the use of such ballots to the infirm, the disabled, and injured citizens who were actually immobile—precisely the policy of American voting law before the politicians began catering to the convenience of voters. Ironically, many of those Ukrainians who braved the bitter cold to demonstrate and threaten violence may have been among those who cast absentee ballots legitimately on grounds that it was too inconvenient to go to the voting station in person.

Nevertheless, American politicians continue to turn a blind eye to the risks to democracy posed by absentee ballots, lamely asserting that convenience of some voters is more important than the integrity of the voting process. It should also be noted that for every fraudulent absentee ballot that is cast, another legitimate voter is effectively disenfranchised.

Provisional Ballots and Voter ID

Nor is the absentee ballot the only means by which politicians have raised the convenience factor above considerations of voting integrity. New provisional ballot laws allow people to vote provisionally despite appearing at a voting booth on election day without registration, valid identification, proof of address, or any other indicia of eligibility to vote. But aside from encouraging illegal voting and fraud, the greatest danger posed by such laws is that the decision to count such votes is determined *after the election* by adversarial representatives of each political party. Such scenarios inevitably lead to interminable lawsuits and litigation. The result is an election decided not by voters but instead by lawyers and judges. Candidates dare not concede an election and let the nation return to normal life as long as provisional ballots are still to be counted, analyzed, and litigated. Candidates who dare to go ahead and concede an election before the interminable process of litigating provisional ballots is completed are lambasted for displaying a callous disregard of the provisional vote and consigning such votes to the dustbin of second-class votes. This happened to John Kerry in the 2004 election when he dared to concede the election to Bush rather than waiting weeks or more for provisional ballots to be counted or litigated, thus leaving the country in limbo as to who actually won the election and who can start forming the government.

Supporters of provisional ballots and opponents of any law that would document voter eligibility lamely maintain that voter ID laws might inhibit certain persons from conveniently voting. The fact that such identification is necessary to cash a check, ride on an airplane, or even show entitlement to welfare reveals that convenience, not ensuring the right to vote, is the overriding concern. Even when voter ID laws provide for issuance of such cards for free, the case is made that their purpose is to prevent people from voting. Is the purpose of the requirement to show ID in order to cash a check or ride in an airplane to prevent people from cashing checks or riding in an airplane?

When opponents to voter ID attempt to make their case by referencing the relatively small number of prosecutions for voter impersonation, the courts have been quick to show the fallacy of such references. As the Seventh District Court of Appeals noted, the sparsity of prosecutions is explained by "endemic under enforcement" and the "extreme difficulty in apprehending a voter impersonator" without the tools of a voter ID card to detect such fraud.[25] When the *New York Times* tried to claim that voting fraud is a myth, it might have wanted to check its own past articles, including one headlined "Boss Tweed Is Gone, but Not His Vote,"[26] in which it documented a grand jury finding of "forgery of voter registration cards with the names of fictitious persons . . . [and] recruitment of people to cast multiple votes on behalf of specified candidates."[27]

While voter fraud poses grave risks to democracy, the greater risk it poses is to the certainty and legitimacy of presidential elections, without which lurks the danger of constitutional crisis, civil upheaval, and instability. In this respect, the Electoral College has done its job too well, leading many Americans into a sense of complacency: what happened in Ukraine, what is happening in Mexico today, and what happened to so many other civilizations in history could not possibly happen to us. NPVIC promoters assume that all the advantages the Electoral College has provided to Americans in the past would also prevail under a Russian-style direct election. In fact, such a system would undermine the very democratic features that give the Framers' vision its substance.

Legitimacy

One might assume that the immediate and decisive effect of the Electoral College would be conceded, even by Electoral College detractors, as

Legitimacy and Certainty

one great advantage of the Framers' vision. Not so. Those hostile to that vision, such as David Abbott and James Levine,[28] claim that the electoral mandates that the Electoral College award to winners are misleading to the American people. They cite the 1936 election in which Franklin D. Roosevelt received 98 percent of the electoral vote but only 61 percent of the popular vote as misleading Americans into believing that Roosevelt was elected in a landside. Why is this bad according to Abbott and Levine? Because, they claim, this "illusion of landside" might enable the president to "push through legislative agendas which are opposed by the majority."[29] It may also "endow the president with excessive power."[30] They also cite the fact that in 1980 Ronald Reagan received 489 electoral votes but only 50.1 percent of the popular votes.

The fallacy in this view rests on the assumption that one bothers to read the newspapers the day after the election. Those old enough to remember the 1960 election are much more likely to remember that the election was one of the closest in American history rather than the fact that Kennedy won in the Electoral College by an overwhelming margin of 303–216. And are members of Congress really likely to roll over and vote for the president's agenda just because he received a healthy margin of electoral votes? As for the loser being demoralized by the lopsided electoral vote, it seems doubtful that Nixon or his party took the view that he had been wiped out. Rather, he was perceived as having come so close that he could win if he tried again (which of course he did in 1968). And does anyone who watched the 2016 election not know that Hillary Clinton won the popular vote even while losing by a significant margin in the Electoral College?

First, even if some voters were deluded in perceiving that Kennedy won a mandate, would the alternative be preferable—that is, that the president lacked a mandate to govern? Would it have been preferable had Kennedy been perceived as lacking a mandate to deal with the Soviets in the Cuban Missile Crisis?

Second, the Abbott and Levine theory fails to recognize that a healthy margin in the Electoral College, even with a narrow popular vote margin, represents support that is *broadly based* across the entire country and not just based on overwhelming popular support in one region, in a few states, or on the coasts. Victory in the Electoral College requires broad support across all major regions and many states, which should be considered as being even more reflective of a mandate since it reflects more than simply receiving concentrated support in one particular region or in a handful of states. In this regard, it has been observed that but for the overwhelming popular vote margin for Clinton in six California counties, Donald Trump would have won the national popular vote.[31]

Third and finally, most Americans are aware that presidential candidates campaign based on the allocation of electoral votes that the Constitution provides. In 2016, lucky New Yorkers and Californians were spared the misery of enduring fatuous campaign television ads because Trump did not waste his time campaigning in states where he knew he could not win. Under a Russian-style election he would surely have concentrated his efforts in high-population areas such as New York City, Chicago, and Los Angeles because that's where the votes are. Instead, he campaigned in the heartland across regions and states where he felt he had a chance and could win—a strategy that resulted in winning the election.

CHAPTER NINE

The Recount Problem

Supporters of National Popular Vote Interstate Compact (NPVIC) are fond of referencing polls that purport to show that the vast majority of Americans support a Russian-style direct election and the abolition of the Electoral College.[1] The most recent edition of the NPVIC manifesto *Every Vote Equal* extols the fact that as of 2010 nine states representing over half the number of electoral votes necessary to approve the NPVIC had adopted the bill.[2] As further proof of the overwhelming support for the NPVIC, it notes with satisfaction that the New York Senate voted 52–7 to adopt the NPVIC.[3]

Even taking into account that the results of such polls inevitably depend upon the wording of the question, they nevertheless raise the question of why, if there truly is such staggering national support for direct election, no constitutional amendment for abolishing the Electoral College has ever even gotten to the state ratification phase for adopting a constitutional amendment.

The answer must concede that the response of the man and woman on the street when asked such questions as "should the presidential candidate who receives the most popular vote be elected president" is quite often "yes." The same "yes" response is often recorded when the question is asked of a generic state legislator or even congressperson. Yet when congressional committees have examined *in detail* the underlying ramifications and consequences of direct election—or worse, of the NPVIC—such attempts to fiddle with the Constitution are stopped in their tracks.

In the case of a number of congressional hearings that have ultimately rejected such bills, it has been the prospect of endless runoffs (French or Russian style) that has caused congressional representatives to pull back from the brink.[4] This was a primary reason why the 1977 Birch Bayh hearings pulled back from the brink. The prospects of a collapse of the two-party system and the likelihood that a direct election would produce a winner with only narrow or minimal support being elected under such a direct election system were among other reasons for rejection.

State legislatures that have rejected the NPVIC have also expressed concern over the number of constitutional amendments that would be necessary to install a Russian-style direct election. The reasons for these states' rejection of the NPVIC are manifold but include the following.

First, Article II, Section 1, Clause 2, which currently grants to each state the power to appoint its own electors, would have to be amended in order to deprive all states of this right they have enjoyed for over 200 years.

Second, Article I, Section 3, Clause 1, which grants to each state equal suffrage in the Senate, would have to be abrogated since it is upon this equal suffrage in the Senate that the Constitution grants moderate extra weight to small states in presidential elections. This comes in the form of two electors to which they would not be entitled under any direct election system, whether imposed directly by constitutional amendment or indirectly by the NPVIC. The denial of states' equal suffrage in the Senate would effectively end the very existence of the Senate as an institution. (It may be recalled, however, that any amendment along these lines, under the guarantee clause of Article V, would require unanimous agreement of all the states.)

Third, Article I, Section 10, Clause 3, would have to be amended to allow states without the consent of Congress to enter into any amalgamations or compacts with other states with the purpose of altering the entire federalist structure of the U.S. government.

But a threshold problem that has caused state legislatures to pull back even without considering the three problems mentioned above is the recount problem. This was the primary reason why in 2007 the Colorado state house committee changed its vote from 10–1 in favor to 10–1 against the NPVIC bill after considering all the nightmarish recount scenarios that would likely occur under that scheme.[5]

Under the current constitutional system, presidential elections have rarely had to endure recounts. This is because even in elections in which the so-called popular vote is very close—or unascertainable as in the 1960 election[6]—a candidate's victory in the Electoral College has rendered moot the need for *any* recount of the entire national popular vote. It will be recalled that in the 1960 election Richard Nixon did not even *ask* for a recount in *any* state, even though in several states (such as Illinois) there was ample evidence of vote fraud, and he would have been entitled

The Recount Problem 87

to demand a recount under the recount laws of several states. This was because a recount in any of those states would not have changed the outcome in the Electoral College for John Kennedy.

For this reason, there has never been a state recount that has affected the outcome of a presidential election.[7] Even the NPVIC manifesto *Every Vote Equal* concedes that under the current system there have been only "five litigated state counts in our nation's 57 elections between 1789 and 2012."[8] In only one of those state recounts *could* the recount have altered the outcome of the election—although it didn't—and that was the election of 2000. The 2000 election was one of those rare presidential elections in which the *electoral* vote, rather than just the popular vote, was actually very close. In that election, a recount of the popular votes in Florida would throw the electoral count to Al Gore and take it away from George Bush if the recount showed that Gore had won the popular vote in that state. Although the Supreme Court finally upheld the popular vote count for Bush in Florida and thus his election, the 2000 election was nevertheless notable in serving as an example of how the Electoral College serves to *isolate* the recount in such cases to a single state.

It remains only to consider how an election in which the popular vote is close—not just on a national level but close in *any* state—would fare under a Russian-style direct election such as the one provided for under the NPVIC. Under that bill, a cabal of state legislatures representing 270 electoral votes would agree to refuse to allocate electoral votes based on the popular vote within their own states if it conflicted with a so-called national popular vote in other states; instead, each signatory state would be required to cast their respective electoral votes for the national popular vote winner. Thus, a recount in *any* state that resulted in winning or losing votes would affect the *national* popular vote total. This would mean that any recounting of the national vote would be meaningless unless *recounts were conducted in each and every state.*

Had the 1960 election been held under an NPVIC regime, Nixon would certainly have requested a national popular vote recount. This would have meant recounts *in every state,* along with the litigation and appeals that go with each of those state recounts. Imagine the 2000 Florida recount trauma magnified by a factor of 50! Imagine further the spectacle of the United States in the middle of the Cold War not knowing who had his finger on the nuclear button until *all 50* recounts and concomitant litigation and appeals had been conducted!

It was precisely this realization that so appalled the members of the Colorado House committee that in 2007 they reversed their vote from 10–1 in favor of the NPVIC to 10–1 *against.*

It is necessary, however, to address how NPVIC lobbyists try to answer these recount concerns:

First, they respond by claiming that "under the current system, a timely recount in a presidential race may be warranted but impossible to obtain in practice,"[9] noting that Title 3, Chapter 1, Section 7, of the U.S. Code requires that a state's counting and recounting be completed prior to the first Monday after the second Wednesday in December after the election.

It is difficult to see how Title 3 would make an NPVIC national recount scenario any less chaotic. The time between the first Tuesday of November and the first Monday after the second Monday can extend to four to six weeks, plenty of time for some states to conduct recounts, as Florida did in 2000. In 2000 Florida conducted recounts over the course of many weeks. The fact that some states might be able to conduct recounts but others might not is not a point in favor of a national recount. In fact, the question must be asked: how could any national recount have any meaning at all if only some states conduct recounts but others do not?

The NPVIC manifesto claims that the fact that "each presidential election under the current state-by-state winner-take-all system is really 51 separate state-level elections means that there is a significant chance of future disputed presidential elections under the current system."[10] However, this assertion is at odds with its concomitant claim that "there have been [only] five litigated state counts in our nation's 57 presidential elections between 1789 and 2012."[11] Assuming the accuracy of the latter and consigning the former as a mere unsubstantiated and self-serving prediction, it can reasonably be concluded that—with the possible exception of the 2000 election—recounts have not been a problem under the current system.[12] Unfortunately, the same cannot be said about what would almost certainly occur under an NPVIC Russian-style regime.

The NPVIC manifesto claims that a recount under the NPVIC would not be a "logistical impossibility or an unimaginable horror."[13] A reasonable person might agree with this assertion, since the horror would be only too imaginable and quite predictable. The crux of the problem is that the NPVIC does not provide for any mechanism *at all* for a national recount. The inconvenient truth facing any NPVIC election is that every state has its own rules and laws regarding recounts and under what circumstances recounts should be conducted.

The NPVIC substitute for a federal entity with the authority to declare and conduct a national recount is some nameless person or newspaper that might conceivably pick up a calculator, tally the popular vote totals released by the chief election official of each state, declare a close national

The Recount Problem

popular vote, and then mandate a national recount—on what national authority the NPVIC does not say. It has already been noted that without a national entity charged with responsibility for determining *how* to tally the popular votes from each state, it would be impossible to calculate a national popular vote. In the 1960 election, for example, many newspapers including the *New York Times* and the Congressional Record only allocated to Kennedy the popular votes cast in Alabama for the Democratic electors pledged to him—a method of counting popular votes that resulted in Nixon winning the hypothetical national popular vote.[14] Other newspapers decided to allocate to Kennedy the popular votes for *all* the Democratic electors (including the unpledged electors who ultimately voted for Senator Harry Byrd of West Virginia in the Electoral College) and thus concluded that Kennedy had won the national popular vote. But under an NPVIC regime, who would determine which method of counting popular votes should be adopted? The NPVIC makes no provision for creating any kind of entity with authority to order individual states to count their popular votes in any particular way. Even if the NPVIC had made such a provision, it would surely be unconstitutional as violating Article II, which gives to each state the plenary power to decide the manner in which electoral votes are to be allocated.

Even if the NPVIC was to make such a provision and even if such a provision could somehow pass constitutional muster, there would remain the insoluble problem of conducting any kind of national recount without all states participating in the recount. Consider a not unlikely NPVIC scenario in which presidential candidate A receives an overwhelming popular vote margin of 10 percent over candidate B in Utah, a state that has not adopted the NPVIC as a signatory; however, candidate B receives a very narrow national popular vote margin of one-tenth of 1 percent over candidate A. Candidate A then demands a national recount; Utah responds by declining to conduct a recount, since Utah law does not provide for any recount unless the popular vote in that state is less than 2 percent. Who is going to force Utah to conduct a popular vote recount in violation of its own laws? Other nonsignatory states would also surely decline to conduct recounts if it would violate their own election laws (especially those states in which the support for candidate B is very strong).

It is not difficult to imagine the horror of a national recount in which only some states participate. Although the spectacle of various political and partisan interest groups lobbying in various states and filing a barrage of court petitions to conduct recounts that might advantage their favored candidate might in itself qualify as a horror, the resulting chaos would be less in the form of a horror than in the simple undeniable fact that *any* such recount without all states participating would be meaningless.

The NPVIC manifesto purports to acknowledge and address this problem: "Let us start with the fact about how rare recounts are in actual practice."[15] The irony of this response is that while it is true that recounts in presidential elections under the current system are relatively rare, *the reason why they are rare is precisely that the current system renders any such recounts unnecessary*. It will be recalled that in 1960, the popular vote margin was so close that had a national popular vote system been in effect, Nixon (and possibly Kennedy had the Congressional Quarterly tally of popular votes been adopted) would surely have demanded a recount—not just in Illinois, where evidence of vote fraud was quite apparent, but *in every state*. The only reason he did not do so was because Kennedy's margin in the *Electoral College* was so substantial that a recount in any state, even one in Illinois, would not have changed the electoral vote. One has only to magnify by a factor of 50 the chaos and spectacle of the Florida recount in 2000 (isolated to but one state because of the Electoral College system) for the word "horror" to come to mind.

Tara Ross made this point in her written testimony to the Delaware Senate in June 2010: "States have different criteria for what does (or does not) trigger recounts within their borders. Those differences could cause a whole host of problems. What if the national total is close—close enough to warrant a recount—but a recount can't be conducted because the margins in individual states were not close?"[16]

The NPVIC's response: "Of course, the ability to obtain a recount in situations close enough to warrant a recount is hardly ensured under the current state-by-state winner-take-all system, as demonstrated by the nation's experience with Florida in 2000."[17] This inadequate response qualifies as misdirection on two counts.

First, it constitutes a complaint not against the Electoral College system but instead against the winner-take-all system, which all states except Nebraska and Maine have by law adopted. Whatever the merits or lack thereof of the winner-take-all system, its abolition would have to be by constitutional amendment, since it would mean amending Article II, which now grants to each state the plenary power to allocate its electoral votes as it sees fit—and that includes adopting a winner-take-all system. Forcing states to abandon their winner-take-all system by constitutional amendment might have arguable merits (it would come very close to achieving the same results as a direct election)[18] and would certainly be a more rational approach than the NPVIC, but the NPVIC has chosen for its

The Recount Problem   91

own reasons not to go the route of amending the Constitution, despite its claim that the vast majority of Americans favor a direct election.

Second, the 2000 Florida recount is hardly an example of how the Electoral College system creates the need for chaotic recounts. The NPVIC's manifesto correctly notes that under the current system there have been only "five litigated recounts in our nation's 57 presidential elections between 1789 and 2012."[19] The reason there have been so few is that it is the very rare election in which the electoral vote is so close that the flip of a single state's electoral votes could alter the result of the presidential election. Florida 2000 was one of those rare elections, but even in that election the recount was isolated to a single state. Under the NPVIC, a close popular vote election would require recounts in every state, not just recounts in a single state.

The NPVIC does make one valid point about recounts under a true direct election regime—namely, that the "probability of recounts would be much lower under a national popular vote because there would [be] a single large national pool of votes (instead of 51 separate pools)."[20] However, even this modest point carries little weight given that a direct election would certainly create a multiparty system—along the lines of France and Russia—that would in turn tend to create closer elections in need of recounts.

Unfortunately, this truism cannot serve as an argument in favor of the NPVIC for the following reasons.

First, the NPVIC is not a proposal for a constitutional amendment that, by abrogating Article II, would impose direct election by depriving the small states of their electoral advantage in the Electoral College. (The very advantage that induced the small states to join the union in 1789.) Such an amendment would also have to deprive all states of their right to promulgate their own state laws regarding terms and triggers for election recounts within their states—rights that states have heretofore enjoyed under the Tenth Amendment of the Constitution, which states that "powers not delegated to the United States by the Constitution, are reserved to the states respectively." (It should be noted that there is no provision in the Constitution whereby states have delegated to the federal government the right to preempt or abolish states laws for conducting elections within each state.) Finally, such an amendment would have to provide for a national entity or institution charged with responsibility for determining how to count and tally popular votes in each state, promulgating uniform regulations for conducting a national recount and enforcing such regulations.

But the NPVIC is not taking this constitutional approach. Rather, the NPVIC is seeking to form a cabal of selected states to circumvent the

Constitution by agreeing among themselves to allocate their electoral votes to a hypothetical national popular vote winner. There is no provision under this scheme for abrogating individual state election or recount laws or even for appointment of any federal or national entity charged with conducting or supervising a national recount (something that could only be done by constitutional amendment).

This brings us to the recount problem inherent in the NPVIC scheme: without any national or federal entity charged with promulgating, regulating, or enforcing terms for a national recount, every state—whether a signatory or not—remains free to promulgate its own election laws and recount triggers. Without all states participating in a national recount and applying uniform recount procedures, no meaningful *national* recount would be possible.

The NPVIC is obviously aware of this problem and purports to solve it by proposing that Congress *should* at some time in the future "enact a federal recount law that would give presidential candidates a right to obtain a recount that would be completed prior to the uniform national date for the meeting of the Electoral College."[21] Its proposed "Presidential Election Recount Act of ___"[22] would require states to prepare a "plan for accelerating the initial count of each ballot given or cast for each . . . presidential elector . . . and a plan for conducting a full recount,"[23] give any presidential candidate a right to request from any state to conduct a "full recount of the votes cast for each candidate for president,"[24] and even empower any citizen of a state to "bring an action against [that] state [in federal court] . . . for such declaratory or injunctive relief to ensure that the State is in compliance with this title."[25]

Implicit in the manifesto's proposed federal recount legislation is that the viability of the NPVIC is dependent on the passage by Congress of such legislation immediately following any adoption of the NPVIC. A better example of putting the cart before the horse cannot be easily imagined: if the viability of the NPVIC rests upon the possible passage of some future act of Congress, then surely such legislation should be passed *before* any states become signatories to the NPVIC. In any case, there is no guarantee that such legislation would ever be passed by Congress. Certainly representative of states that have declined to join the NPVIC cabal would have no incentive to pass legislation that might lay the groundwork for a scheme they oppose in the first place.

However, even if such proposed legislation was somehow to be enacted prior to or immediately after adoption of the NPVIC, it would do little to address the scheme's recount problem.

First, the proposed legislation includes no constitutional saving provision—that is, a provision that purports to preserve those sections of the act should any part of the act be found unconstitutional. As noted, the Constitution does not currently delegate to the federal government any power to vitiate, preempt, or abolish properly promulgated state election laws, including state recount laws. (The only exceptions being the Fifth and Fourteenth Amendments forbidding states to deny to any of their citizens due process or equal protection of the laws and Article IV, Section 4, which guarantees to each state a "Republican form of government.")

Second, the proposed legislation fails to establish any federal entity or department authorized to conduct and supervise a national recount, promulgate recount regulations including uniform recount triggers, enforce provisions of the act, conduct a final tally of popular votes, or even determine how to allocate popular votes for unpledged electors.

Third, the proposed legislation fails to address the problem of reconciling election laws of states that have different rules regarding such matters as voter eligibility and recount triggers; nor does it address the problem of how states must allocate popular votes cast for unpledged electors.

Finally and most disconcertingly, the proposed legislation not only contemplates the necessity for recounts *in every state*—a scenario that would magnify the 2000 election recount trauma by a factor of 50—but even appears to *invite* election chaos by empowering *any* individual state citizen to act as a kind of deputized sheriff to initiate litigation in federal courts to seek declaratory and injunctive relief to ensure compliance with the act. It may be recalled that in the 2000 election, a single state (Florida) barely made it through its own recount procedures, court decrees, appeals to the Florida Supreme Court, and finally the U.S. Supreme Court in time to meet the safe harbor provisions of Title 3.[26] One can only imagine the chaos of 50 separate states attempting to do so simultaneously.

CHAPTER TEN

Myths about the Electoral College

A Response

The final 345 pages[1] of the National Popular Vote Interstate Compact (NPVIC) manifesto *Every Vote Equal*[2] sets forth a litany of no less than 40 purported myths, complete with additional submyths, about the NPVIC. The endorsements on the back page of the manifesto include the testimonials of numerous politicians but interestingly not a single one from a political scientist or constitutional historian. It may be for this reason that many of the myths have never been put forward in the form of assertions by any known constitutional expert or even, as far as can be ascertained, by anyone.

For example, the manifesto sets forth as myth 9.1.17 that "The Due Process Clause of the 14th Amendment[3] precludes the National Popular Vote Compact."[4] However, the manifesto cites no person who has ever made such an assertion. It then purports to rebut this nonmyth by virtuously asserting that the NPVIC "would not deny any person life, liberty or property." (Of course, the NPVIC would violate many other constitutional provisions, just not that one.)

In other instances, the manifesto sets forth a purported myth but then claims to rebut it with a non sequitur. For example, myth 9.1.1 states that "A federal constitutional amendment is necessary for changing the current method of electing the president."[5] The purported rebuttal is that "The shortcomings of the current system of electing the President stem from state winner-take-all statutes."[6] It is of course true that most states have adopted the unit-vote rule, but this hardly rebuts the need for a constitutional amendment to deprive states of the small advantage the Constitution awards the smaller states by virtue of the two extra electoral votes it gains from equal representation in the Senate. In fact, as noted in previous chapters, a routine constitutional amendment promulgated according to the first provisions of Article V (requiring two-thirds of the House and ratification by three-quarters of the states)[7] would not even be sufficient in this case. The last sentence of Article V requires that any bill depriving states of their small two electoral vote advantage in the Electoral College based on "equal suffrage" in the Senate must be ratified by unanimous ratification of *all* the states.[8]

Still other myths dwell on the pedantic or the bizarre, apparently asserted on the basis that someone, somewhere made an assertion, albeit in an entirely different context, but nevertheless making it a myth. Thus, the manifesto's myth 9.36.1: "The state by state winner-take-all rule minimizes the effects of hurricanes and bad weather." Since no actual person has ever claimed such a thing, the manifesto rebuts this myth by noting that Theodore White in his "Making of a President in 1968"[9] noted that "the weather was clear across Massachusetts and New England . . . but from Michigan through Illinois and the Plain States it was cloudy."[10] If the point of this myth and its rebuttal is that weather can indeed affect voter turnout, that is undeniably true, but how the weather would affect voter turnout in a unit-vote such as Colorado more or less than in a non–unit-vote state such as Nebraska is apparently left to the imagination.

For these reasons it is beyond the scope of this chapter to address every such myth and submyth, but the most relevant ones are addressed. Using the format favored by the politicians who contributed to the NPVIC manifesto—including no less than 16 forewords—this chapter addresses the manifesto's myths about the Electoral College.

Myths about the Electoral College

Myth 10.1

Myth: A constitutional amendment is not necessary for challenging the current method of electing the President.[11]

Answer: Article II of the Constitution allocates to each state the number of electors "equal to the whole number of Senators and Representatives to which the state may be entitled in the Congress."[12] This allocation of electoral votes is based on the guarantee that each state is entitled to equal representation in the Senate in the form of two senators regardless

Myths about the Electoral College

of population. This provides the small states with a small but significant advantage in the election of the president, since it gives states with relatively small populations the same number of electoral votes based on Senate representation as states with large populations. The NPVIC would abolish this constitutionally granted advantage by simply ignoring the Article II allocation of electoral votes based on Senate representation in favor of a so-called national popular vote in which the small states' advantage in the Electoral College would be erased.

So concerned were the small states that this advantage might be erased by a future constitutional amendment that they insisted they could only be deprived of this advantage with the unanimous consent of every state (Article V, last sentence). This small but sacred advantage is also reflected in the Electoral College, which allocates two electoral votes based on the two representatives to which each state is entitled in the Senate.

Thus, taking away the electoral advantage that is based on equal suffrage in the Senate requires not just a constitutional amendment but one ratified by all the states.

Interestingly, the 1,000-page NPVIC manifesto *Every Vote Equal* does not even address the constitutional issue of its interstate compact proposal or even the likelihood of every state in the union agreeing to being deprived of its suffrage in both the Senate and the Electoral College.

Myth 10.2

Myth: The Founding Fathers envisioned an Electoral College composed of wise men "who would act as a deliberative body and exercise independent and detached judgment as to the best person to serve as President."[13]

Answer: The Founding Fathers reached no agreement or consensus on the role of electors. Indeed, it would have been remarkable had they reached such a consensus on such an important issue and decided not to include it in the Constitution. Rather, it was precisely because they could *not* reach such a consensus that the Framers wisely gave plenary power to each state to determine such matters in the manner of allocating electors in Article II, Section 1, Clause 2. Despite conflicting inferences that might be drawn from statements made by Framers such as Alexander Hamilton and James Madison,[14] no Framer made any statement suggesting that any provision in the Constitution should preempt the plenary power of the states to determine such critical questions.

In any case, in accordance with the confidence the Framers wisely placed in the states to determine such matters, every state since 1876 has rendered the issue moot by delegating to the people of the state the responsibility for choosing its electors.[15] The NPVIC's assertion that the Framers' vision was to allow wise men to exercise their own independent judgment in derogation of the will of the people of the state to whom they granted plenary power has neither historical nor constitutional basis. The only vision the Framers had on the subject was to leave the question for each state to decide.

Myth 10.3

Myth: "The infamous constitutional provision counting slaves as three fifths of a person for the purpose of apportioning Representatives in Congress (and apportioning electoral votes) was designed to favor Southern states. It is no accident that slave-holding Virginians served as President for 32 of the national's 36 years."[16]

Answer: This particular canard—a true myth—continues to carry weight with the man and woman in the street[17] but reveals a breathtaking misunderstanding of both American and constitutional history.

The constitutional provision to which it apparently refers—Article I, Section 2, Clause 3—did represent a compromise between representatives of the northern and southern states. But it had nothing to do with the Grand Compromise in which every state was granted equal suffrage in the Senate. Rather, it represented a compromise on the question of whether slaves should be included in calculating the number of representatives to which a state was entitled in the House of Representatives. The southern states demanded that *all* the slaves should be counted as whole persons for that purpose. The northern free states quite understandably felt that *none* of the slaves should be so counted, since none of them were considered citizens or had the right to vote. When the southern states insisted on counting slaves as whole persons as their price for joining the union, it appeared that yet another obstacle would make union impossible. As with so many other obstacles that blocked the way to union, the issue was finally resolved by a compromise disliked by representatives of both the North and the South—namely, that the slaves would count as three-fifths of a person. But it was the free North that didn't want slaves to be counted at all. It was the slave South that wanted slaves to be counted as whole persons.

Would John Anderson have preferred that slaves be counted as whole persons so that the South could thereby have gained the benefit of counting its slaves in its population and by so doing magnify its influence in Congress in order to preserve slavery?

Myths about the Electoral College

The Grand Compromise, which Anderson apparently confuses with the three-fifths compromise, was an entirely separate compromise that provided for equal state suffrage in the Senate in order to induce the small states—particularly Delaware and Rhode Island—to join the union. In 1789 the northern state of Delaware had a population of about 40,000, while the southern state of North Carolina had close to 180,000, so the three-fifths compromise would have had little relevance to the Grand Compromise in which equal representation for the smaller states was the primary issue.

It will be recalled that Rhode Island refused even to attend the Constitutional Convention for fear of being bullied into accepting the state's marginalization in a Congress based on population alone,[18] while Delaware delegates came with credentials that absolutely forbade the delegates' participation in any scheme to change the "one state, one vote" provision to which they were entitled under the Articles of Confederation.[19]

It is safe to conclude that without the Framers' concession to the small states guaranteeing equal suffrage in the Senate, the small states would not have joined the union. Without the three-fifths concession, the southern states would not have joined either. It is therefore most probable that without *both* compromises the states would have formed their own amalgamations—and ultimately nations—in much the same way as separate nations have since formed in South America.

Perhaps the most disconcerting aspect of this particular NPVIC myth is the inference that such slaveholder presidents as George Washington and Thomas Jefferson were elected because they owned slaves. In the case of Washington, the fact that he successfully led the American forces' effort in the Revolutionary War that gained American independence had something to do with his election, as did his undisputed status as the father of his country. In the case of Jefferson, the fact that he drafted the Declaration of Independence and commanded the electoral votes of one of the most populous states was crucial to his election.

Myth 10.4

Myth: Democracy would not be undermined by a national popular vote.[20]

Answer: Any election system that does not reflect the will of the people undermines democracy. The description of such popular vote election systems in Russia and France highlights this fact. In the 1993 Russian election, the fascist candidate received 23 percent of the vote, and the communist candidate was barely edged out by the Reform candidate, who received 13 percent. A shift of but 2 percent of the votes for the communist candidate would have given voters the choice in a runoff of either an extreme fascist or a hard-liner communist even though both candidates would have been opposed by two-thirds of the electorate.

In the 2017 French multiparty election, the two runoff candidates were opposed by almost two-thirds of the electorate. The highest vote getter in the runoff was the *ballot blanc* (the blank ballot) in which 600,000 voters expressed their disgust and dismay with the unpalatable choice that this national popular vote system had foisted upon them.

Such elections are hardly poster children for any reasonable concept of democracy. In this regard, it should be noted that the NPVIC does not even provide for a runoff, meaning that a president could be elected with a very small percentage of the vote. Had the Russians in the 1993 election been shackled with an NPVIC national popular vote, the hard-line fascist would have been elected without a runoff (much in the same manner as Hitler was elected in Germany).

NPVIC advocates insist that their version of a national popular vote would somehow be different because the United States has only two major parties. The irony of this position, as explained in Chapter 2, is that the two-party system is the product of the very Electoral College system they seek to destroy.

Myth 10.5

Myth: An entity currently exists for conducting a national recount.[21]

Answer: The rebuttal to this particular myth is contained within the NPVIC's own answer to what it claims is the myth that there is "no mechanism for conducting a national recount."[22] In lieu of actually rebutting this myth, the manifesto instead opines that Congress "should enact [such a mechanism]."[23] Implied therefore is that without such a hypothetical future act of Congress, there indeed does not exist any current mechanism for conducting recounts—thus confirming that the myth is not a myth at all but instead is true. Nevertheless, the NPVIC answer goes on to propose that such a hypothetical future act of Congress should impose upon the states a federal requirement to not only conduct such recounts (upon demand and payment for by candidates) but also accelerate such recounts.[24]

The assumption here is that Congress would have constitutional power to dictate to states how and when to conduct their own internal presidential vote recounts. This is surprising because the entire premise of the NPVIC is that Article II gives states absolute plenary power to "appoint, in

Myths about the Electoral College

such manner as the legislature thereof may direct, a number of electors." Not explained by the NPVIC is what constitutional provision delegates to the federal government the right to override the states' plenary power to choose electors in their own manner. In fact, there is none.

The answer also downplays the risk that recounts under the NPVIC would be necessary, claiming that there have been only "five litigated state counts in a mere 57 presidential elections."[25] Even if true (the NPVIC provides no citation to support this assertion), it fails to take into account that even if rare, a litigated election inevitably creates a constitutional crisis, instability, and uncertainty. Fortunately, under the Electoral College system the trauma of a litigated election is isolated, as it was to just one state, Florida, in the 2000 election. Under the Russian-style popular vote system advocated by the NPVIC, the recount and subsequent litigation would have to take place in all 50 states simultaneously, since a vote in any state—not just 1 state—could alter the outcome of the election.

It may be true that under the Electoral College system there is the rare occasion for a candidate to seek a recount or to initiate litigation. It will be recalled that in the 1960 election, in which the popular vote was so close that not even the Congressional Quarterly or most of the newspapers could agree on the final count,[26] Richard Nixon nevertheless declined to demand a recount or challenge the vote in Illinois despite manifest evidence of voting fraud. This was because the Electoral College vote for John F. Kennedy was so overwhelming that a recount in Illinois, even if successful, would not have changed Kennedy's victory in the Electoral College.[27] Thus, if recounts and litigation are indeed as rare as the NPVIC claims, it is due in large measure to the Electoral College.

The NPVIC claims that under a popular vote election there would rarely be a need for a recount because there would be a "single large national pool of votes."[28] Even if this claim were true—in fact, multiple parties would narrow the voting margins—it assumes that it is even possible to have a national popular vote recount. As noted, this is not possible under the Constitution unless all states agree, because Article II gives each state the right to determine how to allocate its electoral votes. Even if all states were to agree to give up their right to equal voting power in the Senate as reflected in the Electoral College, there would still be the problem of creating a federal entity charged with counting the votes.

In lieu of such an entity, the NPVIC manifesto purports to deputize "the chief election officers of each member state"[29] (nonmember states are excluded from this task) to make a "conclusive statement concerning the number of popular votes in a state for each presidential slate."[30] No provision is made in the NPVIC for conducting a final tally of national popular votes or for creating a national entity to conduct such a final tally. Presumably, someone, somewhere would take out a calculator and add up the popular votes in each state.

The NPVIC purports to address the lack of any entity charged with counting the national poplar vote by claiming that the National Archives and Records Administration publishes the national popular vote totals on a website.[31] What it fails to note, however, is that this website only reports this unofficially by assuming that each state's tally popular votes is correct. The website does not purport to decide whether, for example, the popular votes reported by states for unpledged electors should be counted for the candidate for whom the unpledged electors ultimately voted in the Electoral College or whether such votes should instead be disregarded entirely (as the NPVIC manifesto proposes on grounds that it is impossible to allocate popular votes for unpledged electors). In any case, no provision of the Constitution or any federal law gives the National Archives the responsibility for determining how popular votes are to be counted. This is understandable given that popular votes are constitutionally irrelevant in how a state casts its electoral votes except as provided by individual state laws.

The problem, of course, is that without the creation of such a national or federal entity charged with making a final determination of popular votes (as opposed to making a tally of electoral votes), there is no way to resolve differences in the manner of counting popular votes. It will be recalled that in 1960, some newspapers decided to count all the popular votes for the Democratic slate in Alabama for Senator Kennedy, despite the fact that 6 of the 11 electors on the Democratic slate were pledged to Senator Harry Byrd. This resulted in a narrow national popular vote count for Kennedy. However, the Congressional Quarterly—the closest thing to a federal entity—chose to tally only five-elevenths of the popular votes cast for the Democratic slate, since only 5 of the electors were pledged to Kennedy. This resulted in a national popular vote count for Nixon. While the Congressional Quarterly's manner of counting popular votes was certainly the most logical, the point here is not which method of counting the national poplar votes was the most fair. The point is that there was more than one method for counting national poplar votes, and there was no official federal or national entity charged with deciding which method to use. Had the NPVIC been in effect in that election, the result would surely have been chaos and constitutional crisis.

When asked how the NPVIC would have addressed this crisis, the answer is the same as to so many other questions posed about the how the NPVIC would play out in a future election: litigation.

Myth 10.6

Myth: Federalism would not be undermined by a national popular vote.[32]

Answer: The essential element of federalism was laid out by John F. Kennedy when he stated, "I should hate to see the abolition of state lines. . . . The presidential election is determined on the basis of 48 separate units. I think the election should be decided in each one of them."[33]

The essential feature of the NPVIC would be to adopt, by a circuitous and discursive steeplechase that avoids the constitutional process for amendments, a Russian-style national popular vote that ignores the separate interest each state has in presidential elections. Since the adoption of the Constitution, the way in which the American system of presidential elections has evolved has vindicated the Framers' trust in delegating to each state the manner of appointing electors. Most important in that evolution has been the choice by every state to grant to their own citizens the right to choose their own electors by secret ballot. Also vindicated has been the mistrust and fear expressed by so many of the Framers that future so-called reformers might attempt to undermine not just their federalist vision but even the Grand Compromise that created the United States of America. Nothing in the Constitution so expresses this mistrust than the last sentence of Article V, which sets forth the *one provision of the entire Constitution* that would stand forever immutable against the ravages of those who would someday seek to destroy its federalist foundations: the absolute right of each state to equal representation in the Senate and, by incorporation, the additional weight that equal representation gives to the states in the Electoral College.

The NPVIC manifesto asserts baldly without citation that "the power of state governments relative to the federal government is not increased or decreased based on whether presidential electors are elected along state-boundary lines . . . or national lines."[34]

It was not just such future presidents as John F. Kennedy,[35] constitutional scholars such as Max Farrand,[36] and constitutional historians[37] but also the clear words of the Constitution itself that refute this assertion: "no state, without its consent, shall be deprived of equal suffrage in the Senate"[38]—which equal suffrage is of course in turn reflected in the guarantee of a minimum of three electors (two based on equal Senate suffrage) in the Electoral College. The NPVIC would on its face effectively deprive small states of their effective weight in the Electoral College as provided by Article V's guarantee of equal state representation in the Senate.[39]

The Framers' federalist plan depended upon uniting many separate states—large and small—across a vast geographical territory. With very little to unite these states except perhaps a common language and a hatred of George III, the challenge of unification was so daunting that even George Washington doubted that true unification in a federalist republic would ever be possible.[40] Certainly, the Articles of Confederation provided little confidence that a self-governing federal national republic would ever be possible. George Washington's lack of confidence should be understandable today: who would ever have thought that a sovereign colony such as Delaware with a population of 35,000 in 1776 would have ever agreed to be absorbed by a nation dominated by such colonies as Virginia (with half a million) or Pennsylvania (with a quarter million)? Would the interests of the citizens of Delaware ever have been properly recognized by a Congress dominated by the representatives of millions of citizens of neighboring states?

If there is ever any question about the nature of federalism, the manner in which the U.S. Constitution brought such disparate colonies together provides the answer. Many Americans today take the United States of America for granted—and yet it was just a handful of young men at the dawn of our constitutional history who made it happen when very few observers at the time, including George Washington, thought it could be done.

If there was any doubt about whether Article V's guarantee of equal state suffrage in Senate representation would be sufficient to unify 13 disparate colonies into a true national state, the Tenth Amendment double downed on the Article V guarantee against the tampering and undermining of federalism: "The powers not delegated to the United States by the Constitution, nor prohibited by it to the states, are reserved to the states respectively, or the people."

No right to powers "reserved to the states" is more important than Article II's power to the states to conduct their own internal elections in their own way to appoint presidential electors. A scheme such as the NPVIC would pervert that power to instead coerce nonsignatory states to accept the rules—including voter qualifications, recount triggers, etc.— of other states.

The NPVIC claim that it would "not affect the amount of power that state government possess relative to the federal government"[41] cannot be true when it purports to take away *any* state's weight in the presidential election process, which is currently determined by its 2-vote elector allocation guaranteed by Article V. Nor is it a defense of such claim that "nonsignatory states will still have their extra weight in the Electoral College preserved." Any extra weight carried by the small states would be effectively erased by the NPVIC cabal's casting of 270 electoral votes without

Myths about the Electoral College 105

regard to the nonsignatorys' electoral votes. Any appearance of electors in the nonsignatory states would be an exercise in futility.

Whatever label one wishes to attach to such a scheme, "federalist" is the least descriptive.

Myth 10.7

Myth: The failure to provide a runoff is not a defect in the NPVIC.[42]

Answer: Since 1880 (after which date all states provided for popular election of electors), most Electoral College winners have received popular votes in the mid-40 percent range and many much higher.[43] (Even Warren Harding received 60 percent of the popular vote in 1920.) Contrast this with countries such as Russia and France that are shackled with so-called popular vote schemes. It will be recalled that in the French election of 2017, the two runoff candidates were opposed by two-thirds of the electorate, as expressed by the unprecedented 600,000 votes cast by exasperated and frustrated voters who went to the polls just to vote for the *ballot blanc* (blank ballot).

The Electoral College has never needed a runoff because of two intrinsic elements that do a far better job of narrowing the field. First, in order to win even a single electoral vote, a candidate must win a plurality of votes in at least one state. Second, if any candidate does not receive a majority of electoral votes, the election is referred to the House of Representatives in which each state has an equal vote.

It will be recalled that in the 1932 presidential election, numerous fringe parties—socialists, Trotskyites, Wallacites—vied for the popular vote. However, once these numerous fringe parties realized that the Electoral College only awards electors to those who command a plurality of popular votes in a single state, they strove to make accommodation with one of the two established political parties. As a result, the socialists made accommodation with the Democratic Party, after which the socialists' support in the polls fell from 6 percent to 1 percent. This was the process of accommodation that the Electoral College encourages. There was no need for a runoff.

The NPVIC continues to defend its pursuit of a Russian-style direct election by assuming that the two-party system would persist even after the abolition of the Electoral College. The undemocratic results of such direct elections in other countries reveals that this is not the case. Without the channeling of votes in the Electoral College system, multiparty systems are the inevitable result. This is not to say, however, that one party may not dethrone another party to become a major party, as the

Republican Party replaced the Whig Party. In the months leading up to the 1992 presidential election, polls showed that maverick interloper Ross Perot enjoyed 33 percent of the national popular vote, Bush 28 percent, and Clinton 24 percent. Fortunately, the Electoral College spared the country a runoff between Perot and Bush, as Perot realized that if such a split in the popular vote was reflected in the electoral vote in which no one candidate would receive a majority, the election would be referred to the House, where either Bush or Clinton would surely win.

Contrast such results with the kind of Russian-style popular vote scheme such as the French adopted in 2017. With no incentive for accommodation between the numerous parties vying for the presidency, the popular vote was split, with the two highest polling candidates receiving 24 percent and 21 percent, respectively. Without a runoff, the winner would have attained the presidency with 24 percent, hardly sufficient to govern—a result that the NPVIC says would be completely appropriate without a runoff. The runoff in the 2017 French election, however, was deemed necessary in order to create the illusion of majority support, since in a runoff between two candidates, one candidate was guaranteed to receive a majority—despite the fact that 600,000 braved the weather to show their disgust for the entire national popular vote system by casting their blank votes.

The NPVIC does not provide for a runoff. One would assume that the compact would provide such a runoff if for no other reason than to create the illusion of a democratic result of a 50 percent winner after a runoff. Under the NPVIC scheme, however, no runoff is even possible because instead of achieving their goal of a national popular vote by process of promulgating a constitutional amendment, NPVIC advocates chose instead a scheme to form a cabal of states to accomplish the purpose and thereby marginalize nonsignatory states. Despite the NPVIC's claims that over 70 percent of the men and women on the street support a popular vote, its supporters know that over 400 attempts to abolish the Electoral College have failed dismally once members of Congress recognized that every state must first consent to abolition of the Senate (and thereby deprive smaller states of their modest advantage in the Electoral College). Presumably NPVIC supporters must realize that abolition of the Electoral College would produce results such as were produced in the 2017 French election. It would almost certainly turn our stable two-party system into an unstable multiparty system. It is for this reason that the NPVIC has attempted to circumvent the entire constitutional process for amendments and instead promote its scheme by appearing under the radar of public scrutiny in state legislatures under the banner of "every vote equal." Since the NPVIC

Myths about the Electoral College

scheme necessitates seducing state legislatures to revert to the barbaric practice of reserving the prerogative of choosing electors to themselves rather than to the people of their state, it locks them into preserving the appearance of adherence to the Framers' electoral process while undermining its purpose and intent.

An apt analogy might be the Roman Empire, which after destroying the republican form of government by brute military force tried to preserve the appearance and symbols of the Roman Republic—though even this attempt showed strain when Emperor Caligula appointed his horse as consul.[44]

Myth 10.8

Myth: The two-party system will prevail even under the yoke of the NPVIC.[45]

Answer: Of all the assumptions upon which the NPVIC is based, this one is perhaps the most unsupportable. Proponents of this assumption cannot explain why every other country in the world that has adopted a national popular vote system has degenerated into a multiparty system, such as the one in Russia. Some parliamentary systems such as that in the United Kingdom have managed to preserve a three-major party system, though this often results in unstable coalitions when no one party is able to command a majority in parliament. Most others degenerate into multiparty systems, as in Italy where governments can rise or fall in a matter of months. In Israel, the parliamentary system can depend on coalitions in which one very minor party can command a disproportionate weight in the government by virtue of providing a few pivotal votes necessary for another party to create a coalition. This is true even in Germany, as Chancellor Angela Merkel would be the first to attest. In a German poll conducted on October 10, 2018, by Infratest-Dimap the split of parties in that country demonstrated "Ms. Merkel's conservative bloc at 26%, the Social Democrats at 15%[,] . . . the Green Party at 17% and the Alternative for Germany Party at 16%."[46] This had led to concerns in late 2018 that Merkel's fragile coalition would soon be facing unstable collapse.[47] Given that Germany has no Electoral College system in place, it is puzzling why the NPVIC places so much confidence in its assumption that a similar fracture of parties would not soon plague the United States if its Electoral College was abolished or otherwise marginalized.

It has already been described in detail how the Electoral College performs the critical task of narrowing and channeling the field of candidates in a far better and more democratic way than runoffs. The NPVIC response to this is that even under the yoke of an undemocratic national popular vote system, the two-party system would somehow prevail. It does so by looking at state elections for governor or other state officials and notes that such state elections do not have an internal Electoral College system: "we can refer to the nation's experience in the numerous elections that have been conducted in which the winner was a candidate who received the most popular votes."[48]

The analogy to state elections is particularly inapt in that it fails to acknowledge that the two main current political parties are national organizations. With few exceptions, candidates for statewide office are members of the national party from which they draw support. Where there exists a plethora of parties on the national stage, such factionalism would inevitably exist at both the state and local levels as it does in all other countries lacking an Electoral College or its equivalent.

The history of American elections is littered with both candidates and voters who have had to learn the hard way how the Electoral College serves to produce a leader who enjoys not only deep support in one particular region of the country but also broad support across a number of regions.[49] In 1912, Theodore Roosevelt's breakaway Bull Moose Party split the 50.6 percent Republican vote, thereby enabling the Democrat Woodrow Wilson to win the election with but 41 percent of the vote. In the 2000 presidential elections, the votes cast for Ralph Nader deprived Al Gore of Florida's electoral votes that would have elected him. In 2016 Hillary Clinton's support in areas of high population concentration gave way to the broader support for Donald Trump votes in the heartland, which was reflected in the Electoral College.[50] The Electoral College's success in ensuring broad and not just deep support vindicates the Framers' vision of a federalist and democratic government—one that has endured. Without such stability, freedom, and democracy, the United States, with less than 5 percent of the world's population, would not be producing almost a third of the entire world's GDP.[51] With it, the Electoral College has defied the skepticism of Benjamin Franklin, who in response to a citizen's question about what the Constitution had created answered, "A republic, if you can keep it."[52]

Myth 10.9

Myth: Adding up the popular votes that are cast in each state to obtain the nationwide popular vote total for each presidential candidate is not a difficult task.[53]

Answer: There are several reasons why adding up the popular votes to obtain a nationwide popular vote total would be problematic.

Myths about the Electoral College

The Framers' Electoral College system is not geared to counting national popular votes. Although all states now provide for the popular election of electors, not all states have adopted a requirement that all electors on a party slate must be pledged to that party's national nominee. In 1960, for example, the Democratic elector slate consisted of five electors who had pledged to cast their vote for John F. Kennedy and six electors who had voted to cast their electoral votes for Senator Harry Byrd of Virginia.[54] (Two other states—Louisiana and Mississippi—offered unpledged slates of electors.) Although more Alabama voters had cast their votes for the Democratic slate of electors than the Republican slate of electors, the question of how the popular votes for either Kennedy or Nixon would be counted never had to be considered, since Kennedy had a substantial margin of electoral votes over Nixon. However, this did not stop some newspapers, such as the *New York Times*,[55] from conducting a hypothetical count of national popular votes by "adding up the popular votes that were cast in each state." In doing so, however, the *New York Times* had to decide how to *allocate* the popular votes cast for Kennedy. It should be noted that what the NPVIC now blithely calls the "chief election officer" reported only the number of popular votes cast for the Alabama electors pledged to Kennedy, which was 318,303 (324,050 votes were cast for the Senator Byrd electors). The *New York Times,* followed by the Congressional Quarterly, thereupon pronounced Nixon the popular vote winner by a margin of 112,872 votes.[56] Other newspapers, however, chose to include the 324,050 votes cast for the Democratic electors pledged to Senator Byrd as votes for Kennedy, thus giving Kennedy a popular vote margin the other way. By this method of counting popular votes, these newspapers concluded that Kennedy had actually won the hypothetical popular vote. Interestingly, this latter rather dubious counting method has since found its way into the Kennedy iconography, as reflected by the fact that the average man and woman on the street, when asked who won the popular vote in 1960, often responds that Kennedy won the popular vote.[57]

Fortunately for the nation, the Electoral College rendered moot any dispute as to who won the national popular vote. Had the nation had to count every single popular vote—as the NPVIC would have required—the question would not be a simple question of adding up the popular votes cast in each state but rather what *method* of counting the popular votes would be employed. With 50 different chief election officers around the country making different decisions in this regard, the need for a federal officer or entity to make a conclusive decision becomes glaringly obvious.

It is of note that the NPVIC does not provide for such a federal officer. In truth it could not do so, since the NPVIC is predicated upon each signatory state determining in its own way—without federal or congressional involvement—what method to use in counting the national popular vote. Had these direct election advocates chosen the more honest route of promoting a constitutional amendment to achieve their goal of a national popular vote, this critical defect might have been avoided. But since such a constitutional amendment would require the consent of every state— not just two-thirds of Congress and three-fourths of the states—it now becomes clear why NPVIC advocates would want to avoid the legitimate constitutional amendment process entirely. (For full discussion of why a constitutional amendment abolishing the Electoral College would require the consent of every state, see Chapter 2.)[58]

Myth 10.10

Myth: Under the NPVIC, no coercion would be required to force presidential electors to vote for the national popular vote winner.[59]

Answer: The fallacy of this particular NPVIC assumption is best reflected by the following hypothetical.

Assume that in 2021, a Democratic-controlled legislature in Colorado passes the NPVIC bill, which binds Colorado to appoint a slate of electors pledged to vote for the national popular vote winner in the upcoming 2024 presidential election, even if that so-called popular vote winner happens to be a Republican and even if the Colorado voters overwhelmingly vote for electors pledged to the Democratic candidate. In 2022, a Colorado state election returns an overwhelming Democratic majority to the Colorado legislature. In the 2024 presidential election, a Republican candidate—we'll call him Joe Trump—is the Republican nominee, and a woman—we'll call her Jane Obama—is the Democratic Party nominee. In a contentious national election, Jane Obama wins an overwhelming majority of popular votes in Colorado as well as a slim majority in the Electoral College, but the demagogic Joe Trump manages to eke out a razor-thin national popular vote victory, mainly by concentrating his campaign efforts in highly concentrated population regions. Now, under the NPVIC, the Democratic-controlled Colorado legislature is obliged to appoint electors and direct them to go to the Electoral College and cast their electoral votes for the much-despised Joe Trump, thereby electing him president. Presumably the Democratic-controlled legislature would now appoint electors on the Democratic slate to go to the Electoral College to perform the distasteful task of voting for its archenemy, Joe Trump.

Myths about the Electoral College

Over the course of American history, there have been only a handful of occasions in which electors have defied the will of the people who elected them and violated their pledge, though none of the votes of these faithless electors have ever changed the course of an election.[60] This is in large part because the party whose elector slate received the most popular votes in that state gets to appoint the electors, and they are generally party stalwarts who follow the party line. While some states provide sanctions for electors who violate their pledges, others provide either nominal fines or no sanctions at all.[61] (For purposes of this hypothetical, we'll assume that Colorado is one of the states that has no criminal sanctions for those electors who violate their pledge.)[62]

In the aftermath of the 2016 election, however, the media repeatedly showed enraged protesters outside the Pennsylvania state house attempting to pressure the Republican electors to violate their pledge to cast their elector votes for the popular vote winner in the state. Similar scenes of such protest were reported around the country. None of the protests appear to have persuaded Republican electors to violate their pledges, although several Democratic electors in Colorado did attempt to violate their pledge to vote for Hillary Clinton.[63]

It should be noted, however, that the failure of faithless electors to violate their pledge in a way that affects the outcome of an election in the past does not mean that it could not happen in the future under an NPVIC regime.

The NPVIC manifesto claims that the faithless elector problem would not arise because "the NPVIC compact (like the current system) would result in the election to the Electoral College of presidential electors who are avid supporters of the national popular vote winner."[64]

Really? The Democratic electors appointed by the Democratic-controlled legislature would be "avid supporters" of the Joe Trump they despise? They would happily forfeit the election to their hated opponent just to abide by an unenforceable pledge? Upon what known or unknown fact about the nature of partisan politics is this NPVIC assumption based?

Granted, the NPVIC would oblige its signatory legislatures to appoint the elector slate of the party that won the popular vote in those states, but such pledges are not automatically fulfilled.[65] Indeed, such pledges can be broken, often with no criminal penalty or even sanctions, and in the case of the not unlikely scenario described above, the appointed electors would have every incentive to break their pledges. In such a case, this NPVIC result would create a constitutional crisis that would make the 1876 election look mild by comparison.

The lesson for NPVIC supporters is that if you are convinced that the Framers' plan for presidential elections should be abolished, abrogated, or marginalized, bite the bullet and proceed to go through the legitimate mode for promulgating a constitutional amendment. If support for such an amendment is as overwhelming as you claim, there should be no trouble in getting every state in the union to agree to forfeit both its equal suffrage vote in the Senate and its weight in the Electoral College based on that equal suffrage.

Myth 10.11

Myth: Only 20 percent of the American people support the winner-take-all system of allocating electoral votes.[66]

Answer: Whatever poll this myth is based on, it must be tested by the results of actual referenda in states around the country in which voters have overwhelmingly rejected proposals to end the practice of allocating all of a state's electoral votes to the winner of the popular votes in their state in favor of allocating electoral votes on a percentage basis.[67] Voters in Colorado and California have *soundly rejected such proposals.*[68] As early as 1810, even Thomas Jefferson supported the practice, albeit grudgingly, noting that it would take a fool to not do so when other states were doing so.[69] Today, only Maine and Nebraska have rejected the unit vote, and even they do not cast their electoral votes proportionally but rather by congressional district.[70]

What the NPVIC fails to recognize is that states keep the unit vote only because *most other states do so.* A state with 10 electoral votes is not likely to want to split its electoral votes 5–5—with a net weight in the Electoral College of zero—when most other states are casting all of its electoral votes to that state's popular vote winner, with far greater net weight in the Electoral College.

This variation on the "*Tragedy of the Commons*"[71] lends itself, ironically, to the very solution that the NPVIC is currently pursuing in trying to upend the current constitutional system. If every state or even just most states were to agree by an unenforceable compact to cast their electoral votes proportionally, the myth claimed by the NPVIC might be turned into reality. This is not to say that such a compact would be a desirable one or even a constitutional one, but it would in fact address many of the underlying motivations for the NPVIC. A proportional allocation of electoral votes would carry the same risk of countless recounts, litigation, and uncertainty as direct election. Its benefit would also be marginal: such a proportional plan would have elected at least three popular vote losers to the presidency—Hancock in 1880, William Jennings Bryan in 1896, and Nixon in 1960,[72] or about the same number of winning popular vote

Myths about the Electoral College

losers as the unit vote over the past two centuries. About the best that can said for it is that at least it would not violate either Article I providing for equal suffrage in the Senate, Article II allocating two electoral votes based on equal suffrage in the Senate, or Article V guaranteeing equal suffrage in the Senate except by the consent of all the states.

Perhaps the most humorous analysis of the proportional system was described by Senator Henry Cabot Lodge, who noted that "Even the cleverest surgeon cannot divide one man up—proportionately or otherwise—and expect him to live."[73]

Myth 10.12

Myth: The Electoral College is racist and favors Republicans over Democrats.

Answer: In 1860, the Electoral College elected Abraham Lincoln despite his having won only 39 percent of the popular vote, because the Democrats chose to split their 48 percent support between two factions of the Democratic Party.[74] Lincoln went on to issue his Emancipation Proclamation in 1862.

A hundred years later in 1960, the Electoral College elected the Democrat John F. Kennedy despite the fact that according to the Congressional Quarterly, the *New York Times,* and numerous others newspapers, Richard Nixon won the popular vote.[75] As late as 2000, the *New York Times* continued to support the Electoral College.[76] By 2016, however, when the *New York Times*–favored candidate Hillary Clinton lost in the Electoral College though winning the newspapers' tally of the popular vote, the newspaper had decided that the Electoral College must be racist if it could not elect Hillary Clinton. Its editorial of December 19, 2016, opined that the Electoral College was outdated, racist, and an American vestige that needed to be abolished. As justification for this opinion it raised the old canard that the Framers' created the Electoral College in order to advantage the southern states: "[the Electoral College] . . . is a living symbol of America's original sin [slavery]. . . . When slavery was the law of the land, a direct popular vote would have disadvantaged the Southern states . . . counting [slaves] as three fifths of a person."[77]

Whatever talents the *New York Times* may possess in denigrating the Framers' vision, those do not appear to extend to a knowledge of constitutional history. As described more fully in myth 10.3 above, it was the *southern* states that wanted slaves to be counted as a whole person for purposes of calculating how many representatives they would be entitled to in Congress; the northern states did not think they should be counted at all since they had no civil rights or the right to vote. The three-fifths compromise was the price the North had to pay to include the southern states to sign on to the Constitution and create the United States of America. The entirely separate Grand Compromise, which gave the small northern states such as Rhode Island and Delaware the right to equal representation in the Senate and an extra vote in the Electoral College, was the price the large states of Pennsylvania and New York had to pay to induce the small states to sign and ratify the Constitution.

Without these two separate compromises, no United States of America would ever have been created, and the more natural inclination of a large territory to form separate amalgamations and nations (as occurred in South America) would have occurred.

Given that in only 4 of the 56 presidential elections held since 1789 the Electoral College did not produce an outcome that differed from what a Russian-style popular vote would have elected, it is puzzling how racism could have played any part, especially when one of the electoral vote winners was the Democrat John F. Kennedy, who defeated the Republican popular vote winner.[78] It is also interesting to note that if the country in 1860 had been shackled with a Russian-style popular vote election and the Democrats had not decided to split their vote between the two Democrats, John Breckinridge and Stephen Douglas, Lincoln would have been soundly defeated, doubtless along with his vision and hope for the abolition of slavery.

As late as the 2018 midterm elections, however, the New York Times's "three-fifths" canard has been perpetuated in political rhetoric. In October 2018, for example, the socialist Alexandria Ocasio-Cortez won the Democratic nomination to represent the 14th District of New York, tweeting to 88,000 followers that "It is well past time we eliminate the Electoral College, a shadow of slavery's power on America today that undermines our nation as a democratic Republic."[79]

In fact, if one is to cast even a cursory look at the electoral map, it would appear to be tilted very far in favor of Democrats. As of 2016, both California and New York were considered to be locks for any Democrat, even without the need to spend a single dime on campaigning. Even though the Republican candidate received 40 percent of the popular votes in those two states, he received precisely zero electoral votes out of the 84 electoral votes that those two states cast in the Electoral College. Had the unit-vote rule—much despised by NPVIC advocates—not been in effect, the Republican candidate would have gained an extra 33 electoral votes, and the Democrat Clinton would have received 33 electoral votes less than she actually received, a swing of 66 electoral votes.

Myths about the Electoral College   115

Of course, the fallacy in this observation is that states change their political and demographic leanings over time. It was not so many years after the Republican Ronald Reagan was elected governor of California and only 10 years after Republican Arnold Schwarzenegger was elected governor of California that the state was considered a lock for Democrats. Again, the fact that the imposition of a Russian-style presidential election would not have changed the result in only four elections over a period of two and a quarter centuries belies the notion that the Electoral College favors one party over the other—or that it favors racists over decent people.

Nevertheless, if any NPVIC advocates remain convinced that the Electoral College somehow favors racists—or any demographic or racial group for that matter—it might want to consider the traditional impassioned pleas of representatives of civil rights organizations to preserve the Electoral College. During the 1979 congressional hearings on the Electoral College when Republicans (convinced that Nixon had been cheated in the 1960 election) joined with some Democrats to advocate for abolition of the Electoral College, it was witnesses such as Vernon Jordan, president of the National Urban League (one of the leading civil rights organizations) who testified:

> Take away the Electoral College and the importance of being black melts away. Black, instead of being crucial to victory in major states, simply become 10% of the total electorate, with reduced impact.[80]

An attempt by Congress in 1950 to impose a proportional plan (a stand-in for a Russian-style direct election requiring states to allocate their electoral votes in proportion to the popular vote) was met with even more fierce opposition from minority groups. Clarence Mitchell, the Washington director of the National Association for the Advancement of Colored People, stated that such a plan would

> effectively draw the political teeth of all independent voters, including the Negro votes, as far as presidential electors are concerned. . . . If (this) proposal goes through, the Negro vote and the vote of any minority, national and religious group, will no longer be important. . . . The proposal is anti-urban, interurban, anti-northern, and anti-liberal.[81]

Senator John F. Kennedy was even more impassioned in his defense of the Electoral College:

> The proportional plan has been discredited in the past and promises only doubt and danger in the future. . . . [There has been] no breakdown in the

electoral system, or even widespread lack of confidence in it can be shown. . . . [T]here is obviously little to gain—but much to lose by tampering with the Constitution.[82]

While all of these impassioned pleas by minorities to preserve the electoral system do reveal legitimate concerns about how a Russian-style election might affect their rights, it should ultimately be conceded that over time the effect of the Electoral College has been benignly neutral. Attacks on this venerable institution have come mostly from the loser of a particular election who can think no further than that the result might have been different in a popular vote election—witness the Republicans who attacked the Electoral College after Nixon's loss in 1960 or Democrats who sought to undermine its legitimacy after the loss by Hillary Clinton in 2018.

And it should not be forgotten that the whole notion of abolishing the Electoral College is, for all practical purposes, entirely theoretical, as it would require every state in the union to forfeit its constitutional weight in presidential elections. As America's most renowned constitutional historian has so eloquently pointed out,

> [S]hould an abstract standard of equity require the abolition [of the large state advantage in the Electoral College] . . . then surely it requires the abolition of the small state advantage in the Senate.[83]

Nor should it be forgotten when considering such means for undermining federalism that *Article V of the constitution absolutely forbids any taking away of every state's equal representation of the Senate except by unanimous consent of every state.*

Myth 10.13

Myth: Since 1789, the country has become more centralized; therefore, federalism is no longer important, and no reason exists why states should not be downgraded to superfluous entities in presidential elections.

Answer: Perhaps the best answer to this myth was provided by John F. Kennedy, who famously declared that "I should hate to see the abolition of state lines . . . the presidential election is determined on the basis of 48 separate units. I think the election should be decided in each one of them."[84] In short, federalism requires nothing less.

In many ways—indeed, in most ways—the current debate about the Electoral College and equal suffrage in the Senate is the very same as the

Myths about the Electoral College

debate at the Constitutional Convention between big- and small-state delegates. It will be recalled that Rufus King of Pennsylvania attempted to bully the small-state delegates into giving up their claim to equal suffrage in the Senate and a small advantage in the Electoral College, bellowing to them that he was "filled with astonishment" that the small states would not be willing to sacrifice for the good of all the "phantom of state sovereignty!"[85] But Gunning Bedford of Delaware refused to be bullied and pushed back with equal if not greater outrage:

> The large states proceed as if our eyes were perfectly blinded. Impartiality with them is already out of the question. . . . They insist that although the powers of the general government will be increased, yet it will be for the good of the whole; and although the three great states form nearly a majority of the American people, they will never hurt or injure the lesser states. I do not gentlemen, trust you.[86]

Rhode Island refused even to attend the Constitutional convention, so sure was it that the big states would try to bully the Rhode Island delegates into giving up equal suffrage in any federal legislature.[87] It was only the last-minute compromise that gave states equal suffrage in the Senate that finally brought the contentious 13 colonies together in the form of what we now call the United States of America.

Even this compromise was not a sure thing when it came to ratification by the states. For example, in New York, where antifederalists outnumbered federalists, the state threatened not to ratify because it was outraged that small states would have equal suffrage in the Senate. It was only after Alexander Hamilton threatened to join the union with only New York's southern counties and leave upper New York on its own that New York finally agreed (grudgingly) to ratify the Constitution.[88]

One might have thought—or at least hoped—that the question of equal Senate suffrage and the small-state weight resulting therefrom in the Electoral College would have been settled by now, and so it has been—until it was gratuitously resurrected during the 2000 election when the Green Party USA's plank advocated the abolition of the "disproportional aristocratic U.S. Senate."[89]

In 2018 a left-leaning Google executive, Ken Norton, tweeted that the U.S. Senate should be abolished, citing as justification for its abolition the confirmation of Brett Kavanaugh to the U.S. Supreme Court. Numerous Democrats, though not directly calling for abolition of the U.S. Senate, nevertheless denigrate both the Senate and the Electoral College in numerous ways. A headline by the *Washington Post*'s Philip Bump wrote that the very existence of the Senate violates the concept that "all men are created equal"—a mantra not only of NPVIC advocates but also the very title of the manifesto *Every Vote Equal*.

Columnist George Will has attempted to interject some historical fact and principles of federalism in response to such demands for abolition of the Senate as well as acknowledging the close tie-in between the Senate and the Electoral College. He has correctly noted that it is entirely inconsistent to favor abolishing the Electoral College without also favoring abolishing the Senate.[90] If the equal suffrage of the small states "offends you," writes Will, "so does America's constitutional federalism."[91]

It is indeed a puzzle why NPVIC advocates today do not first advocate abolishing the U.S. Senate before advocating the abolition of the Electoral College to which it is so closely tied. It is after all in the Senate, not the Electoral College, that the NPVIC's *Every Vote Equal* mantra might actually appear to have some force. It is in the Senate that legislation affecting the lives of all Americans is undertaken on a regular basis, treaties with other nations are ratified, and cabinet members and Supreme Court nominees are confirmed. The Electoral College, on the other hand, only produces a non–popular vote winner once or twice a century (in the same manner as the great parliamentary democracies do when more members are elected to parliament from a party that did not win the popular vote as happened in 1974 in the United Kingdom, with no reported outrage about the wrong prime minister being elected).

Is the answer to this question that each state prizes its senators as their celebrity representatives, while the members of the Electoral College are no-name John and Jane Does? Or is it simply that Article V is so clear that abolition of the Senate requires unanimous consent of all the states, while its connection to the Electoral College is somewhat more attenuated and less of a slam-dunk constitutional barrier to abolition of the Electoral College?

Whatever the reason, one suspects that the motivation for abolishing either the Senate or the Electoral College is based more on contemporary political and partisan considerations than on a sound understanding of constitutional history and principles of federalism. This is not only unfortunate but is also almost certainly misplaced even on the partisan level. In 2018 Ocasio-Cortez commented on a tweet by Julia Loffe that said "we are a country where two presidents who both lost the popular vote have now placed four justices on the Supreme Court. Democracy in action." It is not clear that Ocasio-Cortez recognized the close connection between the Electoral College and the Senate by responding "It's time we eliminate the Electoral College, a shadow of slavery's power."[92]

Myths about the Electoral College 119

In 2018, spokespersons of the losing party in the 2018 election appeared to be convinced that both the Senate and the Electoral College are rigged in favor of Republicans—just as Republicans felt that these two institutions were rigged in favor of Democrats back in the 1960s. If so, the facts do not support either of these assertions. As Kyle Sammin has explained in the Federalist, the "focus on small states as Republican strongholds [in the Senate] does not survive even the gentlest scrutiny. The senators from the 10 smallest states are nine Democrats, nine Republicans, and two independents who caucus with the democrats. That's an 11-9 split in Democrats' favor."[93]

Myth 10.14

Myth: The NPVIC would not violate the compact clause of the U.S. Constitution.

Answer: Article I, Section 10, of the Constitution states in no uncertain terms that "No State shall, without the Consent of Congress . . . enter into any Agreement or Compact with another State."

This provision was designed by the Framers to prevent states from engaging in conspiracies among themselves or with foreign powers that might threaten the federalist foundations of the new republic. Fresh in the minds of the constitutional Framers were the recent attempts of some states to conspire among themselves to set up trade barriers against each other, form amalgamations and alliances, or even create separate nations under the loose rubric of the Article of Confederation.[94] Indeed, the breakup of the 13 colonies was considered so imminent that a gloating royal adviser to George III advised his king that America was "breaking apart" and that very soon the warring colonists would "openly concert measures for entering into something like their former connections to Great Britain."[95] Delegate Hugh Williamson warned that if a constitutional compromise was not reached, secession of states into separate amalgamations would occur: "the scene of horror attending civil commotion cannot be described."[96]

With these considerations doubtless in mind, only a small number of states dared to enter into even the most innocuous interstate compacts prior to 1920, and these covered mainly such rudimentary functions as technical boundary disputes and water rights. Over a period of more than 130 years (between 1783 and 1920) states attempted to enter into fewer than 36 such compacts, most of which were bilateral and primarily used to settle boundary or water disputes. Even such minor and benign housekeeping compacts as these have been challenged in the U.S. Supreme Court as violative of the Article I, Section 10, compact clause.[97]

By 1978, however, with the Framers' concerns fading from memories, more states had begun engaging in compacts that pushed the envelope of what was constitutional without congressional approval under Article 1, Section 10. In the 1978 case *U.S. Steel v. Multistate Tax Commission,* plaintiffs challenged the constitutionality of a benign interstate agreement purporting to establish an interstate commission designed simply to help develop uniformity of certain state and local tax laws. Although the court in this instance approved this interstate compact, it nevertheless set forth the standard for any such future state compacts or conspiracies—namely, whether such a compact "enhances state power *quoad* the National government."[98] In upholding this particular contract it noted that "no sovereign power has been delegated to the Commission" and, most important, that "each state is free to withdraw at *any time*."[99] The court reduced these criteria to the following three requirements:

1.   Does the compact give a member state political power that it could not exercise but for the compact?
2.   Does the compact delegate sovereign power to another entity?
3.   Does the compact allow member states to withdraw at any time?

On its face, the NPVIC manages to directly violate all three of these constitutional criteria as set forth in the Multistate Tax Commission.

First, NPVIC IV-2 strictly and arbitrarily forbids any signatory's withdrawal to become effective until "six months or less before the end of a President's term." (Any difference between "actual right to withdraw" and "the date the withdrawal becomes effective" is of course not explained.)

Second, the compact *does* purport to delegate sovereign power to another entity. Because the drafters of the NPVIC were aware that it would have no power to appoint a federal entity to perform the task of counting the votes, Section III-5 of the NPVIC purports to delegate that task to a fictional entity consisting of an unnamed person or entity charged with tabulating the popular votes reported by the "chief election officials of each member state."[100] Remarkably, no provision is set forth providing for how any disagreement between such officials would be resolved. It will be recalled that in the election of 1960 the task of counting popular votes was hypothetically delegated to newspapers and the Congressional Quarterly, which disagreed as to how to count the popular votes for the six Alabama Democratic electors who voted for Senator Byrd. Mercifully for the nation, such a disagreement did not throw the country into constitutional crisis, since the Electoral College gave Kennedy a substantial majority of electoral votes.

Myths about the Electoral College

Third, the NPVIC gives a cabal of signatory states political power that it could not exercise but for the compact—namely, the power to determine who would be the next president of the United States. Most disconcerting of all, this power is given only to the states that sign on to the NPVIC. All other states are excluded. As noted by constitutional and legal historian Tara Ross, "This grant of authority is new and surely impacts horizontal relations among sister states. Today states are free to change their manner of elector allocation at any moment up until voting actually starts. NPV's compact would purport to restrict states and bind them for about six months during presidential elections years."[101]

Constitutional historian Derek Muller has noted that under the NPVIC,

> the non-compacting states' electors would have absolutely no influence in deciding the election—the bloc of electors from the compacting states would always have sufficient incremental power to elect the president, regardless of what non-compacting states did. In ex ante analysis, it is clear that the non-compacting electors could neither add nor take away from the ability of a presidential candidate to win.[102]

Nor will it do for NPVIC advocates to reply that various interstate compacts covering such matters as boundaries, water rights, and coordinating state taxes justifies approval of a compact that directly affects the federalist structure of the nation. Rather, the compact purports, by delegating to a fictional entity, to give a cabal of signatory states the power to alter the federalist structure of the United States.

Myth 10.15

Myth: The NPVIC provides a mechanism for enforcement of the compact.[103]

Answer: The NPVIC provides no procedure or mechanism for enforcing the terms of the compact should any state seek to withdraw from the compact outside the strict limits set by the NPVIC for withdrawal. Instead, it apparently assumes that some extraneous court would enforce it. Unstated is who would have standing to enforce the compact and which court—state or federal—would have jurisdiction to consider such litigation. If a state court had such standing, which state? Is it a state that is withdrawing from the compact or some signatory state that wishes to coerce a withdrawing state to abide by the compact's terms? Would such a court also have the power to interpret and apply the terms of the contract? What if such a court declines to accept subject matter jurisdiction on grounds that any decision would necessarily impinge upon the supremacy clause of the Constitution?[104] How would the presidential election be decided if litigation in any such court extends beyond the time for electors to meet on the first Monday after the second Wednesday of the month after the presidential election? (Note: Litigation in other compact enforcement actions have been known to take many months if not years before winding its way up the Supreme Court.)[105]

Perhaps the best way to visualize the constitutional chaos that would follow the initiation of any such litigation is by way of the same hypothetical set forth in myth 10.10.

Assume that a Democratic-controlled legislature in Colorado passes the NPVIC bill that purports to appoint a slate of electors pledged to vote for the media's tally of the national popular vote winner, even if the so-called popular vote winner is a Republican and even if the Colorado voters overwhelmingly vote for a Democratic slate consisting of electors pledged to the Democratic candidate. Assume further that in the 2024 presidential election the voters of Colorado overwhelmingly vote for the electors pledged to vote for the Democratic candidate Jane Obama. However, the Republican candidate, Joe Trump, ekes out a narrow national popular vote victory. The Colorado legislature announces that pursuant to a little-known bill called NPVIC, it intends to ignore the overwhelming number of votes cast for electors pledged to Jane Obama in Colorado and instead either order the duly elected Democratic electors to violate their pledge to vote for Jane Obama and instead vote for Joe Trump or, failing that, to simply dismiss the duly elected Jane Obama electors and instead nominate a whole new slate of electors who are willing to follow the legislature's order to vote for Joe Trump.

Chaos now reigns.

The electors appointed by the legislature to vote for Joe Trump in the Electoral College simply refuse to do so, saying that it would be contrary to the will expressed by the voters of Colorado. Mobs of outraged voters—many of whom have never even heard of the NPVIC—now gather in protest around the state capitol demanding that Colorado withdraw from the NPVIC compact and instead appoint the electors chosen by the people of Colorado. The Democratic-controlled Colorado legislature is inclined to heed the protests, especially those legislators who despise Joe Trump, and after much deliberation and consultation decide that it will withdraw from the NPVIC compact prior to the meeting of the Electoral College—a meeting that is less than three weeks hence. To make matters worse, if Colorado does withdraw from the NPVIC cabal and allows the duly elected Colorado electors to vote in accordance with their pledges to vote

Myths about the Electoral College

for Jane Obama, the much-despised Joe Trump will lose the election in the Electoral College, and Jane Obama will be duly elected.

Lawyers from the NPVIC consortium now converge on the Colorado capitol to demand that the Colorado legislators reverse their decision to withdraw from the compact, citing an obscure provision in the NPVIC (IV-2), which states that "any withdrawal occurring six months or less before the end of a president's term shall not become effective until a President or Vice-President shall have been qualified to serve the next term." The besieged legislators respond that no president can be elected until the withdrawal issue is resolved in the courts and that therefore they should be allowed to withdraw immediately in order that a president *can* be elected. They buttress their legal argument by relying on Article II, Section 2, which gives them an unrestricted right to cast their electoral votes in any way they wish *without any time restrictions*. In any case, the attorneys for the legislature assert that the NPVIC is unconstitutional in that it purports to forbid the Colorado legislature to allocate its electoral votes as it sees fit—a right guaranteed by the Constitution.

To make matters even more complicated, the Republican governor of Colorado refuses to sign any bill abrogating the NPVIC bill previously passed by the legislature. Lawsuits are now filed against the governor by legislators claiming that they alone have the power under Article II to abrogate interstate compacts.

During this time of chaos, the drop-dead date for the meeting of the Electoral College now looms. In the weeks that follow, other states seeking to follow the example of Colorado also seek to withdraw, throwing the presidential election into even greater chaos.

NPVIC lawyers now go to court trying to coerce Colorado and other states from withdrawing from the compact. Lawyers for Colorado defend vigorously.

When the first Monday after the second Wednesday comes around, no decision by the courts is looming, and civil unrest now erupts all across the United States. What happens next is now anyone's guess. Astonished allies around the world would surely ask what happened to that American electoral system that seemed to always produce a political successor without conflict or civil war.

Myth 10.16

Myth: The NPVIC provides a sound and workable interstate structure for imposing a Russian-style direct election on nonsignatory states without going through a legitimate constitutional amendment process.[106]

Answer: The best that can be said of this myth is that whatever might be its sincerity, it would result in an unsound attempt to fit a round peg (the NPVIC) into a very square hole (the Electoral College system as envisioned in Article II).

There are several preliminary points. First, if Americans' support for a Russian-style direct election is as overwhelming as NPVIC advocates claim,[107] the constitutional amendment process should be far easier to implement than trying to construct a fragile, unstable, and unwieldly conspiracy[108] of a relative handful of states.

Second, once the details, ramifications, and implications of the NPVIC are understood by those states that originally signed on to it, believing that it would be a problem-free means of avoiding the constitutional amendment process, withdrawals are likely to become the rule rather than the exception. Such withdrawals would throw the presidential election process into even further chaos.

Finally, support or opposition to a change in the Framers' vision for presidential elections generally arises during a contentious election or its aftermath—precisely the worst time to consider a dramatic upheaval of the Constitution. During such time, support or opposition is most likely to be based on whose ox was the most recently gored rather than what is good for the country. Thus, in the aftermath of the 1960 election in which, according to the Congressional Quarterly and the *New York Times* Nixon won the popular vote but lost the electoral vote, it was enraged Republicans who demanded abolition of the Electoral College.[109] Democrats, minority groups, and constitutional historians vigorously resisted such attempts.[110] In 2016, it was enraged Democrats who demanded its abolition because it resulted in a loss by their favored presidential candidate. In conducting polls in the aftermath of such elections, any pollster needs to take into account the current passions and partisan leanings of the person polled. Would Democrats in 2016 be as adamant about abolishing the Electoral College if it had resulted in the defeat of Donald Trump? Why did Democrats not join Republicans in opposing the Electoral College system after Kennedy won in the Electoral College but lost the popular vote?

Whatever the merits of and support for a Russian-style direct election, the NPVIC scheme for imposing it must be looked at *sui generis*. Unfortunately, the NPVIC does not reflect an understanding of how the Electoral College—which it purports to work within—actually works.

For example, the scheme is based on the erroneous assumption that when a voter casts a ballot in a presidential election, he or she is implicitly casting a vote for a party-nominated presidential candidate. This is

Myths about the Electoral College

not and never has been the case. Rather, a voter is casting a ballot for an *elector* who either pledges to go to the Electoral College and cast an electoral vote *for* a particular presidential candidate or in some cases an elector who is unpledged.[111] In many states elector pledges are not even legally enforceable or are enforceable only by a nominal fine.[112] (In 1960, for example, no fewer than three states—Louisiana, Mississippi, and Alabama—offered unpledged slates of electors.)[113] Since not a single vote cast by a single voter in any presidential election in American history has ever been for a particular presidential candidate, it follows that there can never be a calculation of popular votes cast for a presidential candidate— the very calculation upon which the NPVIC is based. The NPVIC purports to get around this inconvenient fact in paragraph III-3 by purporting to bind a signatory legislature to certifying the "appointment" of an "elector slate" nominated in that state "in association with" the national popular vote winner.

It is difficult to imagine a more ambiguous phrase in this context than "in association with." If nothing else, the very use of the phrase implicitly concedes that no voter in American history has ever cast a popular vote for a particular presidential candidate but only for persons who may be associated with a particular candidate. What does that really mean? The phrase apparently assumes that when some voters cast their ballots, they are under the impression or illusion that they are in fact voting for a presidential candidate, when of course they are not. The manifesto then goes on to make the conceptual jump that as long as voters are under this illusion, the association is complete, and it is then legitimate to assume that a vote for an elector is the equivalent of a popular vote for a particular candidate—regardless of whether that elector is pledged to that particular candidate, is "bound" to a particular candidate,[114] or is chosen in a state that bothers to enforce pledges at all.[115]

The NPVIC manifesto purports to address this anomaly by the simple expedient of providing that when calculating the popular votes cast in states where ballots only present voters with the names of electors, the popular votes will simply be ignored.[116] It effectively does so by conceding that "there would be no easy way to associate the votes of the various presidential electors with the nationwide tally accumulated by any regular presidential slate running in the rest of the country."[117]

Precisely!

The manifesto even uses as an example of this scenario the ballot presented to voters in the 1960 presidential election in Alabama, in which only the names of the electors of the various parties were listed, not the names of any presidential candidates.[118] In that election, the 11 Alabama electors listed under the Democratic slate were unpledged—in the same way that unpledged electors were listed under the Democratic slate in such other states as Louisiana and Mississippi. Nevertheless, only 5 of the chosen Alabama electors went on to the Electoral College and voted for Kennedy. Thus, had the NPVIC been in effect in 1960, all the popular votes cast for electors who voted for Kennedy in the Electoral College would have been disregarded for purposes of calculating the national popular vote.

Aside from the undemocratic feature of effectively disenfranchising half a million or more voters who cast their vote for electors who went on to cast their electoral votes for Kennedy, the NPVIC exclusion of any votes cast for the unpledged Democratic electors renders it impossible to calculate any meaningful national popular vote. In this regard, it should be noted that after the 1960 election several newspapers assigned over 318,000 popular votes to Kennedy by allocating to him the votes cast for *all* the electors on the Democratic slate. Even the *New York Times* and the Congressional Quarterly assigned to Kennedy only five-elevenths of the popular votes cast for the Democratic slate of electors.[119] The NPVIC would apparently allocate exactly zero popular votes for Kennedy in that scenario because, as it acknowledged, "there would be *no way to associate the vote counts of the various presidential electors with the nationwide tally being accumulated by any regular national popular vote.*"[120]

The drafters of the NPVIC manifesto are aware of the threat to its scheme that might be posed by nonsignatory states that deliberately defy an NPVIC scheme by emulating Alabama and other states that list only unpledged electors under a party slate. The manifesto recognizes that states opposing the NPVIC could sabotage the NPVIC scheme by simply listing unpledged electors on its ballot. This would make it impossible for any unnamed entity to calculate any meaningful national popular vote. In order to defeat any such resistance to its scheme, the manifesto claims that it must mandate the exclusion of all popular votes that are not "cast for each presidential slate in each state of the United States and in the District of Columbia in which votes have been cast in a nationwide popular election."[121]

How this provision would, in the words of the NPVIC manifesto, "deal with the unlikely possibility of a 'one-state veto' preventing the orderly operation of the compact"[122] is not clear. What is clear, however, is that the drafters of the scheme are willing to take the most draconian measures— up to and including disenfranchisement of millions of voters—to prevent any attempt by any nonsignatory state to resist the imposition of a Russian-style direct election in its home state.

CHAPTER ELEVEN

Reform
Proposals and Alternatives

There is no exact account of the number of proposals and alternatives for electoral reform that have been introduced in Congress since the time of the Constitutional Convention. Estimates range from no less than 500 to over 700. These proposals range from the labyrinthine and the bizarre to the simplistic.

An example of the former was a proposal by Senator James Hillhouse in 1808 to have retiring senators choose a president by drawing colored balls from a box.[1] A plan introduced by Senator Lazarus Powell in 1864 proposed that electors meet in groups of six and select the president by lot from among another group of six electors.[2] The most simplistic of all the plans, of course, is the proposal for direct election, despite its obvious danger of selecting a minority president (see Chapters 1 and 5). In between these two extremes has been a variety of other schemes, many of which have been seriously considered. Some have even come close to being adopted and proposed by Congress.

One plan or another has been fashionable at various times in the nation's history, depending on whose interests the proposed plan would favor. In the 1820s the district plan was popular and was proposed as a means of reducing the "present weight of the large states."[3] The plan enjoyed a revival in the 1950s by conservative and rural interests. It was finally killed by opponents who recognized, as stated by Senator Paul Douglas, that the plan was an obvious attempt to "deliver the cities bound hand and foot, into the power of the rural sections of the country."[4] Professor John Dixon warned that the district plan played into the hands of those seeking to entangle the judiciary into presidential elections and that if the plan were adopted "we shall have gerrymandered the Presidency."[5]

The proportional plan has enjoyed periods of high fashion several times in the nation's history, the most recent being during the 1950s when it was introduced in the form of the Lodge-Gossett Plan. Most of the electoral reforms in Congress have been supported by high-sounding rhetoric claiming that the proposed reform would be in the best interests of the country as a whole. Fortunately for the republic, the sponsors of the Lodge-Gossett plan were not very discreet in giving their candid views of what interest groups the plan would favor and whom the plan would harm. On July 17, 1950, Representative Ed Gossett supported his proposed reform in a speech on the House floor in which he asked whether it was right for the present Electoral College system to place a premium on "labor votes, or Italian votes, or Irish votes, or Negro votes, or Jewish votes," claiming that the present system permitted undue influence on Middle East policy because "there are 2.5 million Jews in the city of New York alone."[6] Gossett also claimed that the power the Electoral College gave to African Americans was what had led to the hated fair employment platforms of the major parties.

No opponent to the proposed reform could have asked for a better speech, and support for the proposal quickly evaporated. Since then, most reformers, particularly advocates of direct election, have been much more circumspect about giving their true reasons as to why they want to tamper with the Constitution, since all the arguments in favor of the proportional plan also apply to direct election.

The real problem with proposing a constitutional amendment based on a perceived advantage it will give to one group or another is that demographics and political views change over time. A plan that may favor one group in 1860, for example, may not do so in 1994. The republic is indeed fortunate that a precedent was not set in the earliest days of amending the constitutional plan for electing a president every time there was a perceived political advantage to be gained by doing so. Protected thus far by the formidable constitutional barrier to amending the Constitution, the Electoral College has endured as an impartial arbiter of the presidential election process. One major reason for its long endurance is that it has thus far been impervious to political tampering. It was not adopted by the Framers to favor Democrats or Republicans, conservatives or liberals, cities or towns. Rather, it was adopted as a critical cornerstone of federalism in which a stable democracy could flourish.

Had the earliest reformers been able to amend the Constitution to suit their perceived political goals, numerous other changes would doubtless

Reform

have followed over the years. The process of electing a president might have switched back and forth from direct election to district to proportional, depending upon the prevailing mood. Parties in power would have had every incentive to change the rules of the game to their own benefit. Had an early proposal for direct election been adopted, the proliferation of small parties, the factionalization of the political process, and the election of minority presidents would surely have brought demands for reform. The process would doubtless have been changed periodically to accommodate the fashion or political agenda of the day.

It has been claimed at various times that the Electoral College favors the Republican Party (in the 1980s when the Republicans had an alleged electoral lock in the South and the Midwest) or the Democratic Party (in the 1930s when Franklin D. Roosevelt had the alleged electoral lock). The fact is that over time the Electoral College favors no one. Indeed, the only time when it could possibly have favored any one group was in the election of 1888, the only fairly conducted election in which the electoral vote winner did not match the popular vote winner. To claim that the Electoral College has favored any particular group in any election other than 1888 is to claim that direct election would have favored the same groups.

But the Electoral College has not endured only because of its long acceptance and impartiality. It has also endured because of its success in meeting the needs of the nation. It remains, however, to examine a few of the many hundreds of proposals that have been made to amend the constitutional plan for electing the president.

The District System

There are several varieties of district systems that have been proposed. A common type of district plan would superimpose presidential districts on existing congressional districts. Each district in the nation would elect not only one representative to the House but also exactly one presidential elector. In addition, two electors (representing the two senators to which each state is entitled) would be elected statewide.[7]

A subvariety of the district plan would not superimpose presidential districts on existing congressional districts but rather would create a whole new map of presidential districts by dividing each state into districts equal in number to the total number of senators and representatives to which the state is entitled.

The sole redeeming feature of either type of district system is that it retains the essential feature of federalism agreed to at the Constitutional Convention. That is, each state would continue to have electors equal in number to the total number of senators and representatives to which it is entitled. But it retains this feature at the expense of every other desirable feature of the existing Electoral College system.

All but two states now employ the general ticket system to elect electors to the Electoral College. That is, electors are chosen statewide rather than by district. The general ticket system is thus immune from political attempts to gerrymander districts to the advantage of one party or the other—that is, to alter the geographic boundaries of the area in which a candidate is to be elected. Under the Constitution, state boundaries are simply not subject to political tampering.[8]

The practice of gerrymandering may be illustrated by the following example. Assume that a state has within it 10 districts. About 48 percent of the state's electorate supports party A, and 52 percent supports party B. Unfortunately for party A, however, its support is concentrated in 3 districts where it has 90 percent support. In the remaining 7 districts, it enjoys an average of only 30 percent support. Pursuant to elections held in districts with the existing geographical boundaries, it will therefore elect 3 representatives out of 10. If party B is in power, however, it may attempt to redraw the geographic boundaries so that in each district party A has only 48 percent support. In such a manner, party A can be deprived of any representatives (despite its 48 percent statewide support), and party B will get all 10. In the same manner, if party A can gain control, it may be able to draw the boundaries so that it has 60 percent support in 6 districts but only 20 percent support in the remaining 4. Thus, despite having only 48 percent statewide support, it may elect 6 of the 10 representatives.

The practice of redrawing the geographic boundaries of a district to gain such political advantage has become known as gerrymandering. The enormous incentive to engage in its practice should be apparent from the above example. It is not surprising therefore to learn that its practice has plagued congressional elections since the very earliest time of the republic. It was noted in Chapter 4 that the judiciary began to get heavily involved in this area when it decided *Baker v. Carr*[9] and *Gray v. Sanders*.[10] Fortunately, the Electoral College system and the general ticket ballot have spared the presidential election process from the problems associated with gerrymandering.

It is apparent that there would be enormous incentives for gerrymandering under the district system for electing a president. The incentives for redrawing district boundaries to affect a presidential election would be equal to or even greater than the incentives for redrawing boundaries

Reform

131

to affect congressional elections. Doubtless the courts would be drawn in, as they already have been in the area of congressional elections.

The district system would also not have the discouraging effect on third and extremist parties that the Electoral College has under the general ticket ballot. The chances of an extremist party winning an entire state are relatively small. Its chances of winning a particular district, however, would be substantially greater.

Finally, the district system does not provide the same unambiguous result as the general ticket ballot. By splitting each state's electoral vote, the impact of each state is proportionately decreased. If an election is extremely close in the popular vote, it is likely to be extremely close in the electoral vote as well. Each district might become critical, creating an incentive to recount each challenge and every vote within the close districts. In close elections it would be unlikely that there would be a clear winner, and the final result could be delayed for a long period, thus bringing uncertainty to the entire political process.

So, what is gained from using a district system? The only real claim of its supporters is that such a system would lessen the possibility of electing a wrong president—that is, a president who wins a majority of electoral votes without winning the most popular votes. Without conceding that such a president would in any way be wrong in our federal system, it should be noted that had the district system been in effect in other elections, "the district plan would have had their outcomes reversed."[11] In 1960, for example, John Kennedy would have lost the election under the district plan despite having received the most popular votes.

The district system is not prohibited by the Constitution, and any state is free to adopt it. Maine and Nebraska have already done so. If more states were to follow, the nation could return to the situation that existed in the early 1800s in which states switched back and forth between systems depending upon which party a system favored. Responsible reform would make uniform the general ticket system, which has been adopted by 48 of the 50 states. In the nuclear age the republic can no longer risk the delays, uncertainties, and incentives for political intrigue that are inherent in the district system.

The Proportional System

Even the cleverest surgeon cannot divide one man up—proportionately or otherwise—and expect him to live.

—Henry Cabot Lodge[12]

The proportional system would attempt to award electoral votes in the same proportion as the popular vote. Like the district system, it has the redeeming feature that it would retain the federalist allocation of electoral votes to each state. Unlike the district system, however, there would not be the political incentive to practice gerrymandering. The earliest proposals for a proportional system were introduced in Congress in the late 1800s. They provided that electoral votes would be awarded in the same percentage as the popular vote, with each electoral vote rounded off to the nearest 1 electoral vote. Thus, if a candidate received 59 percent of the popular vote of a state that was entitled to 10 electoral votes, he or she would be awarded 6 votes; if the candidate received 66 percent, he or she would be awarded 7 electoral votes.

Later proposals provided for rounding each elector off to the nearest thousandth of a percentage point. Thus, a candidate could receive a fraction of electoral votes, such as 2.308. A proportional plan introduced in Congress in 1950 would have combined the system with the automatic plan whereby the actual electors would be abolished and each state would automatically be awarded the electoral votes of a state in the same percentage as the popular vote the candidates received.

The proportional plan was supported and opposed—for mostly the wrong reasons. Supporters such as Gossett felt that it would lessen the influence of minorities, particularly that of African Americans and Jews. In this one respect Gossett's interpretation coincided with the views of Clarence Mitchell, the Washington director of the National Association for the Advancement of Colored People, who stated that the proportional plan would

> effectively draw the political eye teeth of all independent voters, including the Negro voter, as far as Presidential elections are concerned. . . . If the Gossett proposal goes through, the Negro vote and the vote of any other minority, national and religious group will no longer be important. . . . The Gossett proposal is antiurban, antinorthem, and antiliberal.[13]

Democrat Paul Douglas observed that

> some of the [proponents of proportional representation] have been frank enough to admit that they are talking about Negroes, Jews, Catholics . . . but to others [they refer] to farmers . . . veterans, the aged. If the Republican Party succeeds in having the Gossett resolution adopted that will put an end to . . . the civil rights issue from national politics. . . . No surer method of introducing confusion and lack of confidence in our electoral system could be devised.[14]

Reform 133

Democratic senator John Kennedy observed that the proportional plan

> has been discredited in the past and promises only doubt and danger for the future. . . . No minority Presidents have been elected in the 20th century; no breakdown in the electoral system, or even widespread lack of confidence in it can be shown. . . . There is obviously little to gain—but much to lose by tampering with the Constitution.[15]

Although both supporters and opponents perceived that one group or another was harmed or favored by proportional representation, for every view that one group was favored by the Electoral College there was a political scientist who claimed that the same group was disadvantaged. (It will be recalled that Abbott and Levine claim that the Electoral College disadvantages African Americans, Mormons, and homosexuals.)[16]

The real problem with the proportional plan is the same as that of direct election—namely, that it would encourage factionalism, discourage compromise, and magnify the problems of ambiguity and delay in cases of close elections. A few senators chose not to base their opposition on perceived political grounds but instead recognized that it would "weaken the two party system."[17]

The only nonpolitical reason given in support of the plan was that it would reduce the chances of a wrong president elected without a majority of the popular vote. Even by this misguided standard, however, the proportional plan fails. Had it been in effect in the elections of 1880, 1896, and 1960, it would have elected popular vote losers Winfield Scott Hancock, William Jennings Bryan, and Richard Nixon.

Indeed, even under this misguided standard put forward by reformers, the Electoral College has proven superior to either the direct or proportional plans.

The Automatic Plan

At first blush, the automatic plan would appear to have none of the evils associated with direct election, the district system, or the proportional plan. The automatic plan would go no further than to eliminate the actual office of elector and would continue to award electoral votes in the present manner. That is, there would no longer be electors who would actually be elected and subsequently meet to cast their votes. Instead, the popular vote winner of a state would simply be automatically credited on the computer with the number of electoral votes allocated to that state.

Ironically, it is the very modesty of this plan that makes it unlikely to be adopted. More radical reformers fear that the adoption of such a plan would "be worse than having no reform at all. Not only would it write into the Constitution the evils of the unit vote system, but its adoption would undoubtedly preclude meaningful reform indefinitely."[18] Others have asserted that "it is hardly worth cranking up the complex and protracted amendment process to accomplish so little—it would be almost like chasing a fly with an elephant gun."[19]

Some opponents of the automatic plan have claimed that it would harm the two-party system by making it easier for splinter parties to get on the ballot.[20] This claim does not appear particularly persuasive in light of the many other factors that are involved in being placed on the ballot.[21]

However, the radical reformers do have a point about whether it is worth going through the process of amending the Constitution for so insignificant a reform. The automatic plan addresses only one small aspect of the Electoral College—the problem of the faithless elector. Despite the fact that faithless electors have cast only 7 out of 17,000 votes cast in the past 150 years and have never come close to affecting an election, it would nevertheless ease anxieties if this problem was addressed.

As will be explained in the final chapter, there are a number of areas in which the Electoral College could use some fine-tuning. The faithless elector is only one of those areas. If the amendment process is to be utilized, all areas should be addressed in one package.

There are several ways in which the faithless elector problem can be dealt with, and the automatic plan is not the only way. It can be argued, of course, that the actual office of elector is unnecessary and that computers can do the job once performed by electors. There is some truth to the claim that the meeting of human electors is an old and archaic ceremony. There is perhaps no conceptual or political rationale for its retention. But the same could be said for many ceremonies of state that commemorate a past tradition. There is certainly no political or conceptual rationale for retaining the tradition of the inaugural address or parade. New presidents could simply put their remarks on a disc and electronically transfer them to a computer network, and the parade itself could certainly be dispensed with.

Doubtless the tradition of the president's State of the Union Address could be dispensed with and put on videotape. The day may even come when meetings of the Senate and the House in the Capitol are considered archaic, and it is suggested that their work can be conducted more efficiently on an electronic computer network. But many Americans would

Reform

consider that something would be lost in such an arrangement. It may well be that some electors consider their appointment and meeting to be a useless exercise. But others consider the office to be an honor and appreciate that their meeting is part of a tradition that began when the first Electoral College met to elect George Washington. If the only real concern is that of the faithless elector, this can be dealt with in other ways. For example, a package of responsible reform could provide that a vote cast by an elector in violation of his or her pledge could be changed to a vote in compliance with the elector's pledge by a majority vote of either house of Congress. It would be rare that such a remedy would be required (perhaps once or twice a century), but its constitutional availability might ease the anxieties of some reformers.

In any case, at least the automatic plan would not tamper with the essential characteristics of the presidential election process that were devised by the Framers and have been refined and developed over 200 years.

Legislative Election

It will be recalled that the Constitution delegates to each state the appointment of electors. With but one or two minor exceptions, all states by the 1830s had provided for appointment of electors by popular election. The most recent election in which a legislature chose electors was in 1944, when the Mississippi legislature chose electors to oppose all the other party slates.[22]

It has been proposed by William Martin, writing for the *American Bar Association Journal*,[23] that state legislatures should again begin selecting electors. Martin has expressed the view that the election of a president has become too centralized and nationalized and that the only way to return to the scheme envisioned by the Framers is to let the state legislatures choose the electors. "Have we the courage," Martin has asked, "to bring this plan out in the open and elect legislatures which will carry it out? It has been tested in our early history and electors then selected their best and most patriotic citizens for President. It is valid. It is Constitutional."[24]

Martin is correct in stating that such a plan would be constitutional. But he is incorrect in suggesting that any particular plan for appointing legislators was envisioned by the Framers. Rather, what the Framers envisioned was a process of development as each state determined what was the best way of selecting electors. The Framers' faith and confidence in the state legislators has been fully vindicated, as each state has chosen popular election as the most democratic and fair method of selecting electors. Indeed, popular election of electors has now become such an integral part of the Electoral College that a responsible reform would enshrine this process in the Constitution.

Hybrids

A few of the more bizarre proposals for electoral reform have already been mentioned, but most others are not worthy of serious attention. In 1861 Representative Clement Vallendigham of Ohio proposed an electoral reform that he hoped might avert the American Civil War. Under his plan, the country would be divided into four large regional districts, one of which would include the South. In order to be elected president, a candidate would have to receive a majority of electors in each of the four regional districts.[25] Other than its general impracticability, this plan's obvious deficiency was that it would be rare for any president to be elected under such a system, and a subsequent election by the Congress would defeat the purposes of the plan.

Other hybrids have included plans to elect presidents alternately from the North and the South[26] and to require a plurality of popular votes and a majority of electoral votes[27] as well as a wide variety of combinations of popular vote, majority vote of electors, pluralities in a majority of states, or pluralities in states having the majority of voters.[28] One hybrid plan, known as the bonus plan, is worthy of special attention.

The Bonus Plan

In 1978 the Twentieth Century Fund enlisted the contributions of a distinguished panel of Americans to study the Electoral College and make recommendations.[29] Members of the task force included historian Arthur Schlesinger, Jeane Kirkpatrick (later to be the U.S. representative at the United Nations), and other distinguished historians, lawyers, journalists, political scientists, and educators.[30] The final recommendation of that group was the bonus plan. Although the plan itself proved to be just another inconsequential and ultimately ignored hybrid, the Twentieth Century Fund study is nevertheless notable for having conducted the most in-depth study of the Electoral College system.

Although the members of the task force represented no political constituency and thus had no federalist interest to protect, they nevertheless represented some of the brightest and most independent thinkers who could have been brought together. Although in the end their study made a recommendation of the bonus plan, the study stands as perhaps the

Reform 137

most persuasive defense of the Electoral College system. The preface to the study states that

> the Electoral College has weathered great changes—demographic and technological as well as political—in the nature of presidential elections, and more than once in the nation's history, has been challenged. Yet it has endured, in part because it stands for some important and cherished principles, in part because proposals for replacing it have threatened those principles.[31]

In explaining how it reached its final recommendations, the task force stated that initially it saw no way of reconciling what was apparently irreconcilable. Several members noted that the probable consequences, some necessarily unforeseen, of changing the system might amount to a cure that was worse than the disease. Others supported direct election. Faced with these opposing choices, the task force appeared to be merely replaying the inconclusive data that had gone on for so long. Nevertheless, the task force's discussions revealed a remarkable degree of consensus on critical issues and on the values to be preserved.

Included on the task force were some hard-core advocates of direct election.[32] In order to achieve any kind of consensus, it was necessary to address their overriding concern of the once every two century possibility of a president being elected without a popular majority. For the rest of the task force, however, it was essential to retain the basic federalist values of the Electoral College as well as preserve those aspects that nurtured the two-party system and provided for a conclusive result.

The necessity of satisfying the advocates of direct election resulted in the bonus factor of the task force's plan. Under this plan, virtually all the essential characteristics of the Electoral College would be retained. That is, each state would continue to be entitled to electors equal in number to its senators and representatives. However, electoral votes would be automatically awarded to the winner of each state's popular votes (the automatic plan), and the winner of the national popular vote would get an extra 102 electoral votes (the bonus).

The sole claimed redeeming feature of the bonus plan (other than retaining the basic apparatus of the Electoral College) appeared to be that it would have provided for the election of Grover Cleveland in 1888. That is, in every election conducted in the United States, the plan would have selected the popular vote winner as the winner in the Electoral College. (According to mathematician Samuel Merrill, however, it would still be possible to elect a popular vote loser under the bonus plan.)[33]

138   *Saving the Electoral College*

However, the concession to the direct election advocates was greater than was perhaps apparent to those who wished to preserve the basic values of the Electoral College. By giving a bonus of 102 electoral votes to the winner of the popular vote, a presidential election was made subject to the same kind of uncertainties and delays that would accompany a close direct election. Thus, in return for giving up the once every two century possibility of a popular vote loser, the bonus plan gave up obtaining a decisive result in close popular vote elections.

For example, if the bonus plan had been in effect in 1960, the winner of the election would have been determined by who received the popular vote bonus of 102 electoral votes. That is because without the bonus, Kennedy received 303 electoral votes and Nixon received 219. Therefore, whichever candidate received the most popular votes (and the 102 bonus electors) would be the winner.

It will be recalled, however, that there was a serious dispute as to which candidate was entitled to claim the most popular votes in Alabama. Although only five of the Democratic electors were pledged to Kennedy, the official count nevertheless awarded to him the popular votes of the unpledged Democratic electors and the electors pledged to Harry Byrd. Under the method of counting popular votes utilized by the Congressional Quarterly, however, Kennedy should have only been awarded six-elevenths of the popular votes cast in Alabama. Under this method of counting popular votes, Nixon would have won the popular vote both in Alabama and nationwide and would have been entitled to the 102 bonus points and the presidency.

There were strong arguments both for and against the method used by the wire services that awarded to Kennedy the popular votes cast for all the Democratic electors. The basic weakness of this method, however, was that it counted the popular votes for the unpledged electors twice— once for the unpledged electors and once for Kennedy! In many respects, the Congressional Quarterly method of counting the votes would have been far more fair.

Fortunately, the nation was spared a divisive argument over which candidate should have been credited with the popular vote majority in Alabama. The dispute faded into a footnote in history, because under the Electoral College system, there was a clear winner regardless of who won the popular vote in Alabama or nationwide. It was for this reason that Nixon did not challenge the popular vote allocation in Alabama. Had the bonus plan been in effect, however, the question would have been absolutely critical to the outcome of the election.

With the entire election hanging on which method was used to count Alabama's popular votes, Congress would probably have been obliged to

Reform

appoint an electoral commission to resolve the dispute. The nation would very likely have had to endure a prolonged period of uncertainty as both parties pressed to have their representatives appointed to the commission. In short, the process would have been very similar to what the nation endured in 1876, with one very important exception.

In 1876 the law provided that the president was not to be inaugurated until March 4 of the following year. Even so, the long process of appointing commissions, listening to testimony, and making decisions took until March 2. In 1960 the law provided that the president was to be inaugurated on January 20. Despite the greater demands for procedural due process that Americans in 1960 would doubtless have demanded, an electoral commission would have had to act even more swiftly than the one appointed in 1876. It should also be recalled that in the Cold War year of 1960, a period of uncertainty and ambiguity in the election of the president would have had far graver consequences than in 1876.

Members of the Twentieth Century Fund Task Force who favored retention of the Electoral College apparently acceded to the bonus plan as the price of retaining the basic apparatus of the Electoral College. Doubtless they did so in order to reach a consensus and head off a more radical demand for popular election. But in doing so they conceded one of the most important features of the Electoral College system—the production of a clear-cut and unambiguous winner. They also proposed to burden the present system with one of the worst features of direct election.

It may be that no one on the task force seriously considered the bonus plan to be a viable alternative to the present system and reached its compromise only to avoid an absolute deadlock. Nevertheless, the distinguished task force's acknowledgment of the basic principles and advantages of the Electoral College system would have been sufficient to justify its hard work.

For example, the task force recognized that "under the election, the states would be deprived of their constitutional role in the election of the President. This might weaken not only state political parties but also the influence of state and local issues in presidential campaigns."[34] In reviewing the track record of the Electoral College in past national elections, the task force acknowledged that "the election of 1888 is the only undisputed example of a runner-up victory,"[35] thus rejecting the claims of some radical reformers that the elections of 1824 and 1876 provide examples of electoral malfunction. The task force also acknowledges that in the 1960 election, the Congressional Quarterly's method of allocating Kennedy only five-elevenths of the Alabama Democratic popular vote would have been a "seemingly fairer method."[36]

Most important, however, the task force rejects the simplistic notion that direct elections result in electing the majority candidate. When "the candidate with the most votes among multiple candidates wins less than 50%," he or she will not necessarily be "the most preferred candidate because, if given another choice, more than half the people may prefer one of his opponents."[37] The study concludes that by "majoritarian standards," the "direct popular vote is somewhat arbitrary."[38] More important, "direct election does not guarantee that the candidate with the most support wins if there are more than two candidates."[39]

On the question of whether a direct election would encourage factionalism and multiple parties, the task force cited a contemporary study conducted by Bradley Canon. According to Canon, the task force states that

> the possibility of a runoff [in a direct election] has a striking effect; it increases the proportion of votes going to the top candidates and lowers the number of candidates receiving significant numbers of votes. [Canon's analysis] generates support for the idea that the existence of run-offs actively encourages more candidates to enter, thus reducing the proportion of the vote going to the top candidates.[40]

Canon's study concludes that direct elections that provide for a runoff encourage more minor parties than even a direct election without a runoff.[41]

The task force concluded that under direct election, state boundaries would become irrelevant in counting votes, and the position of state parties in national campaigns might therefore be weakened. State political parties, once the most vital element of the national of party organization, have already seen their position eroded by the reform of the national nominating process and by the changing nature of political campaigns; direct election might continue that erosion.[42]

But perhaps the most important of the task force's conclusions was that the one point on which the case for direct election seems to be weakest and the case for the Electoral College seems to be strongest is in yielding a clear result: "While no one would create the Electoral College de novo today, it is defended with a vigor that derives from decades of success that are considered satisfactory."[43]

The Contingency Election

There have been many proposals over the years to reform the provision for election of the president by the House when no candidate has received

Reform 141

a majority of electoral votes in the general election. Many of these proposals have been attached to other proposals, such as the American Bar Association (ABA) proposal for a runoff election when no candidate receives 40 percent of the votes in a popular election. Other plans have been proposed to retain the House election but allow each representative to have one vote or to have a vote by a joint session of Congress.[44] Peirce and Longley have claimed that the contingency election has been "almost universally condemned."[45]

The proposals for reform of the contingency election fall into two categories: those that would continue to have Congress elect the president if no candidate receives a majority of electoral votes and those that would bypass Congress and provide for a runoff election. Since the arguments are different for both of these categories of reform, they will be dealt with separately.

Most arguments for a runoff in lieu of an election by Congress are based on the assumption that any election by Congress would be inherently undemocratic. In fact, it should be noted that most of the world's democracies provide for the election of their chief of state in exactly this manner. Nevertheless, the constitutional provision for a contingency election in the House should be examined on its own merits.

The problems with any kind of runoff election have been noted by Judith Best. In her study of runoff elections in other countries, she has noted that such elections result in additional "expense, voter fatigue, and a drop-off in participation."[46] She has also suggested that the uncertainty created during the period between the first and second elections would "foster political intrigue" and "shorten the time available for an orderly transition of power." In addition, it would "necessitate a national recount, and weaken or alter the two party system."[47] It has already been noted that runoffs can reduce the possibility of electing a true majority candidate.

Although such reasons provide a practical reason not to adopt a runoff system, there are more fundamental reasons to reject it. It will be recalled that the manner of electing the president was included in the Great Compromise (see Chapter 3). Indeed, it was the promise of equal state representation in the contingent House election that finally resolved the dispute between small and large states. When it was finally proposed as a means of breaking the deadlock, the Constitutional Convention adopted the idea "with what must have been an audible sigh of relief"[48] that a walkout by the small states had been averted and a final compromise achieved.

It will also be recalled that the small states believed that their right to equal state representation in the House would prove to be a significant concession. Because the Electoral College process has worked so much better than any convention delegate had ever dreamed, the small states have already been deprived of most of the benefits of their bargain. The small states anticipated that many, if not most, elections would be referred to the House, where the small states would have equal representation. In fact, no election has been referred to the House since 1824.

In short, the contingent election in the House is part of the "whole solar system of government power."[49] If this part of the system is to be tampered with, then the other parts of the federalist system must also be looked at, such as the equal representation of the states in the Senate and the equal power of states to ratify constitutional amendments.

Nevertheless, betrayals of federalist principles might be justified in the extreme situation whereby a constitutional provision has 'caused or threatens to cause great harm. So far, the only potential harm that reformers can point to is that once every 200 years or so, this nation might have to employ the method used by most of the world's democracies to elect their heads of state.

In fact, not only has the contingent election not caused or threatened to cause any harm to the republic, it has been a very positive force in the development of the presidential election process. Next to the general ticket ballot, this feature of the electoral process has probably contributed more to the creation of the two-party system and the discouragement of factionalism than any other one feature.

Remember that early in the 1992 presidential election Ross Perot dropped out of the race, despite placing very competitively in the national polls. One of the reasons he gave was that the most he could hope for in the election was to deprive the other two candidates of an electoral majority, thus sending the election into the House, where he would certainly lose. Had the ABA provision for a runoff election been in effect, Perot would have had every reason to stay in the race, hoping for a narrow second-place finish in the general election that would have qualified him for the runoff. In short, it was the provision for a House contingency election that narrowed the field down to two candidates, making it possible for the voters to elect a majority, or large plurality, president.

Perhaps the most attractive feature of the contingent House election is that it has the effect of reinforcing the two-party system without actually having to be implemented. The mere knowledge that this contingency provision exists is usually enough to narrow the field to a number that will permit the election of a president with a majority or large plurality of the popular vote. Without this provision, the country would probably by

Reform

now have had a large number of presidents who received neither a majority nor a large plurality of the popular votes.

Proposals to elect the president in a joint session of Congress or to give each representative a separate vote would only serve to further diminish the value of the federalist bargain made to the small states. It would also create the possibility most feared by the small states—that the vast armies of representatives of just a few large states could overwhelm the election process and dictate a choice to the rest of the country. Federalism was simply not founded on such a basis, and our union would never have existed had such a plan been insisted upon at the Constitutional Convention.

But in the final measure, the contingent House election should be retained because it has so faithfully served the cause of democracy and federalism within which democracy has flourished for 200 years.

Direct Election

The simplest of all the proposed alternatives to the Electoral College is, of course, the direct election. It was first advocated as early as the Constitutional Convention but was voted down by one state in favor and nine states against. It was first proposed in Congress as a constitutional amendment in 1816. However, it was soundly defeated by senators led by Maryland senator Robert Harper, who stated that direct election "threw out of view altogether the federal principle under which the states are represented. It would destroy that influence of the smaller states . . . and thus destroy a very important principle of the Constitution."[50]

Over 100 proposals for direct election have been introduced in Congress since 1816. None have been successful. In 1956 a direct election proposal was defeated by a Senate vote of 28–63. The opposition was led by Senator John Kennedy of Massachusetts, who stated that "I should hate to see the abolition of state lines. . . . The Presidential election is determined on the basis of 48 separate units. I think the election should be decided in each one of them."[51]

The most ambitious assault on the Electoral College was launched in Congress in 1969 under an umbrella of relentless invective. One representative called the Electoral College "barbarous" and "dangerous."[52] In 1970 the assault was continued but was stemmed in part by the testimony of such experts as Theodore White and assistants to former presidents.[53] In the end, however, it was the runoff feature of the direct election plan that caused many members of Congress to pause. "Everyone is much scared of the runoff feature," explained one legislative aide.[54] In 1979 representatives of minority groups testified against a proposal for direct election, claiming that it would "have a disastrous impact . . . on black people."[55]

Although the 1969 proposal came closest to being adopted, all were ultimately defeated. Apparently many members have felt as historian Clinton Rossiter did that "we should hesitate a long time before replacing a Humpty-dumpty system that works for a neat one that will blow up in our faces."[56]

Nevertheless, the quest to abolish the Electoral College continues today. Proposals for direct election constitute the most direct threat, for several reasons. First, unlike most of the other proposed reforms, direct election is simplistic and easy for the man and woman in the street to understand. Pollsters find it easy to ask voters whether they would favor direct popular election of the president instead of the Electoral College, which is not generally understood by the average voter. Often the question is simply asked "do you believe that the presidential candidate who receives the most popular votes should be elected?"

Second, the very term "direct popular election" has an aura of democracy about it. It simply sounds more democratic. Reformers have encouraged this view by perpetuating myths, such as that the Framers were anti-democratic elitists who proposed the Electoral College as a means of insulating the presidency from the people. (In fact, they left the selection of electors to the legislatures, all of which subsequently provided for popular election of electors.)

However, many of those who profess to favor direct election state that they are unaware of the federalist origins of the Electoral College; the role that the Electoral College played in the Great Compromise, which included equal state representation in the Senate; and the fact that direct election may encourage factionalism and produce a minority president. Others are not aware of the delays and ambiguities inherent in the direct election process. Most have heard only arguments in favor of direct election and have heard few if any defenses of federalism.

Advocates of direct election have dismissed virtually all of the concerns of those who favor retention of the Electoral College. Evidence of the Electoral College's contribution to the creation of the two-party system is dismissed—apparently on the theory that the two-party system is a natural state of political affairs.

Despite the specific statements of James Madison that "the little states insisted on retaining their equality in both branches"[57] and the findings by constitutional historian Max Farrand that "the proposed method of electing the President was a compromise,"[58] advocates of direct election persist in taking the view that there was no such compromise.

Reform 145

On the one hand, Peirce and Longley simply assert that the "Great Compromise was devised to settle the dispute over representation in Congress, not the Electoral College."[59] Although acknowledging the many references to the presidential compromise in the Federalist papers and in ratifying conventions, they nevertheless conclude that Madison and the constitutional experts must be wrong and that the argument that the Electoral College was "central to the institution of the presidency . . . is simply false."[60]

On the other hand, Peirce and Longley describe the subject of the "big versus small state interests" at the Constitutional Convention as the "Great Irrelevancy."[61] If it is so irrelevant, one may wonder why the fact that a compromise occurred is so vigorously denied.

Nevertheless, the reformers' vehement rejection of the view that the Electoral College was part of the Great Compromise is intriguing, as it suggests that even the reformers believe that such a compromise, if it existed, would be relevant as revealing a significant aspect of federalism. If such reformers could be convinced that such a compromise did exist, one wonders if they would remain undeterred or would then concede that direct election would be a betrayal of an important federalist principle.

Reformers rarely address the objection, stated by John Kennedy, that "direct election would break down the federal system under which most states entered the union, which provides a system of checks and balances to ensure that no area or group shall obtain too much power."[62] Kennedy's observation that the Electoral College is but one aspect of the "solar system of government power" is dismissed on grounds that such other parts of the system have changed—citing the rise of political parties and the primary system. It is clear, however, that Kennedy was not speaking of parties or primaries but rather the essential ingredients of federalism agreed to as part of the Great Compromise at the Constitutional Convention— that is, the equal representation of states in the Senate and in the ratification of constitutional amendments. Neither of these two latter aspects of federalism has changed in the past 200 years.

In 1977, renowned historian Arthur Schlesinger wrote that "should an abstract standard of equity require the abolition of large-state advantages in presidential elections, then surely it requires the abolition of the small state advantage in the Senate."[63] Reformers Peirce and Longley dismissed this idea as a "red herring" on grounds that under the Constitution, deprivation of equal representation in the Senate requires unanimous consent of all the states.[64] It is true that at the Constitutional Convention the small states did not trust the large states and were prudent enough to insist upon their right to veto any proposal to deprive them of their right to equal suffrage in the Senate. It now appears that their lack of prudence in protecting those same rights in the executive branch is to be used against them. But this does not make Schlesinger's point a red herring.

Reformers put much stock in the fact that some representatives from the small states are willing to forsake the Electoral College birthright won by their forebears at the Constitutional Convention. Presumably the point to be made is that small states are now willing to give up whatever rights were once given to them in the presidential election process. If such a willingness is to be found to forsake suffrage rights in the Electoral College, why not also in the Senate? It would take the consent of all the states, to be sure (rather than just 34), to abolish the Electoral College, but it could be done if all the small states were to recognize the nature of the "undemocratic" Constitution of the U.S. Senate.

Honest reformers have at least been willing to concede that direct election poses severe problems in close elections. Peirce and Longley, for example, have conceded that

> many states are unable to report an official account until several weeks after election day, as local boards of elections languidly carry out their duties. If recounts are necessary or challenges reach the courts, the process of establishing an official count can drag on well into the term of the official who has been elected. It is in this area of the speed in the count and challenge procedure, rather than in obtaining, finally, a conclusive national count, that the direct vote for president raises the most serious problems.[65]

In addressing such problems in a direct election, Peirce and Longley appear to put much faith in a federal takeover of the election process[66] and in "automatic, mandatory retallys." A federal takeover, of course, presents its own problems of federalism. More important, however, it must be recognized that mandatory retallies and technological advances in vote counting will not solve the problem of delays and challenges. First, there are many delays that can not be eliminated simply by advanced computers. Absentee votes cast by Americans overseas must still be tabulated and fed into a computer or vote-counting machine. Allegations of fraud are frequently based on intimidation, denial of access, and other matters totally unrelated to the accuracy of machines. Even total nationwide computerization, which would help somewhat, is a long way off. Even if advanced machines had been available in 1876, it is doubtful that they would have helped very much in resolving the kinds of problems encountered in that election.[67]

Reform 147

An example of the kinds of delays that are encountered with a direct election system was illustrated in the Twentieth Century Fund's 1978 study of the Electoral College. In the 1974 New Hampshire Senate election, official returns showed that the Republican had won by 355 votes. A recount, however, showed that the Democrat had won by 10 votes. An appeal was made to an electoral commission, which ended up having to scrutinize each individual vote. After this scrutiny, the commission determined that the Republican had actually won by a margin of 2 votes out of a quarter of a million cast. This decision was in turn referred to the Senate Rules Committee, which after considerable deliberation determined that it was unable to reach a conclusion. Party politics soon reared its ugly head, and a proposal to hold a new election was filibustered by party opponents. The matter was settled only when the candidates themselves agreed to a new election. But the entire process took almost a year (or about one-sixth of the senatorial term).[68]

The consequences of this delay in seating a senator were not particularly severe (except perhaps for New Hampshire), since no matters of national security or nuclear responsibility were at stake. Had this been a presidential election, such a delay could have created a constitutional crisis of catastrophic proportions. Fortunately, when this country has had presidential elections that have been as close as the New Hampshire election (as in 1880), the Electoral College has provided an instant clear-cut winner. The sole exception was in 1876, when massive fraud across an entire region put the popular vote counts in so many states at issue that a favorable Republican resolution in each of four entire states would have given the Republican an electoral majority of exactly one vote.

It is true that if there is another election involving massive region-wide fraud, a recount might be necessary even under the Electoral College system. This has occurred only once in our history and is unlikely to occur again. However, the delay and uncertainty created in the New Hampshire election are likely to occur in any close presidential election. Close elections in American history have occurred frequently and are likely to occur again. It therefore follows that the chances of a constitutional crisis arising are far more likely under a state of direct election than under the Electoral College.

Under a direct election system, any close election would require the recounting of virtually every vote. Under the Electoral College system, a recount would be required only in that state in which the vote is very close or in which there are challenges to the votes. Votes in states that are not in doubt do not need to be counted.

Historian Theodore White has explained that the Electoral College is

> like a vessel. We have a vessel now with 50 separate containers. They slosh around a bit, but they are contained. If you have this whole pack of 75 million votes cascading in all at once, the sloshing and the temptation to stall here or there will, I think be enormous. This is such a gamble . . . that it appalls me to think of it.[69]

Historians, constitutional scholars, and political scientists have carefully set forth the dangers involved in tampering with the Constitution in the manner of selecting the president. However, as long as direct election is simplistically espoused as a more democratic alternative, without explaining the inherent dangers, it will continue to be a threat to the system that has served our nation so well for 200 years. In the end, only education and dedication to the principles for which this nation stands can save this grand American institution.

CHAPTER TWELVE

Conclusion

The Case for Preserving Federalism[1]

This book has endeavored to catalog the inherent weaknesses of a Russian- or French-style direct election that if imposed upon the United States would undermine not only the federalist foundations of the republic but also democracy itself. It has been submitted that the historical record fully vindicates John F. Kennedy's observation that "direct election would break down the federal system upon which most states entered the union, which provides a system of checks and balances to ensure that no area or group shall obtain too much power." The Constitution's guarantee of equal state suffrage in the Senate and the allocation of electors based on that equal suffrage has served to not only provide the federalist structure that bound the states to a union but also ensure that no one group or area is able to obtain too much power. Without these provisions the original colonies would have formed their own amalgamations and nation-states, as occurred in South America. The United States would have been left to be ruled from one region or area, be it from the South in an era of segregation and Jim Crow during the 1930s–1950s or from the coastal regions in the 2000s—just as John Kennedy recognized and feared should direct election ever be imposed on the American people. The country—like France after the 2017 presidential elections—would be shackled with leaders who enjoyed support from only a minority of the population, making governance both risky and unstable. American voters would have the same complaint about their presidential election system as Christine Poumailloux had with the French popular vote election system in 2017 that produced a leader who enjoyed only 24 percent in the first round: "It was obvious, the choice was either ultraliberalism—that's not good—or ultranationalism, that not good either. For the first time in my life I didn't vote in the second round."[2] Presenting voters with a choice between extreme parties or candidates in a multiparty system undermines not only democracy but also the very federalist foundations of a united republic.

Aside from undermining democracy and federalism, the practical problems of Russian-style direct election would create chaos if some states conducted recounts but others did not. Litigation and recounts in every voting hamlet in every state would create uncertainty and instability. Presidential candidates would devote the focus of their attention to areas of the country with the greatest concentrations of population—where the votes are—thereby increasing the political divide between the coasts and the hinterland of the country. The small states would be marginalized by losing their small but significant electoral advantage in the Electoral College based on equal suffrage in the Senate.

John F. Kennedy's vision of federalism was correct in virtually every respect, but it is difficult to imagine what he would have thought of the National Popular Vote Interstate Compact (NPVIC) cabal of states seeking to impose an unworkable Russian-style direct election on the current Electoral College structure itself. Whatever the democratic weaknesses and deficiencies of direct election, its establishment through a legitimate constitutional amendment process would at least avoid the worst constitutional and practical anomalies that the NPVIC would create.

It should be recalled that direct election was considered by the Framers at the Constitutional Convention. It was not adopted for the same good reasons as exist today. The much maligned unit-vote system was not adopted by the Framers but was adopted individually by every state except Nebraska and Maine.

The district system—which would require each state to allocate an electoral vote based on the winner of each congressional district—does have some precedent in American history, though it too is not reflected in the Constitution. Both Thomas Jefferson and James Madison originally supported such a system but recognized why most states would reject it unless all or most states adopted it as well. Nevertheless, the district system has its merits. Its implementation by constitutional amendment would not require depriving states of equal suffrage in the Senate (which would require consent of all the states) or smaller states' weight in the Electoral College based on equal suffrage. It would also reduce—though not eliminate—the risk of an electoral winner losing the popular vote. It would, however, feature many of the weaknesses of direct election, including recount problems.

Conclusion 151

The proportional plan—requiring states to allocate their electoral votes based on the percentage of popular vote—would also not require depriving the states of either their right of equal suffrage in the Senate or their weight in the Electoral College but, like the district plan, would carry the same risks of recount chaos, delay, and uncertainty.

The recommendation of this study is adoption of a plan that retains the essential features of the current system but would also require a constitutional amendment. Known as the automatic plan, it would do away with the need for human electors. Instead, electoral votes would be automatically allocated to presidential candidates according to the popular vote within each state. While this would preclude states from authorizing their legislatures to appoint electors, it should be noted that no state has reverted to this procedure since 1880. It is therefore unlikely that this preclusion would prove an obstacle to approval by three-quarters of the states. It would not, however, require ominous approval of all the states, since it would not deprive states of either their equal suffrage in the Senate or the weight that suffrage gives to all the states in the Electoral College. Its most important feature would be to eliminate entirely the nagging potential for electoral mischief of the "faithless electors." It is true that in the course of American history only a relative handful of electors have violated their pledge to cast their vote for a particular candidate—by one count only 7 out of 17,000 electors have done so. Since 1876, no state has even hinted at depriving state voters of their right to elect electors.

Nevertheless, the reformers have a point with regard to faithless electors and the right of legislatures under the Constitution to appoint electors. These two problems should be addressed as part of any package of responsible reform. But to many reformers, these potential problems provide a convenient fig leaf for their true agenda: to abolish the Electoral College and undermine the principles of federalism. Indeed, many reformers have actively resisted efforts to specifically address these particular problems for fear that any such minor reform would jeopardize their agenda for a radical change in the electoral process. This is indeed unfortunate, for the Electoral College system has already been refined to the limits permitted outside the Constitution. A constitutional amendment would be required to specifically address the potential problems of the faithless elector and the legislative appointment of electors.

In addition, there are other aspects of the electoral process that should be addressed, such as the disenfranchisement of American citizens who are not citizens of a state.

Retaining the Electoral College, even with its present minor potential problems, would be preferable to the adoption of any of the major radical reforms that have been proposed. It may be that a package of responsible reform will be impossible as long as radical reformers consider such a package to be a threat to their own agenda. Nevertheless, what follows is the outline of a package of six responsible reforms that specifically address the real potential problems and that, if implemented, would undermine neither federalism nor the basic structure of the electoral process.

1. Enfranchising All American Citizens

Under the Constitution, only states and the District of Columbia may appoint electors. This provision effectively disenfranchises American citizens who are not citizens of a particular state or the District of Columbia. It is proposed that the District of Columbia be designated as the electoral repository for all citizens of the United States who are not citizens of states and that the number of electors from the District of Columbia should reflect the total population of such citizens according to the constitutional formula for awarding electoral votes.

2. Legislative Appointment of Electors

Although the Constitution provides that each state shall have plenary power to determine the manner in which electors are chosen, all states have now adopted popular election as the method of choosing electors. Although it is highly unlikely that a state would ever revert to legislative or executive appointment of electors, it is theoretically possible, in a critical election, that a state might be tempted to revert to direct legislative appointment. Therefore, the Constitution should be amended to provide that state electors shall be chosen by popular election in each state.

3. The General Ticket Ballot

All states but two have long adopted the general ticket ballot (unit rule) as the means of casting electoral votes. The two states that have reverted to the district method, Maine and Nebraska, have not been a major factor in recent elections. (Maine, despite its theoretical adoption of the district system, has not ever cast its votes except as a bloc.) The general ticket ballot, developed over two centuries and now adopted by almost all the states, has provided the Electoral College with its most important tool for nurturing and sustaining the two-party system, discouraging factionalism, and producing a clear-cut winner the day after each election. Although the threat to uniformity created by the district systems adopted

Conclusion

by Maine and Nebraska is very small and theoretical, the potential danger of a state being able to manipulate the electoral process for political ends should be eliminated. The Constitution should be amended to require each state to adopt the general ticket ballot.

4. The Faithless Elector

The automatic plan, which eliminates the office of elector, automatically awards electoral votes to candidates receiving a plurality of votes within a state. It is an acceptable means of ensuring that electors, by breaking their pledges, do not thereby frustrate the will of the people who elected them. However, there is an alternative method that would not dehumanize the electoral process or unnecessarily bring to a halt the 200-year tradition of electors meeting in their respective states to cast their votes for president—a uniquely American tradition that has occurred like clockwork every 4 years since George Washington was elected president.

Rather, an amendment could give Congress the right to change any vote cast by a faithless elector to a vote for the candidate to whom the elector was pledged. Such a vote should be limited only to changing the unpledged vote to the candidate to whom the elector was pledged, and no other disposal of the vote should be permitted. The requirement for making this change should be minimal, such as a majority vote of either house of Congress.

It will be recalled that when elector Lloyd Bailey cast his vote for George Wallace rather than Richard Nixon in 1968, Congress attempted to challenge the vote as not having been "regularly given" in accordance with 3 U.S. Code 15. This challenge was not successful, primarily because many members of Congress believed that the Constitution gave an elector the right to vote for any candidate, even in violation of a pledge. Thus, in the view of many members of Congress, Bailey's vote was nevertheless regularly given. The amendment proposed would eliminate this uncertainty and would specifically give Congress the right to reverse any vote cast by an elector in violation of a pledge to the electorate.

5. Congressional Certification of Electoral Votes

It will be recalled that 3 U.S. Code 15 states that if there shall have been any final determination in a state in the manner provided for by law of a controversy or contest concerning the appointment of all or any of 166 electors of such state, it shall be the duty of the executive of such states to communicate under the seal of such state to the archivist of the United States a certificate of such determination.

In addition, 3 U.S. Code 15 then provides that such a certification shall be accepted by Congress unless both houses concurrently determine that such certified electoral votes were nevertheless not regularly given.

There are three problems with these provisions. First, each state should be required to provide a method for resolving electoral controversies, although most states certainly now do so.

Second, a specific statutory choice should be made as to whether the incumbent governor or the governor-elect has the power and duty to certify the electoral slate. It will be recalled that in the election of 1876, the incumbent governor and governor-elect of several states certified different electoral returns to Congress, thereby throwing the entire presidential election into doubt. To avoid delay, the incumbent governor should probably be designated.

Third, the electoral slate as certified by the governor should be absolutely final. The U.S. Code provision permitting Congress to overturn even certified returns if they are found to have not been regularly given is ambiguous and vulnerable to both political intrigue and mischief, which could cause delays and political upheaval similar to what the nation endured in 1876. Congress's power to overturn any electoral vote should be limited to the narrowly defined power to change a specific elector's vote cast in violation of a pledge to the candidate to whom an elector was originally pledged.

It is doubtful that any commission or other body appointed by Congress to second-guess a governor's certification would be any more legitimate than that of a sitting elected state governor. Remember that in 1876 the election appointed by Congress was, by necessity, split along strictly party lines, and the one supposedly nonpartisan member effectively ended up choosing the president. Any advantages in accuracy or procedural due process that might be gained by allowing a lengthy and partisan federal electoral commission to second-guess a properly certified state electoral slate would be more than outweighed by the delay and uncertainty created by such a commission, not to mention the dangers of conflict and upheaval.

This change in the law would not require a constitutional amendment but could be accomplished by amending Sections 6 and 15 of Chapter 3 of the U.S. Code.

6. The Contingent House Election

The importance of retaining the contingent House election has been noted in previous chapters. The contingent election reinforces the Electoral

Conclusion 155

College in nurturing the two-party system and discouraging factionalism and has proved critical in ensuring the election of a president favored by a majority or large plurality of the American people.

However, the procedures for this election should be more specifically set forth. First, a determination should be made as to whether the incumbent House or the new House should elect the president. There is at present no agreement on which House would elect the president. Although it has been argued in Chapter 1 that the incumbent House should elect the president, the most important provision would be to make a clear-cut choice between the old or the new House.

Second, there should be a specific provision clarifying whether the votes within each state delegation should be by majority or plurality vote. Although a majority would be preferred, the best option would be to reduce the number of eligible candidates in the House to the two top electoral vote getters in the Electoral College. In this case, all votes within a delegation would either be a majority or a tie vote, in which case a state's vote would still be lost. Reducing the number of candidates in the House to two would also reduce considerably the possibility that a vice president would be chosen in the Senate who was of a different party than the candidate chosen to be president by the House.

Third, the quorum requirements in both the contingent House and Senate elections should be eliminated. This would reduce the incentive for political mischief by one party deliberately refusing to attend the election in the hope that the election would thereby be delayed for some ulterior political purpose. With no quorum requirement, it is assumed that few if any members of Congress would choose not to attend a House election of the president or Senate election of the vice president.

Fourth, a specific date should be chosen for both the contingent House election of the president and the contingent Senate election of the vice president. This date should be no more than one or at the most two weeks after the general election. The House election should preferably be held first. Such a provision would limit delay and uncertainty and inhibit political mischief that might be caused by delaying tactics of either party.

Fifth, it should be provided that all votes in a House election should be by open rather than secret ballot. Although the proposed changes with regard to the contingent House and Senate elections could be made by statute, incorporation of the changes in a constitutional amendment would be preferable.

None of these six proposed changes would alter the basic federalist structure of the electoral process or reduce the substantial advantages the present system provides. They would, however, eliminate the possibility of conflict and uncertainty in the event of unusual and unanticipated occurrences in the electoral process. It is submitted that all of the proposed changes would further refine the electoral process, and it is hoped that the fear of preventing a radical restructuring would not prevent the adoption of such reforms. Even without such reforms, the plan of the constitutional Framers remains far superior to the hundreds of plans that have been proposed since the Constitutional Convention.

APPENDIX A

National Popular Vote Interstate Compact: California's Bill

Assembly Bill No. 459

Chapter 188

An act to add Chapter 1.5 (commencing with Section 6920) to Part 2 of Division 6 of the Elections Code, relating to presidential elections.

[Approved by Governor August 08, 2011. Filed with Secretary of State August 08, 2011.]

LEGISLATIVE COUNSEL'S DIGEST

AB 459, Hill. Electoral college: interstate compact.

Existing law provides for statewide election of a slate of electors to vote in the electoral college for President and Vice President of the United States. Under existing law, each political party selects its slate of presidential electors in accordance with statutory procedures that differ by party.

This bill would ratify a specified interstate compact that requires the chief election official of each signatory state to appoint the slate of presidential electors that was nominated in association with the presidential ticket that received the largest national popular vote total. This compact would only become effective if states cumulatively possessing a majority of the total electoral votes have ratified the compact.

DIGEST KEY

Vote: majority Appropriation: no
Fiscal Committee: yes
Local Program: no

BILL TEXT

THE PEOPLE OF THE STATE OF CALIFORNIA DO ENACT AS FOLLOWS:

SECTION 1.

Chapter 1.5 (commencing with Section 6920) is added to Part 2 of Division 6 of the Elections Code, to read:

CHAPTER 1.5. Voting Compact

6920.

The Legislature of the State of California hereby ratifies the Agreement Among the States to Elect the President by National Popular Vote as set forth in Section 6921.

6921.

The provisions of the Agreement Among the States to Elect the President by National Popular Vote are as follows:

Article 1. Membership

Any state of the United States and the District of Columbia may become a member of this agreement by enacting this agreement.

Article 2. Right of the People in Member States to Vote for President and Vice President

Each member state shall conduct a statewide popular election for President and Vice President of the United States.

Article 3. Manner of Appointing Presidential Electors in Member States

Prior to the time set by law for the meeting and voting by the presidential electors, the chief election official of each member state shall determine the number

Appendix A   159

of votes for each presidential slate in each state of the United States and in the District of Columbia in which votes have been cast in a statewide popular election and shall add such votes together to produce a "national popular vote total" for each presidential slate.

The chief election official of each member state shall designate the presidential slate with the largest national popular vote total as the "national popular vote winner."

The presidential elector certifying official of each member state shall certify the appointment in that official's own state of the elector slate nominated in that state in association with the national popular vote winner.

At least six days before the day fixed by law for the meeting and voting by the presidential electors, each member state shall make a final determination of the number of popular votes cast in the state for each presidential slate and shall communicate an official statement of such determination within 24 hours to the chief election official of each other member state.

The chief election official of each member state shall treat as conclusive an official statement containing the number of popular votes in a state for each presidential slate made by the day established by federal law for making a state's final determination conclusive as to the counting of electoral votes by Congress.

In event of a tie for the national popular vote winner, the presidential elector certifying official of each member state shall certify the appointment of the elector slate nominated in association with the presidential slate receiving the largest number of popular votes within that official's own state.

If, for any reason, the number of presidential electors nominated in a member state in association with the national popular vote winner is less than or greater than that state's number of electoral votes, the presidential candidate on the presidential slate that has been designated as the national popular vote winner shall have the power to nominate the presidential electors for that state and that state's presidential elector certifying official shall certify the appointment of such nominees.

The chief election official of each member state shall immediately release to the public all vote counts or statements of votes as they are determined or obtained.

This article shall govern the appointment of presidential electors in each member state in any year in which this agreement is, on July 20, in effect in states cumulatively possessing a majority of the electoral votes.

Article 4. Other Provisions

This agreement shall take effect when states cumulatively possessing a majority of the electoral votes have enacted this agreement in substantially the same form and the enactments by such states have taken effect in each state.

Any member state may withdraw from this agreement, except that a withdrawal occurring six months or less before the end of a President's term shall not become effective until a President or Vice President shall have been qualified to serve the next term.

The chief executive of each member state shall promptly notify the chief executive of all other states of when this agreement has been enacted and has taken effect in that official's state, when the state has withdrawn from this agreement, and when this agreement takes effect generally.

This agreement shall terminate if the electoral college is abolished.

If any provision of this agreement is held invalid, the remaining provisions shall not be affected.

Article 5. Definitions

For purposes of this agreement, "chief executive" shall mean the governor of a state of the United States or the Mayor of the District of Columbia; "elector slate" shall mean a slate of candidates who have been nominated in a state for the position of presidential elector in association with a presidential slate; "chief election official" shall mean the state official or body that is authorized to certify the total number of popular votes for each presidential slate; "presidential elector" shall mean an elector for President and Vice President of the United States; "presidential elector certifying official" shall mean the state official or body that is authorized to certify the appointment of the state's presidential electors; "presidential slate" shall mean a slate of two persons, the first of whom has been nominated as a candidate for President of the United States and the second of whom has been nominated as a candidate for Vice President of the United States, or any legal successors to such persons, regardless of whether both names appear on the ballot presented to the voter in a particular state; "state" shall mean a state of the United States and the District of Columbia; and "statewide popular election" shall mean a general election in which votes are cast for presidential slates by individual voters and counted on a statewide basis.

Source: California State Assembly Bill AB-459, "An Act to Add Chapter 1.5 (Commencing with Section 6920) to Part 2 of Division 6 of the Elections Code, Relating to Presidential Elections," State of California Legislature.

APPENDIX B

Selected Provisions of the U.S. Constitution Relating to the Electoral College*

Article I

Section 2, Clause 3:

. . . Each state shall have at least one representative. . . .

Section 3 Clause 1:

The Senate of the United States shall be composed of two senators from each state . . . and each senator shall have one vote.

Article II:

Section 1, Clause 2:

Each state shall appoint, in such manner as the Legislature thereof may direct, a number of Electors, equal to the whole number of Senators and Representatives to which the state may be entitled in the Congress. . . .

*Capitalizations and spelling have been changed to modern form.

Section 1, Clause 3:

The electors shall meet in their respective states, and vote by ballot. . . . The person having the greatest number of votes shall be the President if such number be a majority of the whole Number of Electors appointed . . . and if no person have a majority, then from the five highest on the list the said House shall in like manner choose the president. But in choosing the President, the votes shall be taken by states, the representation from each state having one vote. . . .

Article V

. . . No state, without its consent, shall be deprived of its equal suffrage in the Senate. . . .

Source: U.S. Constitution, Article I, Sec. 2 and Sec. 3, and Article II, Sec. 1.

Notes

Preface

1. Congressional Record—Senate (March 20, 1956), 5159.
2. Ibid., 5162 (cited by Senator John F. Kennedy).
3. Ibid., 5137–5167.
4. Ibid., 5163.
5. Ibid., 5150.
6. Ibid., 5152.

Chapter 1

1. See Chapter 1 for an explanation as to why the 1960 election is included on this list.
2. Neal Peirce and Lawrence D. Longley, *The People's President: The Electoral College in American History and Direct Vote Alternative,* rev. ed. (New Haven, CT: Yale University Press, 1981).
3. Final report of the Commission on National Elections, Georgetown University, *Electing the President: A Program for Reform,* ed. Robert E. Hunter (Washington, DC: Center for Strategic and International Studies, 1986).
4. William Peters, *A More Perfect Union: The Making of the United States Constitution* (New York: Crown Publishers, 1987), 110.
5. Robert M. Hardaway, *The Electoral College and the Constitution: The Case for Preserving Federalism* (Westport, CT: Praeger, 1994), 70.
6. Peters, *A More Perfect Union,* 97.
7. Burton J. Hendrick, *Bulwark of the Republic: Biography of the Constitution* (Boston: Little, Brown, 1937), 32 (statement of Edward Bancroft).
8. Cited in Peters, *A More Perfect Union,* 99.
9. Ibid.
10. Hearings on S.J. Res. 1, 8, and 18 before the Subcommittee on the Constitution of the Committee of the Judiciary, U.S. Senate, 95th Cong., 1st sess. (July 22, 1977).

11. National Popular Vote!, accessed December 15, 2018, https://www.national popularvote.com.

12. The NPVIC proposal is explained and defended in detail in John R. Koza et al., *Every Vote Equal: A State-Based Plan for Electing the President by National Popular Vote* (Los Altos, CA: National Popular Vote Press, 2013).

13. *Williams v. Rhodes,* 393 U.S. 23.

14. Jessica Chasmar, "Alexandria Ocasio-Cortez: We Must 'Eliminate the Electoral College,'" *Washington Times,* October 7, 2018, accessed December 15, 2018, https://www.washingtontimes.com/news/2018/oct/8/alexandria-ocasio -cortez-we-must-eliminate-the-ele/.

15. Koza et al., *Every Vote Equal,* 258.

16. *United States Steel Corp. v. Multistate Tax Com.,* 434 U.S. 452.

17. See, e.g., Tara Ross, *The Indispensable Electoral College: How the Founders' Plan Saves Our Country from Mob Rule* (Washington, DC: Regnery Gateway, 2017).

Chapter 2

1. Congressional Record—Senate (July 22, 1977), 102 (statement of Sen. John F. Kennedy).

2. G. F. Webb, "Precinct Size Matters—The Large Precinct Bias in U.S. Presidential Elections," PhD dissertation (Vanderbilt University, 2014), 1.

3. Martin Diamond, "The Electoral College and the Idea of Federal Democracy," *Publius* 8, no. 63 (1978).

4. William Schneider, "Electoral College's Archaic Ritual," *National Journal* 20 (December 10, 1988): 3164.

5. "Electing the President: Recommendations of the American Bar Association's Commission on Electoral College Reform," *American Bar Association Journal* 53 (March 1967): 219.

6. Congressional Record—Senate (March 20, 1956).

7. John R. Koza et al., *Every Vote Equal: A State-Based Plan for Electing the President by National Popular Vote* (Los Altos, CA: National Popular Vote Press, 2013), xxxvii.

8. Why a national popular vote is best characterized as a Russian-style election will be explained in the chapters below.

9. William Peters, *A More Perfect Union: The Making of the United States Constitution* (New York: Crown Publishers, 1987), 9, 11.

10. Ibid., 5.

11. Ibid., 31.

12. Ibid.

13. Martin Diamond, "The Electoral College and the Idea of Federal Democracy," *Publius* 8, no. 1 (Winter 1978): 63–77.

14. Jill Karson, ed., *Great Speeches in History* (Farmington Hills, MI: Greenhaven, 2003).

15. National Archives and Records Administration. *Presidential Election Laws.* National Archives and Records Administration. 2018.

16. Peters, *A More Perfect Union,* 81.

Notes 165

17. Ibid., 28.

18. Burton J. Hendrick, *Bulwark of the Republic: A Biography of the Constitution* (Boston: Little Brown, 1937), 65.

19. Peters, *A More Perfect Union,* 99.

20. Ibid., 103.

21. Ibid., 104.

22. Original source: *The Papers of George Washington,* Confederation Series, Vol. 5, *1 February 1787–31 December 1787,* ed. W. W. Abbot (Charlottesville: University Press of Virginia, 1997), 257.

23. John F. Banzhaf, "One Man, 3,312 Votes: A Mathematical Analysis of the Electoral College," with comments by the Honorable Birch Bayh, the Honorable Karl E. Mundt, the Honorable John J. Sparkman, and Neal R. Peirce, *Villanova Law Review,* 13 (Winter 1968): 304. See also John F. Banzhaf III, "Weighted Voting Doesn't Work: A Mathematical Analysis," *Rutgers Law Review,* 16 (1965): 317; John F. Banzhaf III, "Multi-Member Electoral Districts—Do They Violate the 'One Man, One Vote' Principle?," *Yale Law Journal* 75 (1966): 1309.

24. Peters, *A More Perfect Union,* 97.

25. Ibid.

26. Koza et al., *Every Vote Equal,* 53.

27. Robert Ernst, *Rufus King: An American Federalist* (Chapel Hill: University of North Carolina Press, 2012), 103.

28. Koza et al., *Every Vote Equal.*

29. Joe Setyon, "Alexandria Ocasio-Cortez: 'Eliminate' Electoral College, It 'Undermines' Democracy," Reason.com, October 8, 2018, accessed January 11, 2019, https://reason.com/blog/2018/10/08/alexandria-ocasio-cortez-we-should -elimi.

30. Koza et al., *Every Vote Equal.*

31. Pew Research Center Poll focusing on "40% of Millennials OK with Limiting Speech Offensive to Minorities." See also Brookings Institution survey focusing on "Views among College Students regarding the First Amendment."

32. Robert M. Hardaway, *The Electoral College and the Constitution: The Case for Preserving Federalism* (Westport, CT: Praeger, 1994).

33. Alexander Hamilton, James Madison, and John Jay, "Federalist No. 68," The Federalist Papers.

34. Cited in Lucius Wilmerding Jr., *The Electoral College* (Boston: Beacon, 1958), 19.

35. Hardaway, *The Electoral College and the Constitution,* 122–125.

Chapter 3

1. David Robertson, *The Debates of the Convention of Virginia, 1788* (2nd ed., 1805), 351, cited in Max Farrand, ed., *The Records of the Federal Convention of 1787,* Vol. 1 (New Haven, CT: Yale University Press, 1966), 135.

2. *Williams v. Rhodes,* 393 U.S. 23 at 28.

3. Congressional Record—Senate (May 28, 1974), 23.

4. Maine actually elects two of its electors on a statewide basis, since its two senators are also elected on a statewide basis; the other Maine electors are elected by congressional district.

5. 3 U.S.C.A. §7.

6. 3 U.S.C.A. §15.

7. U.S. Constitution, Article II, §1, clause 2.

8. Alexander Hamilton, Federalist Paper 68.

9. James Madison, Madison Debates, July 19, 1787, avalon.law.yale.edu.

10. William Peters, *A More Perfect Union: The Making of the United States Constitution* (New York: Crown Publishers, 1987).

11. Ibid., 31.

12. Ibid.

13. Thomas M. Durbin, "The Anachronistic Electoral College," *Federal Bar News & Journal* 39 (October 1992): 510.

14. Peter Applebome, "George Wallace Rues and Relishes the Past," *New York Times,* February 1994.

15. U.S. Constitution, Article II, and Amendment XII.

16. Peters, *A More Perfect Union,* 30.

17. Ibid., 5.

18. Burton J. Hendrick, *Bulwark of the Republic: Biography of the Constitution* (Boston: Little, Brown, 1937), 35.

19. Robert Hardaway, "Misunderstanding Of Electoral College Clouds Debate and Obstructs Reform," Huffington Post, December 01, 2017, accessed January 11, 2019, https://www.huffingtonpost.com/robert-hardaway/misunderstanding-of-electoral-college-clouds-_b_13327082.html.

20. Joe Setyon, "Alexandria Ocasio-Cortez: 'Eliminate' Electoral College, It 'Undermines' Democracy," Reason.com, October 08, 2018, accessed January 11, 2019, https://reason.com/blog/2018/10/08/alexandria-ocasio-cortez-we-should-elimi.

Chapter 4

1. Neal Peirce and Lawrence D. Longley, *The People's President: The Electoral College in American History and Direct Vote Alternative,* rev. ed. (New Haven, CT: Yale University Press, 1981), cited in Robert M. Hardaway, *The Electoral College and the Constitution: The Case for Preserving Federalism* (Westport, CT: Praeger, 1994), 165.

2. Ibid.

3. Final report of the Commission on National Elections, Georgetown University, *Electing the President: A Program for Reform,* ed. Robert E. Hunter (Washington, DC: Center for Strategic and International Studies, 1986).

4. Ibid., 142.

5. Statement of Democratic senator Paul Douglas of Illinois, cited in Peirce and Longley, *The People's President,* cited in Hardaway, *The Electoral College and the Constitution,* 141.

Notes 167

6. Ibid.

7. Report of the Twentieth Century Fund Task Force in Reform of the Presidential Election Process, *Winner Take All,* background paper by William R. Keech (New York: Holmes and Meier, 1978).

8. Peirce and Longley, *The People's President,* 185.

9. Ibid., cited in Hardaway, *The Electoral College and the Constitution,* 156.

10. Ibid., 165.

11. Peirce and Longley, *The People's President,* 203.

12. Peirce and Longley, *The People's President,* cited in Hardaway, *The Electoral College and the Constitution,* 10.

13. Ibid.

14. Ibid.

15. Ibid.

16. National Archives and Records Administration, accessed January 11, 2019, https://www.archives.gov/federal-register/electoral-college/print_friendly .html?page=faq_content.html&title=NARA, Federal Register, U.S. Electoral College, cited in Hardaway, *The Electoral College and the Constitution,* 22.

17. *Congressional Quarterly Guide to the American Government* (Washington, DC: Congressional Quarterly, 1979), 78; cited in David Abbott and James Levine, *Wrong Winner: The Coming Debacle in the Electoral College* (New York: Praeger, 1991), cited in Hardaway, *The Electoral College and the Constitution,* 23.

18. Ibid.

19. Vanessa Miller, "Smaller States Get Bigger Say in Electoral College," *The Gazette,* November 26, 2016, accessed January 11, 2019, https://www.thegazette .com/subject/news/government/elections/smaller-states-get-bigger-say-in-elec toral-college-20161126.

20. Abbott and Levine, *Wrong Winner,* 83–84. See also Dale R. Durran, "Whose Votes Count the Least in the Electoral College?," *The Conversation,* November 08, 2018, accessed January 11, 2019, http://theconversation.com /whose-votes-count-the-least-in-the-electoral-college-74280.

21. Abbott and Levine, *Wrong Winner,* 90.

22. Ibid., 93.

23. Ibid., 91.

24. Ibid., 94–95.

25. Ibid., 94.

26. Ibid., 87–88.

27. Ibid., 88–89.

28. Ibid., 89.

29. Cited in Martin Diamond, "The Electoral College and the Idea of Federal Democracy," *Journal of Federalism* (Winter 1978): 63.

30. John F. Banzhaf, "One Man, 3.312 Votes: A Mathematical Analysis of the Electoral College," with comments by the Honorable Birch Bayh, the Honorable Karl E. Mundt, the Honorable John J. Sparkman, and Neal R. Peirce, *Villanova Law Review* 13 (Winter 1968): 304. See also John F. Banzhaf III, "Weighted Voting Doesn't Work: A Mathematical Analysis," *Rutgers Law Review* 19 (1965): 317;

John F. Banzhaf III, "Multi-Member Electoral Districts—Do They Violate the 'One Man, One Vote' Principle?," *Yale Law Journal* 75 (1966): 1309.

31. Robert J. Sickels, "The Power Index and the Electoral College: A Challenge to Banzhaf's Analysis," *Villanova Law Review* 14 (Fall 1968): 92. See also Carleton W. Sterling, "Electoral College Misrepresentation: A Geometric Analysis," *Polity* 13 (1981): 425–449.

32. John R. Koza et al., *Every Vote Equal: A State-Based Plan for Electing the President by National Popular Vote* (Los Altos, CA: National Popular Vote Press, 2013).

33. John D. Feerick, "The Electoral College—Why It Ought to be Abolished," *Fordham Law Review* 37 (1968): 54n10. An election occurred in the 1974 parliamentary election in Great Britain in which the Labour Party lost the nation popular vote but nevertheless formed the government because three more of its members were elected to Parliament.

34. Stephen Bush, "What Happened in the 1974 Election?," New Statesmen, accessed January 1, 2019, https://www.newstatesman.com/politics/2015/04/what-happened-1974-election.

35. Jazmine Ulloa, "Hundreds Protest the Electoral College at Capitol Building in Sacramento," *Los Angeles Times,* December 19, 2016, accessed January 11, 2019, https://www.latimes.com/nation/politics/trailguide/la-na-trailguide-updates-hundreds-protest-at-capitol-building-in-1482178769-htmlstory.html.

36. Abbot and Levine, *Wrong Winner,* 144.

37. Koza et al., *Every Vote Equal,* 474.

38. Peirce and Longley, *The People's President,* 172 (my emphasis).

39. See generally Hardaway, *The Electoral College and the Constitution*, 43–65.

40. Ibid.

41. See generally Hardaway, *The Electoral College and the Constitution,* chap. 5.

42. Hearings on S.J. Res. 1, 8, and 18 before the Subcommittee on the Constitution of the Committee of the Judiciary, U.S. Senate, 95th Cong., 1st sess. (July 22, 1977); transcription set forth in Diamond, "The Electoral College and the Idea of Federal Democracy," 75–76.

43. Ibid.

44. Ibid.

Chapter 5

1. John Stuart Mill, *Utilitarianism: On Liberty, and Representative Government* (New York: Dutton, 1920), 102–28, cited in David Shultz, "Rethinking Drug Criminalization Policies," *Texas Tech Law Review* 25 (1993): 152.

2. Hearings on S.J. Res. 1, 8, and 18 before the Subcommittee on the Constitution of the Committee of the Judiciary, U.S. Senate, 95th Cong., 1st sess. (July 1977), cited in Robert M. Hardaway, *The Electoral College and the Constitution: The Case for Preserving Federalism* (Westport, CT: Praeger, 1994), 19–20.

Notes 169

3. Michael J. Glennon, *When No Majority Rules: The Electoral College and Presidential Succession* (Washington, DC: Congressional Quarterly, 1992), 76, citing Congressional Record, Senate Bill 150, 84th Cong., 2nd sess., March 20, 1956.

4. John R. Koza et al., *Every Vote Equal: A State-Based Plan for Electing the President by National Popular Vote* (Los Altos, CA: National Popular Vote Press, 2013).

5. Ibid.

6. Lynn Bartels, "Bill to Toss Electoral System Dies in Committee," *Rocky Mountain News,* March 9, 2007.

7. Koza et al., *Every Vote Equal,* 259.

8. Ibid., 524–624.

9. Ibid., 622.

10. Gordon Tullock, "JFK's Popular Vote Myth—Capital Research Center," *New York Review,* November 10, 1988.

11. Steven T. Allen, "JFK's Popular Vote Victory: The Myth," November 12, 2013, https://capitalresearch.org/article/jfks-popular-vote-victory-the-myth/.

12. Koza et al., *Every Vote Equal*, 264.

13. *Rocky Mountain News* (Denver), December 24, 1993, 36A.

14. See, e.g., *Pennoyer v. Neff* 95 U.S. 714 (1877).

15. "When Do Presidential Candidates Get Recounts," CBS News, November 9, 2016, https://www.cbsnews.com/news/when.

16. Koza et al., *Every Vote Equal,* 609.

17. 434 U.S. 452 (1978).

18. 434 U.S. 452 at 472.

Chapter 6

1. John R. Koza et al., *Every Vote Equal: A State-Based Plan for Electing the President by National Popular Vote* (Los Altos, CA: National Popular Vote Press, 2013), 474–476.

2. Ibid., 475.

3. Ibid.

4. Ibid.

5. Koza et al., *Every Vote Equal,* 645–646, objects to my use of the word "conspiracy" to describe the NPVIC on grounds that conspiracy is defined as "an agreement to commit a crime." According to Webster's New Collegiate Dictionary, however, definitions of "conspiracy" include "scheme" and "to act in harmony." However one might describe the NPVIC, it is certainly an agreement, or scheme.

6. "From Thomas Jefferson to James Monroe, 12 January 1800," Founders Online, National Archives, last modified June 13, 2018, Original source: *The Papers of Thomas Jefferson,* Vol. 31, *1 February 1799–31 May 1800,* ed. Barbara B. Oberg (Princeton, NJ: Princeton University Press, 2004), 300–301.

7. Ibid.

8. Testimonial of Donald Scott, chairman of the Chamber Study Group on Electoral College Reform, March 6, 1966, unpublished dissertation.

9. Congressional Record, 1956, 5644–5646; Statement of Democratic senator Paul Douglas of Illinois, cited in Neal Peirce and Lawrence D. Longley, *The People's President: The Electoral College in American History and the Direct Vote Alternative*, rev. ed. (New Haven, CT: Yale University Press, 1981), 173n17.

10. David W. Abbott and James P. Levine, *Wrong Winner: The Coming Debacle in the Electoral College* (New York: Praeger, 1991), 127.

11. H-145.

12. H-147.

13. Ibid.

14. Ibid.

15. Congressional Record, 1950, 886, cited in Peirce and Longley, *The People's President*; statement of Democratic senator Paul Douglas of Illinois, cited in Peirce and Lawrence, *The People's President*, 173.

16. Congressional Record, 1956, 5644–5646, cited in Peirce and Longley, *The People's President*, 156.

17. Ibid.

18. Ibid.

19. Ibid., 152.

Chapter 7

1. John R. Vile, *The Constitutional Convention of 1787: A Comprehensive Encyclopedia of America's Founding* (Clark, NJ: Lawbook Exchange, 2005).

2. Ibid.

3. Burton J. Hendrick, *Bulwark of the Republic: Biography of the Constitution* (Boston: Little, Brown, 1937), 97.

4. See discussion, paragraph one of Chapter 1.

5. John R. Koza et al., *Every Vote Equal: A State-Based Plan for Electing the President by National Popular Vote* (Los Altos, CA: National Popular Vote Press, 2013), 434.

6. Ibid., 435.

7. Ibid., 461.

8. Ibid.

9. Ibid., 457

10. Ibid., 451.

11. Michael J. Glennon, *When No Majority Rules: The Electoral College and Presidential Succession* (Washington, DC: Congressional Quarterly, 1992), 76, citing Congressional Record, Senate Bill 150, 84th Cong., 2nd sess., March 20, 1956.

12. Koza et al., *Every Vote Equal*, 434.

13. John Kennedy was elected by a vote of 303–219 in the Electoral College.

14. Nathanial Persily, Robert F. Bauer, and Benjamin L. Ginsberg, *Campaign Finance in the United States: Assessing an Era of Fundamental Change*, January 2018.

15. See Chapter 3.

Notes

16. Persily, Bauer, and Ginsberg, *Campaign Finance in the United States.*

17. Ari Shapiro, "No Big Money Or TV Ads—What's with the U.K.'s Low-Key Election?," National Public Radio, March 10, 2015.

Chapter 8

1. See Tara Ross, *The Indispensable Electoral College: How the Founders' Plan Saves Our Country from Mob Rule* (Washington, DC: Regnery Gateway, 2017), showing the number of elections in which the popular vote of the winning candidate has been within 2 percent of the losing candidate.

2. "The 1960 Election Results," in *CQ Almanac 1961,* 17th ed., 1025–1026 (Washington, DC: Congressional Quarterly, 1961).

3. See chapter 2 for a full discussion.

4. Edmund F. Kallina, *Was the 1960 Presidential Election Stolen? The Case of Illinois* (n.p.: Center for the Study of the Presidency, 1985).

5. Patrick C. Valencia, "Combination among the States: Why the National Popular Vote Interstate Compact Is an Unconstitutional Attempt to Reform the Electoral College," *Harvard Journal on Legislation,* October 26, 2018.

6. John R. Koza et al., *Every Vote Equal: A State-Based Plan for Electing the President by National Popular Vote* (Los Altos, CA: National Popular Vote Press, 2013), III-5.

7. U.S.C. Code, Title 3, Section 1.

8. Koza et al., *Every Vote Equal,* 614.

9. Ibid.

10. "Florida Supreme Court Ruling: Election 2000," National Public Radio, 2000.

11. Roy Morris Jr., "Master Fraud of the Century: The Disputed Election of 1876," *American History Illustrated* 23 (July 1988): 28.

12. Michael J. Glennon, *When No Majority Rules: The Electoral College and Presidential Succession* (Washington, DC: Congressional Quarterly, 1992), 18.

13. Sidney I. Pommerantz, "Election of 1876," in *The Coming to Power: Critical Presidential Elections in American History,* ed. Arthur M. Schlesinger Jr. and William P. Hansen (New York: Chelsea House Publishers in association with McGraw-Hill, 1972), 213.

14. Ibid.

15. Neal R. Peirce and Lawrence D. Longley, *The People's President: The Electoral College in American History and the Direct Vote Alternative,* rev. ed. (New Haven, CT: Yale University Press, 1981), 66–68.

16. Morris, "Master Fraud of the Century," 32.

17. Ibid., 31.

18. Pommerantz, "Election of 1876."

19. "Florida Supreme Court Ruling: Election 2000."

20. See generally John Fund and Hans Von Spakovsky, *Who's Counting? How Fraudsters and Bureaucrats Put Your Vote at Risk* (New York: Encounter Books, 2012).

21. Ibid.

22. Ibid., 115.

23. Ibid., 118.

24. Ibid., 119.

25. Ibid., 49.

26. Ibid., 50.

27. Ibid.

28. David W. Abbott and James P. Levine, *Wrong Winner: The Coming Debacle in the Electoral College* (Westport, CT: Praeger, 1991), 103.

29. Ibid., 108.

30. Ibid.

31. Larry J. Sabato, Kyle Kondik, and Geoffrey Skelley, "16 For '16: Bite-Sized Observations on a Wild Election," Larry J. Sabato's Crystal Ball RSS, November 17, 2016.

Chapter 9

1. John R. Koza et al., *Every Vote Equal: A State-Based Plan for Electing the President by National Popular Vote* (Los Altos, CA: National Popular Vote Press, 2013), 691.

2. Ibid., xii.

3. Ibid.

4. See generally the discussion in Robert M. Hardaway, *The Electoral College and the Constitution: The Case for Preserving Federalism* (Westport, CT: Praeger, 1994), 19–21.

5. Lynn Bartels, "Bill to Toss Electoral System Dies in Committee," *Rocky Mountain News,* March 9, 2007.

6. Michael Levy, "United States Presidential Election of 1960," Encyclopaedia Britannica, accessed January 11, 2019, https://www.britannica.com/event/United-States-presidential-election-of-1960.

7. It could be argued that the 1876 election was one in which a recount of the popular vote in several southern states might have affected the outcome, but in fact that election was not decided by recounts at all; it was decided by an 8–7 vote of a special electoral commission whose decision had very little to do with recounts. See Hardaway, *The Electoral College and the Constitution,* 128–137.

8. Koza et al., *Every Vote Equal,* 606.

9. Ibid., 604.

10. Ibid., 613.

11. Ibid., 606.

12. The one exception might be the 2000 election. In that case the Florida recount was conducted because of a close national popular vote. It was the very rare election in which the electoral vote was so close that the turning of the electoral votes of a single state—Florida—would change the result of the entire election.

Notes   173

13. Koza et al., *Every Vote Equal,* 599.

14. Steven F. Allen, "JFK's Popular Vote Victory: The Myth," Capital Research Center, November 12, 2013, accessed January 11, 2019, https://capitalresearch.org/article/jfks-popular-vote-victory-the-myth/.

15. Koza et al., *Every Vote Equal,* 589.

16. Quoted in ibid., 603.

17. Ibid., 602.

18. But see Chapter 4, which reviews the democratic weakness of a Russian-style direct election.

19. Koza et al., *Every Vote Equal,* 599.

20. Ibid., 612.

21. Ibid., 610.

22. Ibid., 613–622.

23. Ibid., 620.

24. Ibid.

25. Ibid., 621.

26. "On This Day, Bush v. Gore Settles 2000 Presidential Race," National Constitution Center, December 12, 2018, https://constitutioncenter.org/blog/on-this-day-bush-v-gore-anniversary.

Chapter 10

1. John R. Koza et al., *Every Vote Equal: A State-Based Plan for Electing the President by National Popular Vote* (Los Altos, CA: National Popular Vote Press, 2013), not counting the epilogue, appendix, and index.

2. Ibid.

3. The Due Process clause of the Fourteenth Amendment provides that no "state shall deprive any person of life, liberty, or property without due process of law."

4. Koza et al., *Every Vote Equal,* 401.

5. Ibid., 351.

6. Ibid.

7. The first sentences of Article V also provide for a constitutional convention to propose amendments, but such amendments also require only ratification by three-quarters of the states, not unanimous consent of all the states.

8. U.S. Constitution, Article V.

9. Koza et al., *Every Vote Equal,* 700n618.

10. Theodore Harold White, *The Making of the President* (New York: Harper Perennial Political Classics, 2010), 7.

11. Koza et al., *Every Vote Equal,* 349.

12. U.S. Constitution, Article II.

13. Koza et al., *Every Vote Equal,* 366.

14. See Chapter 2 for discussion of these differing statements.

15. Robert M. Hardaway, *The Electoral College and the Constitution: The Case for Preserving Federalism* (Westport, CT: Praeger, 1994), 45–46.

16. Koza et al., *Every Vote Equal*, xvii–xviii.

17. Ibid., xxvii.

18. William Peters, *A More Perfect Union: The Making of the United States Constitution* (New York: Crown Publishers, 1987), 12.

19. Ibid., 28.

20. Koza et al., *Every Vote Equal*, 384.

21. Ibid., 610.

22. Ibid.

23. Ibid., 610–611.

24. Ibid., 611.

25. Ibid.

26. Ibid., 26–29.

27. Paul Von Hippel, "Here's a Voter Fraud Myth: Richard Daley 'Stole' Illinois for John Kennedy in the 1960 Election," *Washington Post*, August 08, 2017, https://www.washingtonpost.com/news/monkey-cage/wp/2017/08/08/heres-a-voter-fraud-myth-richard-daley-stole-illinois-for-john-kennedy-in-the-1960-election/?noredirect=on&utm_term=.988b32e06ca0.

28. Koza et al., *Every Vote Equal*, 611.

29. Ibid., 269.

30. Ibid., 259.

31. Ibid., 581.

32. Ibid., 384.

33. Robert Hardaway, "History Upholds Reasons for the Electoral College," *Deseret News*, December 10, 2000, https://www.deseretnews.com/article/797343/History-upholds-reasons-for-the-Electoral-College.html.

34. Koza et al., *Every Vote Equal*, 384.

35. 102 Congressional Record 5150 (1956) (statement of Senator John F. Kennedy).

36. Max Farrand, ed., *The Records of the Federal Convention of 1787*, Vol. 2 (New Haven, CT: Yale University Press, 1911), https://oll.libertyfund.org/titles/1786.

37. Luis Fuentes-Rohwer and Guy-Uriel Charles, "The Electoral College, the Right to Vote, and Our Federalism: A Comment on a Lasting Institution," *Florida State University Law Review* 29 (2001): 879–923, https://scholarship.law.duke.edu/cgi/viewcontent.cgi?article=5565&context=faculty_scholarship.

38. U.S. Constitution, Article V.

39. Ibid.

40. Herbert Mitgang, "New Light on 1787 and Washington's Doubts," *New York Times*, July 4, 1987.

41. Koza et al., *Every Vote Equal*, 385.

42. Ibid., 490.

Notes

43. U.S. Census Bureau, Statistical Abstract of the United States, 2002, Table 370, http://www.census.gov/prod/2003pubs/02statab/election.pdf; U.S. Census Bureau, Statistical Abstract of the United States, 2010, Table 389, http://www.census.gov/prod/2009pubs/10statab/election.pdf; Federal Election Commission, http://www.fec.gov/pubrec/electionresults.shtml.

44. Elizabeth Nix, "Did Caligula Really Make His Horse a Consul?," History.com, June 21, 2016, https://www.history.com/news/did-caligula-really-make-his-horse-a-consul.

45. Koza et al., *Every Vote Equal,* 491.

46. Bojan Pancevski, "Merkel, Already Wobbling, Faces Fresh Blow in Historical Stronghold," *Wall Street Journal,* October 12, 2018, https://www.wsj.com/articles/german-voters-set-to-punish-merkels-conservative-bloc-1539336600.

47. Tobias Buck, "Fate of Merkel's Spy Chief Exposes Fragility of Coalition," *Financial Times,* September 19, 2018, https://www.ft.com/content/bba510c4-bc0a-11e8–94b2–17176fbf93f5.

48. Koza et al., *Every Vote Equal,* 492.

49. "United States Presidential Election of 1912," Encyclopædia Britannica, November 5, 1912, https://www.britannica.com/.

50. Andy Kiersz, "Here's the Final 2016 Electoral College Map," *Business Insider,* November 28, 2016, https://www.businessinsider.com/final-electoral-college-map-trump-clinton-2016-11.

51. Mark J. Perry, "Putting America's Enormous $19.4T Economy into Perspective by Comparing US State GDPs to Entire Countries," AEI, May 8, 2018, http://www.aei.org/publication/putting-americas-enormous-19–4t-economy-into-perspective-by-comparing-us-state-gdps-to-entire-countries/.

52. Richard R. Beeman, "Perspectives on the Constitution: A Republic, If You Can Keep It," National Constitution Center, https://constitutioncenter.org/learn/educational-resources/historical-documents/perspectives-on-the-constitution-a-republic-if-you-can-keep-it.

53. Koza et al., *Every Vote Equal,* 503.

54. Patrick Novotny, "John F. Kennedy, the 1960 Election, and Georgia's Unpledged Electors in the Electoral College," *Georgia Historical Quarterly* 88, no. 3 (Fall 2004): 394.

55. See Gordon Tullock, "Did Nixon Beat Kennedy?," The New York Review of Books, November 10, 1988, http://www.nybooks.com/articles/1988/11/10/did-nixon-beat-kennedy/.

56. "The 1960 Election Results," in *CQ Almanac 1961,* 17th ed., 1025–26 (Washington, DC: Congressional Quarterly, 1961).

57. Steven J. Allen, "JFK's Popular Vote Victory: The Myth," Capital Research Center, November 12, 2013, https://capitalresearch.org/article/jfks-popular-vote-victory-the-myth/.

58. Koza et al., *Every Vote Equal,* 511.

59. Ibid., 514.

60. Hardaway, *The Electoral College and the Constitution,* 165.

61. "Faithless Elector State Laws," FairVote.org, 2018.

62. In fact, a Colorado law, CRS 1-4-304(5) does currently provide for such sanctions, though that law is currently being appealed. In that case some Democratic electors who wanted to violate their pledge to vote for Hillary Clinton are appealing the Colorado law, claiming it is unconstitutional. (10th Cir. No. 18-1173-2018). This author wrote an amicus brief in that case on behalf of the State of Colorado arguing that the statute is indeed constitutional as an exercise of the Article II powers granted to the state to appoint electors.

63. Ibid.

64. Koza et al., *Every Vote Equal,* 514.

65. This author has proposed a constitutional amendment that would indeed make electoral votes automatic without the requirement that actual human electors go through the hapless exercise of going to the state house to cast votes that are usually no more than a formality. For this and other proposed housekeeping reforms of the Electoral College, see Chapter 12.

66. Koza et al., *Every Vote Equal,* 515.

67. History, Art & Archives, U.S. House of Representatives, Electoral College Fast Facts, January 03, 2019.

68. Ibid.

69. National Historical Publications and Records Commission, Founders Online: From Thomas Jefferson to George Washington, 9 September 1792, National Archives and Records Administration, January 24, 2002.

70. "Maine & Nebraska," FairVote.org, 2018.

71. Garrett Hardin, "The Tragedy of the Commons," *Science* 162, no. 3859 (December 13, 1968): 1243–1248.

72. Robert Hardaway, "Hands Off the Electoral College," *Denver Post,* February 8, 2007.

73. S. De Lesseps, *Electoral College Reform: Editorial Research Reports 1976,* Vol. 2 (Washington, DC: CQ Press, 1976).

74. Koza et al., *Every Vote Equal,* 517.

75. Allen, "JFK's Popular Vote Victory."

76. K. Jost and G. Giroux, "Electoral College," *CQ Researcher,* December 8, 2000, 977–1008.

77. The Blaze, December 20, 2016.

78. Allen, "JFK's Popular Vote Victory."

79. Jessica Chasmar, "Alexandria Ocasio-Cortez: We Must 'Eliminate the Electoral College,'" *Washington Times,* October 7, 2018, accessed December 15, 2018, https://www.washingtontimes.com/news/2018/oct/8/alexandria-ocasio-cortez-we-must-eliminate-the-ele/.

80. *Congressional Quarterly Guide to American Government* (Washington, DC: Congressional Quarterly, 1979), 78, and cited in David W. Abbott and James P. Levine, *Wrong Winner: The Coming Debacle in the Electoral College* (Westport, CT: Praeger, 1991), 127.

Notes

81. Congressional Record, 5644–5646, 1956, cited in Neal R. Peirce and Lawrence D. Longley, *The People's President: The Electoral College in American History and the Direct Vote Alternative*, rev. ed. (New Haven, CT: Yale University Press, 1981), 73.

82. Ibid.

83. Peirce and Longley, *The People's President*, 73.

84. Michael J. Glennon, *When No Majority Rules: The Electoral College and Presidential Succession* (Washington, DC: Congressional Quarterly, 1992), 76, citing Congressional Record, Senate Bill 150, 84th Cong., 2nd sess., March 20, 1956.

85. Peters, *A More Perfect Union*, 97.

86. Ibid.

87. Hardaway, *The Electoral College and the Constitution*, 77.

88. Ibid., 89.

89. The Green Party USA supported Ralph Nader for president in 2000 but should not be confused with Nader's Association of State Green Parties, which did not directly advocate the abolition of the U.S. Senate.

90. George Will, "Defending the Electoral College," ABC News, November 2, 2000.

91. Ibid.

92. Chasmar, "Alexandria Ocasio-Cortez."

93. Howard Kurtz, "Change the Rules? Why the Left Is Slamming the Senate and Electoral College," Fox News, October 12, 2018.

94. Koza et al., *Every Vote Equal*, 209.

95. Robert McGuire, "Economic Interests and the Adoption of the United States Constitution," EH.Net Encyclopedia, edited by Robert Whaples, August 14, 2001.

96. Oliver Joseph Thatcher, *The Library of Original Sources: The Era of Revolution* (New York: University Research Extension, 1907), 342.

97. Tara Ross and Robert M. Hardaway, "The Compact Clause and National Popular Vote: Implications for the 'Federal Structure,'" *New Mexico Law Review* 44, no. 2 (2014): 428.

98. Koza et al., *Every Vote Equal*, 970.

99. Ibid., 1014 (my emphasis).

100. Ibid., 259.

101. Ross and Hardaway, "The Compact Clause and National Popular Vote," 428.

102. Ibid.

103. Koza et al., *Every Vote Equal*, 257.

104. See Supremacy Clause, U.S. Constitution, Article VI, Clause 2.

105. *United States Steel Corp. v. Multistate Tax Commission*, 434 U.S. 452 (1978).

106. Based on NPVIC myth 6.3.3.

107. Koza et al., *Every Vote Equal*, xxix.

108. NPVIC advocates have indicated that they don't prefer the word "conspiracy" to describe their compact, claiming that the dictionary definition of a

conspiracy is "an agreement to conduct a criminal act." While this is one of the dictionary definitions, another definition of conspiracy (according to *Webster's Collegiate Dictionary*) is simply "an agreement."

109. Kurtis Lee, "In 1969, Democrats and Republicans United to Get Rid of the Electoral College. Here's What Happened," *Los Angeles Times,* December 19, 2016.

110. *Congressional Quarterly Guide to American Government,* 78, and cited in Abbott and Levine, *Wrong Winner.*

111. Hardaway, *The Electoral College and the Constitution,* 26–29.

112. "Faithless Elector State Laws."

113. Tara Ross, *The Indispensable Electoral College: How the Founders' Plan Saves Our Country from Mob Rule* (Washington, DC: Regnery Gateway, 2017).

114. Koza et al., *Every Vote Equal,* 259.

115. Ibid.

116. Ibid., 264.

117. Ibid.

118. Ibid., 108.

119. Ibid., 26–29.

120. Ibid.

121. Ibid., 268.

122. Ibid., 264.

Chapter 11

1. Final report of the Commission on National Elections, Georgetown University, *Electing the President: A Program for Reform,* ed. Robert E. Hunter (Washington, DC: Center for Strategic and International Studies, 1986).

2. Ibid.

3. Ibid., 138.

4. Statement of Democratic senator Paul Douglas of Illinois, cited in Neal Peirce and Lawrence D. Longley, *The People's President: The Electoral College in American History and the Direct Vote Alternative,* rev. ed. (New Haven, CT: Yale University Press, 1981), 173.

5. Ibid.

6. Ibid., 138.

7. See, for example, Thomas M. Durbin, "The Electoral College Method of Electing the President and Vice President and Proposals for Reform," *Congressional Research Service* (August 8, 1988): 22.

8. Section 3 of Article IV of the Constitution states that no "state shall be formed or erected within the jurisdiction of any state; nor any state be formed by the junction of two or more states, or parts of states, without the consent of the Legislators of the States concerned as well as of the Congress."

9. 369 U.S. 186 (1962).

10. 372 U.S. 368 (1963).

Notes 179

11. David W. Abbott and James P. Levine, *Wrong Winner: The Coming Debacle in the Electoral College* (New York: Praeger, 1991), 127.

12. Congressional Record, 1950, 886, cited in Peirce and Longley, *The People's President*, 148.

13. Congressional Record, 1956, 5644–5646, cited in Peirce and Longley, *The People's President*, 152.

14. Ibid.

15. Ibid.

16. Abbott and Levine, *Wrong Winner*, 90–95.

17. Congressional Record, 1956, 5644–5646, cited in Peirce and Longley, *The People's President*, 152.

18. Testimonial of Donald Scott, chairman of the Chamber Study Group on Electorial College Reform, March 6, 1966, cited in Peirce and Longley, *The People's President*, 160.

19. Congressional Record, 1966, 3764 (daily ed.), cited in Peirce and Longley, *The People's President*, 160.

20. View of Arthur Vandenburg of Michigan, Congressional Record, 1934, 8944–8945, 9127, cited in Peirce and Longley, *The People's President*, 158.

21. See Chapter 5.

22. Act of November 4, Ex. Sess. ch. 2 (Miss. 1944).

23. William Logan Martin, "Let the State Legislators Choose Them," *American Bar Association Journal* 44 (December 1958): 1182.

24. Ibid., 1185.

25. A. O'Neill, *The American Electoral System* (New York, 1887), 257–258, cited in Peirce and Longley, *The People's President*, 173.

26. Ibid.

27. Ibid.

28. Ibid.

29. Report of the Twentieth Century Fund Task Force in Reform of the Presidential Election Process, *Winner Take All*, background paper by William R. Keech (New York: Holmes and Meier, 1978).

30. Ibid., 3.

31. Ibid., 38.

32. For example, Neil R. Peirce, journalist, *The National Journal*, Washington, D.C.

33. Samuel See Merrill, "Imperial Estimates for the Likelihood of a Directed Verdict in a Presidential Election," *Publics Choice* 33, no. 2 (1978): 127–133, cited in Peirce and Longley, *The People's President*, 176–177.

34. Report of the Twentieth Century Fund Task Force in Reform of the Presidential Election Process, *Winner Take All*, 11.

35. Ibid.

36. Ibid., 43.

37. Ibid., 45.

38. Ibid.

39. Ibid.

40. Ibid., 63.

41. Ibid., 64.

42. Ibid., 66.

43. Ibid., 69.

44. Peirce and Longley, *The People's President*, 178.

45. Ibid., 177.

46. Judith Best, cited in Report of the Twentieth Century Fund Task Force in Reform of the Presidential Election Process, *Winner Take All*, 53.

47. Ibid.

48. William Peters, *A More Perfect Union: The Making of the United States Constitution* (New York: Crown Publishers, 1987), 192.

49. Michael J. Glennon, *When No Majority Rules: The Electoral College and Presidential Succession* (Washington, DC: Congressional Quarterly, 1992), 76, citing Congressional Record, Senate Bill 150, 84th Cong., 2nd sess., March 20, 1956.

50. Peirce and Longley, *The People's President*, 161–162.

51. Ibid., 165.

52. Representative Emmanuel Celler, cited in ibid., 185.

53. Ibid., 189.

54. Ibid.

55. Ibid., 203.

56. Ibid., 205.

57. David Robertson, *The Debates of the Convention of Virginia, 1788* (2nd ed., 1805), 351, cited in Max Farrand, ed., *The Records of the Federal Convention of 1787*, Vol. 1 (New Haven, CT: Yale University Press, 1966), 135.

58. Ibid.

59. Peirce and Longley, *The People's President*, 215.

60. Ibid.

61. Ibid., 215.

62. Glennon, *When No Majority Rules*, 76.

63. Peirce and Longley, *The People's President*, 172.

64. Article V of the Constitution provides that "no state shall, without its consent," be deprived of its equal suffrage in the Senate.

65. Peirce and Longley, *The People's President*, 231.

66. Peirce and Longley, *The People's President*, 232, cite with approval the work by Kinvin Wroth, "Election Contests and the Electoral Vote," *Dickenson Law Review* 65 (October 1960–June 1961): 321, in which Wroth suggests, in Longley's words, that "federal courts be given exclusive jurisdiction in the event of contested presidential vote returns."

67. Report of the Twentieth Century Fund Task Force in Reform of the Presidential Election Process, *Winner Take All*, 231, recommending that "federal law require an automatic, mandatory retally of all votes cast."

68. Ibid., 59.

69. 1979 Senate Hearing, 347, cited in Peirce and Longley, *The People's President*, 202.

Notes

Chapter 12

1. Adapted from Robert M. Hardaway, *The Electoral College and the Constitution: The Case for Preserving Federalism* (Westport, CT: Praeger, 1994).

2. See Christine Poumailloux, "Macron and Le Pen Face Off in French Election Pitting Vision of Globalization against Nationalism," *Wall St. Journal,* May 7, 2017.

Bibliography

Books

Abbott, David W., and James P. Levine. *Wrong Winner: The Coming Debacle in the Electoral College.* New York: Praeger, 1991.

Bemis, Samuel Flagg. *John Quincy Adams and the Union.* New York: Alfred A. Knopf, 1956.

Best, Judith. *The Case against Direct Election of the President: A Defense of the Electoral College.* Ithaca, NY: Cornell University Press, 1975.

Brams, Steven J. *The Presidential Election Game.* New Haven, CT: Yale University Press, 1978.

Claud, Richard. *The Supreme Court and the Electoral Process.* Baltimore: Johns Hopkins University Press, 1970.

Commission on National Elections, Georgetown University. *Electing the President: A Program for Reform,* Robert E. Hunter, ed. Washington, DC: Center for Strategic and International Studies, 1986.

Dougherty, John Hampden. *The Electoral System of The United States: Its History, Together With a Study of The Perils That Have Attended Its Operations, an Analysis of the Several Efforts by Legislation to Avert These Perils, and a Proposed Remedy by Amendment of the Constitution.* New York: Putnam, 1906.

Farrand, Max. *The Framing of the Constitution of the United States.* New Haven, CT: Yale University Press, 1987 (originally published in 1913).

Gibson, A. M. *A Political Crime: The History of the Great Fraud.* New York: William S. Gottsberger, 1969.

Glennon, Michael J. *When No Majority Rules: The Electoral College and Presidential Succession.* Washington, DC: Congressional Quarterly, 1992.

Hargrove, Erwin C., Donald R. Mathews, et al. *Choosing the President,* ed. James David Barber. Englewood Cliffs, NJ: Prentice Hall, 1974.

Hendrick, Burton J. *Bulwark of the Republic: Biography of the Constitution.* Boston: Little, Brown, 1937.

Longley, Lawrence D., and Alan G. Braun. *The Politics of Electoral College Reform.* Foreword by U.S. senator Birch Bayh. New Haven, CT: Yale University Press, 1972.

MacBride, Roger Lea. *The American Electoral College.* Caldwell, ID: Caxton Printers, 1963.

Madison, James, Alexander Hamilton, and John Jay. *Federalist Papers: A Commentary on the Constitution of the United States, Being a Collection of Essays.* New York: M. Walter Dunne, 1901.

Memoirs of John Quincy Adams: Comprising Portions of His Diary from 1795 to 1848. Ed. Charles Francis. New York: J. B. Lippincott, 1875.

Michener, James A. *Presidential Lottery: The Reckless Gamble in Our Electoral System.* New York: Random House, 1969.

Nevins, Allan. *Letters of Grover Cleveland.* New York: Houghton Mifflin, 1933.

Peirce, Neal R., and Lawrence D. Longley. *The People's President: The Electoral College in American History and the Direct Vote Alternative.* Rev. ed. New Haven, CT: Yale University Press, 1981.

Peters, William. *A More Perfect Union: The Making of the United States Constitution.* New York: Crown Publishers, 1987.

Polsby, Nelson W., and Aaron Wildavsky. *Elections: Strategies of American Electoral Politics.* New York: Scribner, 1964.

Pommerantz, Sidney I. *The Coming to Power: Critical Presidential Elections in American History.* Ed. Arthur M. Schlesinger Jr. and William P. Hansen. New York: Chelsea House Publishers, in association with McGraw-Hill, 1972.

The Records of the Federal Convention of 1787, Vols. I–IV, ed. Max Farrand. New Haven, CT: Yale University Press, 1966.

Schlesinger, Arthur M. *The Age of Jackson.* Boston: Little, Brown, 1945.

Twentieth Century Fund Task Force on Reform of the Presidential Election Process. *Winner Take All.* Background paper by William R. Keech. New York: Holmes and Meier, 1978.

Wells, Gideon. *The Diary of Gideon Wells,* Vol. 3. New York: Houghton Mifflin, 1911.

Wilmerding, Lucius, Jr. *The Electoral College.* Boston: Beacon, 1958.

Woodward, C. Vann. *The Compromise of 1877 and the End of Reconstruction.* Boston: Little, Brown, 1951.

Yunker, John H., and Lawrence D. Longley. *The Electoral College: Its Biases Newly Measured for the 1960s and 1970s.* Ed. Randall B. Ripley. Beverly Hills, CA: Sage Publications, 1976.

Periodicals

"ABC's of How America Chooses a President." *U.S. News & World Report* 96 (February 20, 1984): 39.

Amar, Vik, and Reed Akhil. "Split Decision." *Washington Monthly* 24 (November 1992): 22.

Bibliography

American Law Division, Congressional Research Service. "Majority or Plurality Vote within State Delegations When House of Representatives Votes for the President." Unpublished document. Washington, DC: Library of Congress, June 10, 1980.

Archer, J. Clark, Fred M. Shelly, Peter J. Taylor, and Ellen R. White. "The Geography of U.S. Presidential Elections: Enduring Geographic Cleavages Divide the Electorate; They Weigh Heavily in the Electoral College System and Demand That a Winning Candidate Build a Geographic Coalition." *Scientific American* 259 (July 1988): 44.

Banzhaf, John F. "One Man, 3.312 Votes: A Mathematical Analysis of the Electoral College." With comments by the Honorable Birch Bayh, the Honorable Karl E. Mundt, the Honorable John J. Sparkman, and Neal R. Peirce. *Villanova Law Review* 13 (Winter 1968): 304.

Banzhaf, John F., III. "Multi-Member Electoral Districts—Do They Violate the 'One Man, One Vote' Principle?" *Yale Law Journal* 75 (1960): 1309.

Banzhaf, John F., III. "Weighted Voting Doesn't Work: A Mathematical Analysis." *Rutgers Law Review* 19 (1965): 317.

Barnes, Fred. "College Counseling." *New Republic* 199 (July 18, 1988): 13.

Barnes, Fred. "A Donkey's Year: All the Signs Point to a Democratic Victory in November." *New Republic* (February 29, 1988): 16.

Bartels, Lynn. "Bill to Toss Electoral System Dies in Committee." *Rocky Mountain News,* March 9, 2007.

Bates, Stephen: "How Dukakis Can Still Be President; and You Thought Dan Quayle Was Next in Line." *Washington Monthly* 20 (December 1988): 34.

Bayh, Birch. "Electing a President—The Case for Direct Popular Election." *Harvard Journal on Legislation* 6 (January 1969): 127.

Bickel, Alexander M. "Is Electoral Reform the Answer?" *Commentary* 46 (December 1968): 41.

Corn, David. "Beltway Bandits." *Nation* 254 (June 29, 1992): 884.

Cusak, Michael. "Eight Elections That Made Political History." *Scholastic Update* 117 (October 5, 1984): 22.

Diamond, Martin. "The Electoral College and the Idea of Federal Democracy." *Journal of Federalism* (Winter 1978): 63.

Dolan, Joseph, and Frank Chmelik. "Role of the Courts in Election '80: A 3-Ring Circus for a 3-Way Race." *National Law Journal* (August 18, 1980): 24.

Duffy, Michael. "The 34% Solution." *Time* 139 (June 1, 1992): 34.

Dunn, Katheryn A. "Time for Fairness in the Presidential Electoral Process: Major and Minor Party Candidates in Competition." *Journal of Law & Politics* 6 (Spring 1990): 625.

Durbin, Thomas M. "The Anachronistic Electoral College." *Federal Bar News & Journal* 39 (October 1992): 510.

Durbin, Thomas M. "The Electoral College Method of Electing the President and Vice President and Proposals for Reform." *Congressional Research Service* (August 8, 1988).

Durbin, Thomas. "Presidential Primaries: Proposals before Congress to Reform Them and Congressional Authority to Regulate Them." *Journal of Law & Politics* 1 (Spring 1984): 381.

"Electing the President: Recommendations of the American Bar Association's Commission on Electoral College Reform." *American Bar Association Journal* 53 (March 1967): 219.

"The Electoral Battle Map." *Scholastic Update* 125 (October 9, 1992): 8.

Evans, Michael K. "Democrats Are Boxed in Wrong Electoral Corner." *Industry Week* 223 (December 10, 1984): 112.

Fallows, James. "Plains Talk: What Jimmy Carter's First Bid for Public Office Tells Us about Politics Today." *Washington Monthly* 24 (November 1992): 43.

Feerick, John D. "The Electoral College—Why It Ought to be Abolished." *Fordham Law Review* 37 (1968): 1.

Feerick, John D. "The Electoral College: Why It Was Created." *American Bar Association Journal* 54 (March 1968): 249.

Forbes, Malcolm S., Jr. "Election Prediction: Michael Dukakis Will Win." *Forbes* 142 (November 14, 1988): 33.

Forbes, Malcolm S., Jr. "Helpful, Useful Antique." *Forbes* 143 (February 6, 1989): 27.

Forbes, Malcolm S., Jr. "Politically Paralyzing Ploy." *Forbes* 150 (July 6, 1992): 26.

Forbes, Malcolm S., Jr. "Talking about Politics." *Forbes* 136 (September 16, 1985): 31.

Gewirtz, Paul. "House Party: How Not to Elect a President." *New Republic* 207 (July 27, 1992): 38.

Gewirtz, Paul. "Jackson's Hole." *New Republic* 207 (July 27, 1992): 40.

Goode, John. "The Electoral Commission of 1877." *American Law Review* 38 (January–February 1904): 1.

Gossett, William T. "Electing the President." *Detroit College of Law Review* 4 (1983): 1283.

Gossett, William T. "Electing the President: New Hope for an Old Ideal." *American Bar Association Journal* 53 (December 1967): 1103.

Harmon, Mark D. "The *New York Times* and the Theft of the 1876 Presidential Election." *Journal of American Culture* 10 (1987): 35.

House, Lolabel. "A Study of the Twelfth Amendment." PhD dissertation, University of Philadelphia, 1901.

Kefauver, Estes. "The Electoral College: Old Reforms Take on a New Look." *Law and Contemporary Problems* 27 (Spring 1962): 188.

Kirby, James C., Jr. "Limitations on the Power of State Legislatures over Presidential Elections." *Law and Contemporary Problems* 27 (Summer 1962): 495.

Kirkpatrick, Jeane J. "Martin Diamond and the American Idea of Democracy." *Journal of Federalism* (Summer 1978): 7.

Kleber, Louis C. "The Presidential Election of 1876." *History Today* 20 (1970): 806.

Levinson, Sanford. "Gerrymandering and the Brooding Omnipresence of Proportional Representation: Why Won't It Go Away." *UCLA Law Review* 33: 257.

Bibliography

Marshman, D. M., Jr. "Who Really Elects the Presidents?" *American Heritage* 24 (February 1973): 103.

Martin, William Logan. "Let the State Legislator Choose Them." *American Bar Association Journal* 44 (December 1958): 1182.

Mayhew, David, and Bruce Russett. "How the Democrats Can Win in '92." *New Leader* 72 (January 9, 1989): 13.

McKay, Robert B. "Reapportionment: Success Story of the Warren Court." *Michigan Law Review* 67 (December 1968): 223.

McLaughlin, John. "The Electoral-Vote Lock." *National Review* 40 (August 5, 1988): 26.

Mikva, Abner J. "The Electoral College: How Democratic Was and Is the Constitution?" *Prologue* 19 (Fall 1987): 177.

Milius, Albert J. "The Electoral College—Should Anything Be Done about It?" *New York State Bar Journal* (February 1982): 84.

Morris, Roy, Jr. "Master Fraud of the Century: The Disputed Election of 1876." *American History Illustrated* (July 23, 1988): 28.

Nelson, Michael C. "Partisan Bias in the Electoral College." *Journal of Politics* 37 (November 1974): 1033.

"No Margin for Error (An American Survey)." *Economist* 325 (November 7, 1992): 27.

O'Sullivan, Michael J. "Artificial Unit Voting and the Electoral College." *Southern California Law Review* 65 (July 1992): 5.

Parshall, Gerald. "The Feuding Fathers." *U.S. News & World Report* 114 (February 1, 1993): 54.

"Population Shifts Could Increase Democratic Woes in 1992 Election." *National Journal* 20 (April 16, 1988): 1024.

Reidinger, Paul. "Still Ticking after All These Years." *ABA Journal* (September 1, 1987): 42.

Reuven, Frank. "Election Night." *New Leader* 75 (October 5, 1992): 20.

Roberts, Charley. "Electoral College Placed under Rare Scrutiny." *Los Angeles Daily Journal* (May 27, 1992): 10.

Roberts, Charley. "The Perot Factor at Work." *Los Angeles Daily Journal* (May 27, 1992): 1.

Rose, Jonathon. "The Rapid Rise of Special Interest Groups." *Scholastic Update* 117 (October 19, 1984): 31.

Rosenthal, Albert. "The Constitution, Congress, and Presidential Elections." *Michigan Law Review* 67 (November 1968): 1.

Rosenthal, Albert J. "Some Doubts Concerning the Proposal to Elect the President by Direct Popular Vote." *Villanova Law Review* 14 (Fall 1968): 87.

Schneider, William. "Electoral College's 'Archaic Ritual.'" *National Journal* 20 (December 10, 1988): 3164.

Schneider, William. "An Insider's View of the Election." *Atlantic* 262 (July 1988): 29.

Seligman, Daniel. "The Old College Tie, the Economics of Light Bulbs, Streetwalker Distribution, and Other Matters." *Fortune* 110 (September 3, 1984): 105.

Sickels, Robert J. "The Power Index and the Electoral College: A Challenge to Banzhaf's Analysis." *Villanova Law Review* 14 (Fall 1968): 92.

Sindler, Allan P. "Presidential Election Methods and Urban-Ethnic Interests." *Law & Contemporary Problems* 27 (Spring 1962): 213.

Smith, Hedrick. "The Power Game: How Washington Works (Book Review), by Barry Gewen." *New Leader* 71 (May 2, 1988): 17.

Spering, Howard S. "How to Make the Electoral College Constitutionally Representative." *American Bar Association Journal* 53 (August 1968): 763.

Sterling, Carleton W. "The Electoral College Biases Revealed: The Conventional Wisdom and Game Theory Models Notwithstanding." *Western Political Quarterly* 31 (June 1978): 159.

Sterling, Carleton W. "Electoral College Misrepresentation: A Geometric Analysis." *Polity* 13 (1981).

"Swings and Roundabouts." *Economist* 324 (September 19, 1992): 30.

"Unpicking the Republican Lock: The Campaign." *Economist* 324 (August 15, 1992): 20.

U.S. Bureau of the Census. *Statistical Abstract of the United States.* 112th ed. Washington, DC: U.S. Government Printing Office, 1992.

"The Votes That Really Count." *Time* 132 (October 17, 1988): 20.

Walsh, Kenneth T. "California Picks the President: The Golden State Is the Pivotal Electoral Battleground." *U.S. News & World Report* 111 (December 30, 1991): 44.

Walsh, Kenneth T. "The Key States: The Longhorns of Texas and Laidbacks of California Will Be Kingmakers." *U.S. News & World Report* 105 (August 29, 1988): 42.

Wechsler, Herbert. "Presidential Elections and the Constitution: A Comment on Proposed Amendment." *American Bar Association Journal* 35 (March 1949): 181.

Weinhagen, Robert F. "Should the Electoral College Be Abandoned?" *American Bar Association Journal* 67 (July 1981): 852.

Weisberger, Bernard A. "The Stolen Election." *American Heritage* 51 (July–August 1990): 18.

Wildenthal, John. "The Role of the Electoral College." *Southwest Review* 43 (1968): 113.

Wilkinson, Donald M. "The Electoral Process and the Power of the States." *American Bar Association Journal* 47 (March 1961): 251.

Wilmerding, Lucius. "The Electoral College." *Columbia Law Review* 59 (1959): 838.

Wroth, Kinvin. "Election Contests and the Electoral Vote." *Dickinson Law Review* 65 (October 1960–June 1961): 321.

Index

Abbott, David, 83, 133
Adams, John, 20
"Agreement among the States to Elect the President by National Popular Vote," 49
Alabama: automatic recount, 56–57; Democratic slate in 1960, 17, 50, 53, 73–74, 102; popular vote in 1960, 51, 53, 71, 89, 109, 120, 138–139; unpledged electors in 1960, 120, 125–126
Alaska, 67, 77
Allen, Steven, 53
Alternative for Germany Party, 107
American Bar Association, 38–39, 141–142
American Bar Association Journal, 135
American Civil War, 75, 79
Anderson, John, 98–99
Annapolis Convention, 19
Arkansas, 80
Articles of Confederation, 2, 18, 20, 99, 104, 119
Athens, 79
Automatic plan, 133–135, 151

Bailey, Lloyd, 153
Baker v. Carr, 130

Ballot: absentee, 80–81, 146; general ticket, 131, 152–153; provisional, 81–82; requirements, 31, 53–54
Ballot blanc, x, 6, 44, 54, 100, 105
Banzhaf, John, 39–40
Bayh, Birch, xii, 6–8, 45–47, 54, 86
Bedford, Gunning, 2, 22, 34, 65, 117
Best, Judith, 141
Bonus plan, 136–140
Breckinridge, John, 114
Bryan, William Jennings, 6, 121, 133
Bull Moose Party, 108
Bump, Philip, 117–118
Bush, George H. W., 7, 44, 106
Bush, George W., 57, 82, 87
Byrd, Harry, 17, 51, 53, 71, 73, 89, 102, 109, 120, 138

California, 39, 41, 48, 61, 67, 83–84, 112, 114–115
Caligula, 78, 107
Canon, Bradley, 140
Cleveland, Grover, 137
Clinton, Bill, 7, 44, 106
Clinton, Hillary, 83, 108, 111, 113–114, 116
Cold War, 87, 139
Colorado, 13, 61, 110, 112, 122–123; House Committee Hearing, xiii–xiv, 49, 86–87

190   *Index*

Communist Party, 5, 43
Confederation Congress, 18, 20–21
Congressional Quarterly: method of
counting popular vote in 1960,
51, 53, 73, 90, 102, 126, 138–139;
1960 election, 1, 8, 17–18, 38, 71,
90, 109, 113, 120, 124
Constitutional Convention of 1787,
117, 127, 129, 143, 146, 150, 156;
direct elections, 4; Grand/Great
Compromise, 3, 19–24, 32–33,
42–43, 65, 72, 98–99, 103, 114,
141–142, 144–145; Grand/Great
Compromise, myths about, 59–63;
Grand/Great Compromise, purpose
of, 23–24; proposal to abolish the
Electoral College, 2–3
Cuban Missile Crisis, 83

Dayton, Jonathan, 21
Declaration of Independence, 20, 99
Delaware, 20, 34, 99, 104, 114, 117;
Senate, 90
Democratic Party, 51–53, 57, 73, 75,
102, 105, 108, 126, 138–139, 147;
Electoral College and, 38, 61, 113,
115–117, 119, 124, 129; platform
concessions made to, 6, 13, 44–46,
105; post-Civil War, 75; Pre-Civil
War, 113–114, 128
Democracy, 44, 143, 150; federalism
and, 5–8; national popular vote
and, 99–100
Denver Post, xiv
Dilanian, Ken, 25
Direct elections, ix, 16, 29, 37–46,
50, 110, 125–126, 137, 143–148;
Constitutional Convention, 4;
factionalization caused by, 7, 12,
45, 48, 55, 62, 91, 100, 105–107,
129; France, x–xi, 6, 11–12, 34, 47,
54–55, 85, 100, 105–106, 149–150;
proportional plan and, 127, 133;
racial discrimination and, 39,

113–116, 128, 132–133, 144, 149;
runoffs in, 140; Russia, 12, 43, 47,
48, 55, 91, 99, 107; weakness of,
47–48
Dirksen, Everett, ix
Disenfranchisement, 10, 68, 74, 151
District of Columbia, 73, 126, 152
District Plan/system, 30, 37, 127–128,
129–131–132, 151–152
Dixon, John, 37, 127–128
Douglas, Paul, 37, 62, 127, 132
Douglas, Stephen, 114

Election(s): 1800, 43; 1824, 43; 1860,
15; 1876, 15, 75–76, 139; 1880,
56–57, 61, 133; 1888, 27, 52; 1896,
61, 133; 1932, 105; 1936, 83; 1960,
8, 16–18, 27, 50–53, 57, 71, 79,
83, 86–87, 89–90, 101–102, 109,
113, 119, 124, 131, 133, 138–139;
1992, 7, 44, 106; 2000, ix, 7, 16,
27, 35, 52, 57, 73–74, 76–77, 79, 87,
90–91, 101; 2004, 81–82; 2016, 27,
52, 83, 111, 124; automatic plan,
133–135, 151; banana republic, 38;
conceding, 81–82; contingency,
140–143, 154–156; direct, ix–xi,
5–7, 9, 11–12, 16, 29, 33, 37–48,
44, 50, 52, 54–55, 82, 85–88,
110, 115, 123–126, 129, 137, 140,
143–150; District Plan/system, 30,
37, 127–128, 129–131–132, 151–
152; Framer's vision for, 29–35;
legislative, 135–136; legitimacy
and certainty, 71–84; proportional
system, 60–62, 113, 128, 131–133,
151; recounts, 11, 56–57, 62, 71,
73–74, 77, 85–93, 100–102, 147,
151; reform, 127–148, 152–156;
runoff, 6, 12, 34, 38, 44, 48,
54–56, 62, 85, 100, 105–107,
140–142; sui generis, 75; unit
rule vote, 30, 59–63, 68, 96,
134, 152

Index

191

Elector(s), 57, 101, 125; allocation of, 5, 30, 32, 40, 121; appointing, 27, 29–31, 34, 49, 51, 53–54, 98, 103, 105, 130, 135–136, 152; chief election officers, 49, 50, 73–74, 109; coercion of, 110–112; faithless, 111, 134, 151, 153; pledged, 26–27, 51, 73, 89, 125, 153; role of, 26–27, 97–98; unpledged, 51, 58, 102, 109, 126

Electoral College, 15, 52, 72, 76, 79, 83, 124, 133, 150; calls to abolish, 1, 4, 10, 12, 17, 24–25, 33, 35, 37–39, 41, 43–44, 85, 105, 118, 124, 143–144, 146, 151; Birch Bayh hearings to abolish, xii, 6–7, 8, 45–47, 54, 86; channeling effects of, x, 7; Constitutional origins of, 18–19; creation of, 2–3, 5–6, 32, 45, 109; criticisms of, 27–28, 39–42, 82–83; equal suffrage for states in, xi, 4–5, 10–11, 20, 24–25, 35, 60–61, 65–67, 91, 96–97, 103, 112, 114, 117–118, 150; majority support for a presidential candidate, 33–34, 42–46; margin, 83, 90; myths about, 96–126; public support of, 16, 38; purpose of, xiv, 4–7, 32–33, 46; race and, 39, 113–116; reform, 127–148; runoffs, provisions for, 12, 54–55, 105–106; studies of, 38–42, 136–140, 147; winner-take-all system of allocating votes, 112–113

Electoral votes: congressional certification, 153–154; counting, 34, 61, 132; fractional, 61

Electoral College and the Constitution: The Case for Preserving Federalism, xii, xv

Emancipation Proclamation, 113

Enfranchisement of all citizens, 152

Every Vote Equal: A State–Based Plan for Electing the President by National

Popular Vote, xiii–xiv, 4, 8, 10, 16, 40, 67, 74, 87; Democracy and, 59; Electoral College and, 67, 85; Federalism and, 59; Myth 9.4.5, 41; Myth 10.1, 96–97; Myth 10.2, 97–98; Myth 10.3, 98–99; Myth 10.4, 99–100; Myth 10.5, 100–102; Myth 10.6, 103–105; Myth 10.7, 105–107; Myth 10.8, 107–108; Myth 10.9, 108–110; Myth 10.10, 110–112; Myth 10.11, 112–113; Myth 10.12, 113–116; Myth 10.13, 116–119; Myth 10.14, 119–121; Myth 10.15, 121–123; Myth 10.16, 123–126; recounts, 74; Section III–1, 50; Section III–3, 125; Section III–5, 120; Section IV–4, 56; Section 9.15, 50; tallying votes, 54

Federalism, xii, xv, 34–35, 47–48, 116–119, 121, 129, 132, 142–144; democracy and, 5–8; Founding Fathers and, 25–28; Kennedy's vision of, 1–14; national popular vote and, 103–105; preserving, 149–156

Federalist Papers, 145; No. 68, 27, 32

Federalist Party, 7

Ferrand, Max, 23, 29, 103, 144

Florida, 74–77, 80, 87, 90–91, 101, 108; Supreme Court, 93

France, 12, 20; direction elections, x–xi, 6, 11, 44, 47, 54, 85, 100, 105–106, 149–150; multiparty system, 55, 91, 99; runoff elections, 34

Franklin, Benjamin, 20–21, 108

Garfield, James, 56–57

General ticket system, 130–131

George III, 2, 4, 104, 119

George Mann's Tavern, 19

George Mason University, 53

Index

Germany, 55, 100, 107
Gerrymandering, 130
Goodwin, Doris Kearns, 53
Google, 117
Gore, Al, ix, xii, 87, 108
Gossett, Ed, 62, 128, 132
Gossett Plan, 62
Grand/Great Compromise, 3, 103,
114, 141–142, 144–145; Articles,
43, 72, 98–99; Constitutional
Convention of 1787 and, 3–4,
19–24, 32–33, 42–43, 65; myths
about, 59–63; purpose of, 23–24;
unit vote and, 59–63
Gray v. Sanders, 130
Great Britain, xiv, 119
Green Party, 107, 117

Hamilton, Alexander, 18–22, 27, 32,
97, 117
Hancock, John, 20
Hancock, Winfield Scott, 61, 112, 133
Harding, Warren, 105
Hayes, Rutherford, 75–76, 79
Henry I, 78
Herblock, 16
Hillhouse, James, 1, 37
Hitler, Adolf, 55, 100

Illinois, 72, 84, 86, 90, 101
Indiana Supreme Court, 80
Infratest-Dimap, 107
Italy, 55

Jefferson, Thomas, 20, 30, 60–61, 99,
112, 150
"JFK's Popular Vote Victory: The
Myth," 53
Jim Crow, 149
Jordan, Vernon, 115

Kavanaugh, Brett, 117
Kennedy, John F., 68, 72–73, 114, 126,
150; defense of the Electoral College,

ix–xi, 24–25, 34, 37, 48, 62, 103,
115–116, 143, 145, 149; federalism,
vision of, 1–17; 1960 election, 1, 8,
16–18, 27, 50–53, 57, 71, 79, 83,
86–87, 89–90, 101–102, 109, 113,
119, 124, 131, 133, 138–139
Kenya, 79
Kerry, John, 81–82
King, Rufus, 3–4, 22–23, 34–35, 117
Kirkpatrick, Jeane, 38, 136
Klu Klux Klan, 75
Koza, John, 8

Lansing, John, 20
Labour Party, xiv, 28, 40
Le Pen, Marine, 6, 44
Levine, James, 83, 133
Liberal Democratic Party, 43
Lincoln, Abraham, 7, 15, 75, 113–114
Lodge, Henry Cabot, 61–62, 113, 131
Lodge-Gossett Plan, 128
Loffe, Julia, 118
Longley, Lawrence D., 38, 145
Louisiana, 75, 109, 126

Macron, Emmanuel, 6, 44
Madison, James, ix, 18–21, 32, 37, 60,
97, 144–145, 150
Maine, 30, 60–61, 90, 112, 131, 150,
152–153
"Making of a President in 1968," 96
Martin, Luther, 2, 21
Martin, William, 135
Massachusetts, 96
Matilda, 78
Merkel, Angela, 107
Merrill, Samuel, 137
Mexico, 79, 82
Miami Herald, 80
Mill, John Stuart, 47
Mississippi, 109, 126, 135
Mississippi Revolution, 75
Missouri, 80
Mitchell, Clarence, 115, 132

Morris, Robert, 26
Mr. Smith Goes to Washington, x
Muller, Derek, 121
Multiparty systems, 7, 12, 45, 48, 55, 62, 91, 100, 105–107
Multistate Tax Commission, 120

Nader, Ralph, 10, 25, 35, 108
National Archives and Records Administration, 102
National Association for the Advancement of Colored People, 115, 132
National Popular Vote, 8, 48
National Popular Vote Interstate Compact (NPVIC), 10–13, 18, 22, 25, 30, 33–35, 44, 47–60, 65, 72–76, 82; enforcement of, 121–123; lobbyists, 8, 13, 48, 50, 88–89; manifesto, xiii–xiv, 4, 8, 10, 16, 40–41, 50, 59, 67, 74, 85, 87, 96–126; myths about the Electoral College in, 95–126; nonsignatory states, 10–11, 24, 54–56, 58, 74, 89, 92, 104–106, 123, 126; one-state veto, 126; primary textual issues, 50–54; provisions of bill, xii–xv, 49–50; public scrutiny of, 13–14, 48; recounts, 56–57, 74, 77, 85–93, 100–102; runoffs, 105–107; signatory states, 9, 17, 58, 62, 66, 87, 89, 92, 110–111, 120–121, 125
National Urban League, 39, 115
NBC, 25
Nebraska, 30, 60–61, 90, 112, 131, 150, 153
Nero, 78
New England, 96
New Hampshire, 56; Senate, 147
New York, 20–21, 25, 39, 41, 67, 75, 84, 114, 117; Senate, 85
New York Review of Books, 53
New York Times, 1, 51–53, 82, 89, 109, 113–114, 124, 126

Nixon, Richard, 16, 31, 50, 72–73, 102, 112, 116, 153; 1960 election, 1, 8, 17–18, 38, 51–53, 71, 86–87, 90, 102, 109, 113, 120, 124, 133
North Carolina, 80, 99
North Dakota, 25, 67, 77
North Korea, 78
Norton, Ken, 117

Ocasio-Cortez, Alexandra, 10, 35, 114, 118
Ohio, 68
Oklahoma, 80
"One Man, 3.312 Votes: A Mathematical Analysis of the Electoral College," 39–40

Parliament, xiv, 12, 40
Peirce, Neal, 38, 145
Pennsylvania, 21, 26, 80, 104, 111, 114, 117
People's Choice party, 5–6, 43
Perot, Ross, 7, 44, 106
Popular vote, 16–17, 26, 28, 33–35, 44, 49, 51–52, 75, 77, 114, 139; allocating, 58, 83, 112–113; democracy and, 99–100; of electors, 152; federalism and, 103–105; loser, x, xiv, 1, 61, 71, 74, 83, 89, 112–113, 116, 133, 137–138, 141; national, 5, 8, 24, 37, 47, 50, 52–53, 61, 66–67, 73, 75, 87–90, 99–102, 106, 108–110, 126; primaries, 31; state, 133–135, 147; tabulating, 8, 17–18, 41, 50–54, 57–58, 73–74, 79, 89, 91, 100–102, 108–110, 126, 147, 151; weakness of, 47–48
Poumailloux, Christine, 149–150
Powell, Lazarus, 37
Presidential: campaign commercials, 68–69, 84; campaigns and incentives, 65–69; candidates, choosing, 42–43

"Presidential Election Recount Act of ___, " 50
Proportional system, 60–62, 113, 128, 131–133, 151

Racial discrimination and racism, 39, 75, 113–116, 128, 132–133, 144, 149
Reagan, Ronald, 83, 115
Records of the Federal Constitution of 1787, The, 29
Recounts, 11, 56–57, 62, 71, 73–74, 77, 147, 151; problems with, 85–93, 100–102
Reform Party, 99–100
Regis University, xiii, 13
Republican Party, 7, 44, 62, 75–76, 106, 109–111, 113–116, 119, 124, 128–129, 132, 147
Rhode Island, 20, 99, 114, 117
Riley, Jim, xiii–xiv, 13, 49
Roman Empire, 78–79, 107
Roosevelt, Franklin D., 83, 129
Roosevelt, Theodore, 108
Ross, Tara, 90, 121
Rossiter, Clinton, 38, 144
Runoff elections, 6, 34, 38, 44, 48, 56, 62, 85, 100, 140–142; Electoral College provisions for, 12, 54–55, 105–106; NPVIC provisions for, 105–107
Russell, Francis, 53
Russia, 12, 43, 47, 48, 55, 91, 99, 107
Rutledge, John, 22

Schlesinger, Arthur, 38, 42, 136, 145–146
Schwarzenegger, Arnold, 115
Segregation, 33, 149
Seventh District Court of Appeals, 82
Slavery, 75, 98–99, 113–114, 118
Social Democrats, 107
Socialism, 13, 45–46, 114
Socialist Party, 45

Society of Cincinnati Convocation, 19
South Carolina, 21, 75, 80
St. Albans School, ix
State of the Union Address, 134
Stephen, 78
Stewart, Jimmy, x
Sutton, Willie, 66

Thomas, Norman, 6
Three-fifths compromise, 99
Tilden, Samuel, 75, 79
Tragedy of the Commons, 112
Trump, Donald, 83–84, 108
Tulloch, Gordon, 53
Tures, John A., 68
Twentieth Century Fund, 38, 136–137, 147; Task Force, 139
Two-party system, 6, 55, 107–108, 133–134, 152, 155

Ukraine, 81–82
Unit rule vote, 30, 59–63, 68, 96, 134, 152
United Kingdom, xiv, 12, 28, 107, 118
United Nations, xiv, 28, 38, 71, 136
U.S. Code: 15, 153–154; Title 3, 15, 31, 50, 93; Title 5, 31
U.S. Congress, 9, 12
U.S. Constitution, 33, 43, 72, 76, 133–134, 136; amending, xii, 16–17, 28, 54, 55, 57, 61, 85, 91, 95–97, 103, 106, 110, 123–126, 128–129, 142; Article I, xii, 3, 5, 11, 23–24, 57–58, 63, 72, 86, 98, 104, 119–121; Article II, xii, 3–6, 9–12, 15, 23–24, 26–27, 29, 31–32, 34–35, 40–43, 49, 50, 55–56, 60, 72, 86, 91, 96–97, 100–101, 113, 123–124; Article IV, 93; Article V, xi, 4, 11, 23–24, 33–35, 41–42, 47, 58, 60, 62, 65, 72, 96–97, 103–104, 113, 116, 118; checks and balances in, ix, xi, 5, 21, 48, 145, 149; equal suffrage for states in, 21–23, 35,

Index

91; enfranchisement of all citizens, 152; federalist structure of, xii, 3, 8; Fifth Amendment, 10, 25, 31, 93; First Amendment, 25; Fourteenth Amendment, 10, 25, 31–32, 93, 95; ratification of, 29–30, 35, 37, 114, 117; Sixth Amendment, 25; separation of powers in, 21; Tenth Amendment, 26, 56, 91, 104; Twelfth Amendment, 30–31, 34

U.S. House of Representatives, 12, 22–23, 27, 34, 43, 55, 98, 134; contingent power in, 140–143

U.S. Justice Department, 80

U.S. Senate, 40–41, 134; abolishment of, 4, 10, 25, 35, 40, 106, 117–118; Birch Bayh hearings, xii, 6–7, 8, 45–47, 54, 86; Committee on Privileges and Elections, 29; equal representation for states in, xi, 2, 4–5, 8, 10–11, 23–25, 32–35, 40–42, 47, 60, 62, 65–67, 72, 96–99, 103–104, 112–114, 116, 117, 145–146, 151; Joint Resolution 31, x; president, 31; Rules Committee, 147; voting disparity, 40

U.S. Steel v. Multistate Tax Commission, 11, 57, 120

U.S. Supreme Court, 29, 40–41, 79, 93, 117, 119

Utah, 89

Virginia, 98, 104

Voter fraud, 15, 71, 80–81, 86

Voter I.D., 81–82

Voter impersonation, 82

Wallace, George, 31, 33, 153

Washington, George, 1–2, 4, 18–21, 34, 42, 99, 104, 135, 153

Washington Post, 16, 117–118

West Virginia, 51, 89, 109

Whig Party, 7, 106

White, Theodore, 38, 96, 148

Will, George, 118

Williamson, Hugh, 21, 119

Wilson, Woodrow, 108

Wyoming, 10

Yates, Robert, 20

Zhirinovsky, Vladimir, 5, 43

About the Author

Robert M. Hardaway is professor of law at the University of Denver Sturm College of Law, where he teaches evidence and civil procedure and election law. He is the author of numerous law review articles and books on the Electoral College and election law, including *The Electoral College and the Constitution: The Case for Preserving Federalism* (Praeger, 1994) and *Crisis at the Polls* (Greenwood, 2008, foreword by Richard D. Lamm, former governor of Colorado). Hardaway has been voted best professor by his students. He has contributed to public media such as CNN, MSNBC, and numerous public television and radio stations as well as the *Chicago Tribune,* the *Los Angeles Times,* Huffington Post, AOL News, and local news publications. He has also written amicus legal briefs to district and appellate courts on issues relating to the Electoral College. Professor Hardaway is the author or coauthor of 37 law review articles and reviews as well as over 325 published articles in publications ranging from *New York Times Upfront* to the *Chicago Tribune* and the *Los Angeles Times.*

Printed in the USA
CPSIA information can be obtained
at www.ICGtesting.com
LVHW051933120524
779928LV00002B/233

9 798765 119020